POPE AND
HUMAN NATURE

POPE AND
HUMAN NATURE

By
GEOFFREY TILLOTSON

OXFORD
AT THE CLARENDON PRESS

Oxford University Press, Ely House, London W. 1

GLASGOW NEW YORK TORONTO MELBOURNE WELLINGTON
CAPE TOWN SALISBURY IBADAN NAIROBI LUSAKA ADDIS ABABA
BOMBAY CALCUTTA MADRAS KARACHI LAHORE DACCA
KUALA LUMPUR HONG KONG

FIRST PUBLISHED 1958
REPRINTED LITHOGRAPHICALLY AT THE
UNIVERSITY PRESS, OXFORD
FROM CORRECTED SHEETS OF THE FIRST EDITION
1963, 1966

PRINTED IN GREAT BRITAIN

PREFACE

READERS of the preface to my earlier book, *On the Poetry of Pope*, in its second edition will be prepared for a further book on him from me, but not for the one I have written. All that needs to be said in explanation is that the present book, which is mainly about the material Pope expresses, was originally intended as part of a book designed to enlarge and replace its predecessor, which was mainly about Pope's methods of expression. When, having turned to other fields, I looked at what had been done towards the new book, I saw that it could be enlarged and related to the former, which was then again in print, as a supplement.

A point about the method of the book. I am aware that I have sometimes given quotations so long that they may be thought to weaken the pace of the argument. They make of my book something more like a stained-glass window than a picture. Pope is not so well known, I think, that the quotations are stale, and if they get in the way of the argument, they may be glanced at rather than read, till the reader finds more leisure to attend to them. All told, they amount to an anthology of passages of special interest.

Two other observations. Throughout the book I have given the words 'nature' and 'natural' a capital N when I use them in what I think to be the sense defined on p. 1 below. Conversely I have deprived 'nature' of a capital when in a passage quoted it means merely the material universe. Any annotations of Pope's text are intended to supplement the annotations in the Twickenham edition, which may also be consulted.

Four passages of my book have appeared before: (*a*) much of Chapter X was published in the *Sewanee Review*, 1958; (*b*) Chapters III and XI include, in revised form, much of a lecture, *The Moral Poetry of Pope*, delivered before the Literary and Philosophical Society of Newcastle upon Tyne in 1945, and printed in 1946; (*c*) Appendixes 1 and 2 include parts of reviews published in the *Times Literary Supplement* for 30 December 1955 and 1 June 1956. I wish to thank the editors of these periodicals for their kind permission to republish. Thanks are also due to Messrs. Methuen for allowing me to quote from the Twickenham edition of Pope, and to Mrs. F. M. Cornford and the Cresset Press for allowing me to quote the poem on p. 9 below.

I have the pleasure of thanking my wife and Dr. Aubrey Williams for reading the book, or a version of it, in manuscript, Miss Joy Russell-Smith for reading Chapter X, and Dr. Frances Mayhew Rippy for compiling the index.

G. T.

University of London
Birkbeck College
15 August 1957

CONTENTS

ABBREVIATIONS AND REFERENCES

Abbott, Edwin, *A Concordance to the works of Alexander Pope, with an Intro-duction by Edwin A. Abbott, D.D.*, New York, 1875. [This concordance does not take in the translations from Greek and Latin, or the imitations of Chaucer and the English poets, or certain of the minor poems.]

Boswell, *Life of Johnson*, ed. G. B. Hill, revised and enlarged, L. F. Powell, 6 vols., Oxford, 1934–40.

Byron, *Works, Letters and Journals*, ed. R. E. Prothero, 6 vols., 1898–1901.

Coleridge, *Biographia Literaria*, ed. J. Shawcross, 2 vols., Oxford, 1907.

De Quincey, *Collected Writings*, ed. D. Masson, 14 vols., Edinburgh, 1889–90.

Dryden, *Essays*, selected and ed. W. P. Ker, 2 vols., Oxford, 1900.

Griffith, R. H., *Alexander Pope: A Bibliography*, I. i–ii, Austin, Texas, 1922–7.

Hazlitt, *Complete Works*, ed. P. P. Howe, 21 vols., 1930–4.

Hobbes, *English Works*, ed. W. Molesworth, 11 vols., 1839–45.

Pope, *The Twickenham Edition of the Poems*, general ed. John Butt, 7 vols. The first is still awaited.

    Vol. II: *The Rape of the Lock and Other Poems*, ed. Geoffrey Tillotson, 1940.

    Vol. III (i): *An Essay on Man*, ed. Maynard Mack, 1950.

    Vol. III (ii): *Epistles to Several Persons (Moral Essays)*, ed. F. W. Bateson, 1951.

    Vol. IV: *The Imitations of Horace with An Epistle to Dr. Arbuthnot and The Epilogue to the Satires*, ed. John Butt, 1939.

    Vol. V: *The Dunciad*, ed. James Sutherland, 1944.

    Vol. VI: *Minor Poems*, ed. Norman Ault and John Butt, 1954.

Pope, *The Correspondence*, ed. George Sherburn, 5 vols., Oxford, 1956.

Pope, *The Best of Pope*, ed. George Sherburn, New York, revised ed. 1946.

Reid, Thomas, *Works*, ed. William Hamilton, 2 vols., Edinburgh, ed. 1863.

Sherburn, George, *The Early Career of Alexander Pope*, Oxford, 1934.

Spence, J., *Anecdotes, Observations, and Characters, of Books and Men*, ed. S. W. Singer, 1820.

Spingarn, J. E. (ed.), *Critical Essays of the Seventeenth Century*, 3 vols., Oxford, 1908–9.

Swift, *A Tale of a Tub*, ed. A. C. Guthkelch and D. Nichol Smith, Oxford, 1920.

I

'NATURE'

I

CRITICS are often found dividing writers into this group and that. Some writers, they discover, aim at simplicity, others at complexity; some prefer to write in well-known forms, others encourage each work to make a new form for itself; some write at great length, others in 'swallow-flights'; some are perfectionists, others confound a pen with a pitchfork; some cover a wide and others a narrow field of subject-matter. On the present occasion I am aware of a division of writers according to a quality in their subject-matter. I am aware of Pope as a poet who subscribed to the old belief that poets put as much human nature as possible into their poems, that they look to mankind—or Nature, as it was called in Pope's day—for their theme, or if not squarely to that, relate their narrower theme to it as closely as possible. Nature, when it was not human hands and feet, was, and of course is still, that quantum of the mind-and-heart which all men—past, present, and in theory future—hold in common.

This abstraction exists in any one mind-and-heart as a mixture of experience, direct and indirect, and conjecture. We can just attain to imagining a man capable of grasping it without recourse to conjecture, with no other aid than a higher power of experience; for, being a human object, Nature offers only such obstacles to being known as inhere in the *res extensa*. By finite persons, however, the obstacles are unsurmountable. Writers who have tried to generalize men into man have ignored the obstacles as far as possible— philosophers, anthropologists, and psychologists are as much concerned with finding and guessing about man as physiologists and doctors are,[1] and, when they generalize, have

---

[1] Cf. 'Doctors from Everywhere', *The Times*, 31 Oct. 1956, p. 9: 'Medicine recognizes neither frontiers, race nor creed. The antibiotics which control tuberculosis in Europe are equally effective in Asia and Africa. The insecticide which

learned the habit of resting content if enough human beings
agree with them to give a sense that they speak for all.
That they are at most speaking for many is attested by the
persistence of change, even if also of development, throughout the long course of their thinking—by the persisting
change that overtakes all matters not independent of conjecture. Nature is inaccessible to us but tempts us towards
forcing some sort of access to it. It is as if each one of us said:
'I am a man among my fellows; I cannot but compare myself
with them, forming general views that I continue to trim as
experience widens and deepens; this activity seems part of
my nature; I often keep these general views to myself, but if
I do offer some of them to others it is on the understanding
that their limited source in myself precludes any confidence
that they do not presume; I offer them for what they are
worth.' Of the truth of some of these general views we can all
be fully confident. All men agree that, as Locke put it,
'Wormwood and Sugar-Plumbs, are not the same thing.'[1] It
is also universally agreed that all men must die—or, if some
have dissented, those very few have not proved to be exceptions. All men agree further that the certain mortality of men
has an effect—of whatever sort—on the way they live their
lives, and on the way they look back on them. About the
truth of certain would-be universal statements we are not so
sure. No doubt there is an almost universal assent to the remark of Sterne's that it is good to have the company of a
friend if only to remark that the shadows lengthen as the day
declines.[2] Sometimes our assertions about Nature become
subjected to scrutiny in the interests of making them more
accurate: to snatch another instance at random, John Stuart
Mill remarked that:

destroys disease-transmitting flies in England is equally effective against the
malaria-transmitting mosquitoes of Africa. The management of a sick patient in
a London teaching hospital is based upon exactly the same principles as the management of a sick patient in Singapore.'

[1] *Essay concerning Human Understanding*, bk. i, chap. ii.

[2] 'Let the torpid Monk seek heaven comfortless and alone—GOD speed him!
for my own part, I fear, I should never so find the way: let me be wise and religious
—but let me be MAN: wherever thy Providence places me, or whatever be the
road I take to get to thee—give me some companion in my journey, be it only
to remark to, How our shadows lengthen as the sun goes down . . .' (*The Sermons
of Mr. Yorick*, ed. 1927, i. 207 f.).

When the Psalmist 'said in his wrath that all men are liars', he enunciated what in some ages and countries is borne out by ample experience; but it is not a law of man's nature to lie; though it is one of the consequences of the laws of his nature, that the habit of lying is nearly universal when certain external circumstances exist universally, especially circumstances productive of habitual distrust or fear.[1]

Sometimes what men nowadays assert about Nature was not known, or not so confidently known, to men of former days: for instance, it was not until the nineteenth century that time was ripe for this statement:

since men differ more in their social relations than in their physiological relations, it is in the former that we should first seek the explanation of intellectual and moral differences not obviously assignable to differences of physiological structure.[2]

Sometimes a statement about Nature arouses dispute on a wide scale: to take a small instance from the field of literature, on p. 20 below, Samuel Daniel gives it as his opinion that all men—or at least all Europeans, of which distinction more later—like rime, a proposition assented to by Dryden. If such a proposition is to establish itself, it will be by argument —and there was nothing that Dryden liked better. It can be argued, acceptably I think, that (European) man likes rime, and that if he had always had it, he would always have liked it. But we cannot be sure—the proposition is not so infallible as that all men must die. Indeed, at the very time Dryden was arguing on these lines, Milton brought back the ancient Greeks and Romans into the heart of the argument, dubbing modern rimers 'vulgar' and 'barbarous' eccentrics:[3] his appeal, like that of Daniel and Dryden, was still to Nature, but to a different interpretation of it.

It is obvious that the nature of Nature is partly conjectural, and, admitting that I prefer to write of what I have more chance of grasping, I apologize in advance for any of my own conjectural generalizations that seem too wild, or for any

---

[1] *A System of Logic*, 1843, ii. 512.

[2] George Henry Lewes, *Problems of Life and Mind. Third Series. Problem the First. The Study of Psychology*, 1879, p. 164. Cf. the declaration made by the scientists called together by UNESCO (see *Civil Liberty*, vol. x, no. 6, Sept. 1950).

[3] 'The Verse', prefixed to a reissued first edition of *Paradise Lost*, meeting the objections of those many readers who were 'stumbled' because 'the Poem Rimes not'.

implied acceptance of a general statement of Pope's that may
be open to question. There was some scepticism about
Nature in Pope's own day—indeed La Rochefoucauld had
gone so far as to remark that 'Il est plus aisé de connoître
l'homme en général, que de connoître un homme en parti-
culier'.[1] Nevertheless, there was also confidence; which on
the solid authority of W. P. Ker was not misplaced:

> There is one idea common to Dryden and all his contemporaries
> which, in spite of its ambiguity, is seldom misleading; that is the idea
> of Nature: 'At once the source, and end, and test of Art.' Pope could
> not help himself in the *Essay on Criticism*; he had to say 'first follow
> Nature', because all the critics and poets had been saying the same thing
> for generations past, and it was not his business to disagree with them.
> Nor was it Dryden's wish in this respect to avoid conforming with the
> rest of the guild. 'Nature' means whatever the author thinks right;
> sometimes it is the reality that is copied by the artist; sometimes, and
> much more commonly, it is the principles of sound reason in poetry;
> and sometimes it is the Ideal. Thus Dryden refers to Nature to justify
> heroic couplets in serious drama; 'heroic rhyme is nearest Nature, as
> being the noblest kind of modern verse'. It might seem as if there were
> little value in a conception so vague, so mutable, so easily turned to
> sophistry and fallacy. Yet it would be a mistake to think so.[2]

Sophistry and fallacy there could not but be: when the
subject was something so general as Nature, their existence
was itself Natural! Nevertheless, my reader will find himself
agreeing with much, probably most, of what I quote from
eighteenth-century writers.

The concept of man was much held in mind in the eighteenth century, and by poets as well as others. It is a useful
concept for a poet, if only because it will save him from a too
close attention to himself. We do not want him to forget himself, of course: he is precious to the rest of us just because he
is himself. But if he is too closely self-concerned we can too
easily lose sight of him, as he of us. Many eighteenth-century
poets—and some seventeenth- and nineteenth-century poets
also—believed that the best material for poetry did not spring
from what was unique in the constitution and contents of any
one man's mind, but from what was common to all minds.

---

[1] *Œuvres,* ed. D. L. Gilbert and J. Gourdault, Paris, 1883, i. 193 (maxim 436).
[2] *Essays of John Dryden,* I. xxiv f.

From this belief it did not follow that the best material lay elsewhere than in individual experience. How could it? We are each ourselves, and cannot assume the mind of others any more than their bodies. It was agreed, for instance, that one difficulty in the way of reading the mental and moral nature of men was that

> There's some Peculiar in each leaf and grain,
> Some unmark'd fibre, or some varying vein:
> Shall only Man be taken in the gross?
> Grant but as many sorts of Mind as Moss.[1]

Each man's mind was seen as unique, but rather as anything is unique, however much it resembles something else. Poets were not encouraged to show much uniqueness outside that category. In the *Dunciad* Pope laughed at the maze-like brain of a poet shown up by the written account of his thinking:

> Nonsense precipitate, like running Lead,
> That slip'd thro' Cracks and Zig-zags of the Head;[2]

and speaking of tropes in the *Peri Bathous* he ironically recommended that they

must be so turn'd, as to manifest that intricate and wonderful *Cast* of *Head*, which distinguishes all Writers of this Genius; or (as I may say) to refer exactly the *Mold* in which they were form'd, in all its *Inequalities*, *Cavities*, *Obliquities*, odd *Crannies*, and *Distortions*.[3]

(We may note that in the mid-seventeenth century Sir Thomas Browne had had constant recourse to the obliquities of his own mind, which in the nineteenth were again delighted in, Lamb calling them 'beautiful obliquities'.)[4] In the eighteenth century it was granted that the experience of each man is inalienably his own, even when experiencing 'the same thing' as others experience, but it was claimed that there are some sorts of things that give any one man an experience as nearly like that of any other as matters: for instance, the love of a native land is similar enough, the world over and throughout historic time, to be counted as roughly the same, whatever land it happens to be.

---

[1] Pope's *Moral Essays*, i ('Of the Knowledge and Characters of Men'), 15 ff. There are some six hundred varieties of moss in England, and nine hundred if liverworts are counted in.   [2] *Dunciad*, i. 123 f.
[3] Chap. x.   [4] 'Mackery End, in Hertfordshire', *Essays of Elia*, 1823.

How did any one man discover what was Natural? The answer is suggested by the sort of thing Pope said of one department of Nature. In the fourth *Moral Essay*, 'Of the Use of Riches', which he addressed to Burlington, he considered the reason why one man makes a satisfactory garden and another not, and concluded it was by the use or neglect of 'Good Sense'. Good sense, a light which lighteneth every man that cometh into the world, was another name for common sense, sense common to all, or, to use the term that Dugald Stewart offered as an expressive approximation, 'mother-wit'.[1] Pope appraised this human endowment in a delightful outburst in a letter to James Craggs:

> We talk much of fine sense, refin'd sense, and exalted sense; but for use and happiness give me a little common sense.[2]

When Thomas Reid came to devote a chapter to common sense in his essay on judgement, he found help in the philosophers of Pope's time and later, drawing on Berkeley, Shaftesbury (whose 'Sensus Communis' forms part of his *Characteristicks of Men, Manners, Opinions, Times*),[3] and others. Reid also appealed to Pope:

> We may take Mr Pope as good authority for the meaning of an English word. He uses it ['sense' meaning common sense] often, and, in his 'Epistle to the Earl of Burlington', has made a little descant upon it.
>
> > Oft have you[4] hinted to your brother Peer
> > A certain truth, which many buy too dear:
> > Something there is more needful than Expence,
> > And something previous ev'n to Taste—'tis Sense:
> > Good Sense, which only is the gift of Heav'n,
> > And tho' no science, fairly worth the seven:[5]
> > A Light, which in yourself you must perceive;
> > Jones and Le Nôtre have it not to give.[6]

---

[1] See *The Works of Thomas Reid*, p. 28.

[2] *Correspondence*, i. 306.

[3] *The Fifth Edition, Corrected*, 1732, i. 57 ff.

[4] Burlington.

[5] The seven liberal arts as systematized in the medieval universities—the quadrivium (arithmetic, geometry, astronomy, music) along with the inferior trivium (grammar, rhetoric, logic).

[6] *Moral Essays*, iv ('Of the Use of Riches', To Burlington), 39 ff. The text is that of the Twickenham ed.

This inward light or sense is given by heaven to different persons in different degrees. There is a certain degree of it which is necessary to our being subjects of law and government, capable of managing our own affairs, and answerable for our conduct towards others: this is called common sense, because it is common to all men with whom we can transact business or call to account for their conduct. . . . Men rarely ask what common sense is; because every man believes himself possessed of it, and would take it for an imputation upon his understanding to be thought unacquainted with it.[1]

Men do not possess this light in uniform measure, and so differ in the degree to which they find it readily perceptible when needing to draw on it. Whatever its measure in any one man, the process of perceiving it was usually a process of penetrating beyond what had been acquired too accidentally. Johnson sometimes saw Nature in negative terms—in terms of absent, stripped-off, or escaped acquirements. Man for him is 'uninstructed by precept, and unprejudiced by authority', and the description of the 'common reader' is of a man 'uncorrupted with literary prejudices' and blessedly exempt from 'all the refinements of subtilty and the dogmatism of learning'.[2] You sought within your own simplified head and heart, but—a further restriction—only for what you saw others to have found in theirs. Even Inigo Jones and Le Nôtre[3] could not endow you with good sense in the practical way that they could endow you with a garden, but if you discovered what you thought your own good sense about gardens and compared it with what of theirs they had embodied in their gardens, the process would help to confirm yours as the right thing. By 1731, the date of the fourth Moral Essay, both these garden-makers were dead. They survived, however, in what they had left, and so were on a footing with

---

[1] Op. cit., pp. 422 f.

[2] See below, p. 56, and *Lives of the Poets*, iii. 441. Cf. Pope on false education, p. 109 below, and A. O. Lovejoy, *Essays in the History of Ideas*, Baltimore, 1949, p. 93.

[3] In the first edition a note identifies Jones by giving him his full name, 'Inigo Jones'. Pope cites him as an architect. The note on Le Nôtre reads in the same edition: 'The famous Artist who design'd the best Gardens in *France*; and plann'd *Greenwich* and St. *James*'s Parks, &c.' Pope's taste in gardens was for something less formal than the gardens at Versailles. Later in the poem, at l. 70, he exclaimed: 'Without it [good sense], proud Versailles! thy glory falls.' There was a question whether Le Nôtre's formalism was not overdone and therefore open to the satire that the poem directed against Timon's garden. All the same Pope's note recognizes Le Nôtre's genius.

living specimens of Nature. What remained in books and in
report was not to be discarded out of hand: it had to be
searched and tested in accordance with the principles used
on living stuff. Johnson—to take an instance—thought that
books had been too much thrown over by the French theorists: Voltaire had counselled men to discard the fancy-
driven reasonings of the theologians, and to rely instead on
the self:

> Et pour nous élever descendons dans nous-mêmes.[1]

But this sort of advice might end, as Johnson thought, in
something that was too flimsy to be Nature:

> Human experience, which is constantly contradicting theory, is the
> great test of truth. A system, built upon the discoveries of a great many
> minds, is always of more strength, than what is produced by the mere
> workings of any one mind, which, of itself, can do little. There is not
> so poor a book in the world that would not be a prodigious effort were
> it wrought out entirely by a single mind, without the aid of prior
> investigators. The French writers are superficial, because they are not
> scholars, and so proceed upon the mere power of their own minds; and
> we see how very little power they have.[2]

Nature was a simple possession, but its simplicity was solid
and satisfactory because the result both of introspection and
as wide a comparison as possible. As Wordsworth was to say,
prosily but with one touch of his best poetry:

> The human nature unto which I felt
> That I belonged, and reverenced with love,
> Was not a punctual presence, but a spirit
> Diffused through time and space, with aid derived
> Of evidence from monuments, erect,
> Prostrate, or leaning towards their common rest
> In earth, the widely scattered wreck sublime
> Of vanished nations, or more clearly drawn
> From books and what they picture and record.[3]

Voltaire was right in turning away from the elaborations of
superfine theologians, but not if he took as the better alternative a sole reliance on the contents of the mind and heart
of a man untutored and in isolation.

[1] 'Exorde' to *Poème sur la loi naturelle*, l. 42.
[2] Boswell's *Life*, i. 454.   [3] *Prelude*, viii. 608 ff.

The typical eighteenth-century poet believed that men read poetry to discover—with the delight, of course, that poetry promises, as well as with profit—that they were like their. fellows, or to remind themselves of themselves. That was their object in the first place, and only in the second to enlarge their curious sense of the sports and varieties possible for human nature as it existed amid all the accidentals that befringed the individual. Nature made for social solidarity. It formed the heart of that social thing literature. They saw that the Bible (the Old Testament in particular) and the literature of Greece and Rome showed it in abundance—the stories of Abraham and Isaac, of Hector and Andromache, or of Aeneas and Dido. Johnson declared that

the poems of *Homer* we yet know not to transcend the common limits of human intelligence, but by remarking, that nation after nation, and century after century, has been able to do little more than transpose his incidents, new-name his characters, and paraphrase his sentiments.[1]

We of the twentieth century still see the force of all this. The parting on the walls of Troy, when the little son is frightened at the plumes in Hector's helmet, has yielded in its turn to other people in other clothes and in other places; but the more it changes, the more it remains the same:

> How long ago Hector took off his plume,
> Not wanting that his little son should cry,
> Then kissed his sad Andromache goodbye—
> And now we three in Euston waiting-room.[2]

An Anglo-Saxon riddle ends by naming food and one's country as deeply loved by man. A present-day story for children shows a Mr. J. Smith addressing his wife on the point of buying a monkey:

'There are five things . . . all things breathing—buffaloes to bullfinches—*need*, like you and me, Amy: food, shelter, sleep, company, and freedom.' And he gave his animals nearly as much as they could wish of them all except the last.[3]

---

[1] Johnson's Preface to *Shakespeare*, para. 3.
[2] Frances Cornford, 'Parting in War-Time', in *Travelling Home and Other Poems*, 1948, p. 30.
[3] Walter de la Mare, 'The Old Lion', in *Collected Stories for Children*, 1947.

To fly to another extreme, Joyce's *Ulysses* is, as it were, a huge bale of Nature—unfortunately the less acceptable because of a false sophistication: Joyce does not convince us that he has managed to reproduce in words that Natural thing, the stream of human consciousness. And there is the latest and sharply pointed addition to the literature of Nature in Mr. Samuel Beckett's plays for stage and radio.

Great literature, which the world is unwilling to let die, and less-than-great literature, which dies without being willed to die and which is capable of sporadic revival—these repositories of Nature are read by adult mankind. When they are also read by youngsters it is because youngsters feel themselves growing into men; when also by the superannuated, because of their need to stay among men. Reading or listening lasts longer than undiminished power to act, and while life lasts the words that are constantly used or implied in literature—*love, common sense, duty, vice, home, sacrifice, envy*, and the hundreds, but not the thousands, more—go on accumulating their sacred meaning for us. It was Newman, as we might expect, who gave this experience its best written form: coming late in a long tradition, he spoke with the more authority:

> Let us consider, too, how differently young and old are affected by the words of some classic author, such as Homer or Horace. Passages, which to a boy are but rhetorical commonplaces, neither better nor worse than a hundred others which any clever writer might supply, which he gets by heart and thinks very fine, and imitates, as he thinks, sucessfully, in his own flowing versification, at length come home to him, when long years have passed, and he has had experience of life, and pierce him, as if he had never before known them, with their sad earnestness and vivid exactness.[1]

The words of those who write of Nature lie in wait for us till our lives have collected, silently and at last, the material their writings express. They speak to us as we stand among our fellows holding the sum of our experience. If their writings surprise us with their meaning, they surprise the 'guilty thing' that has forgotten, or the callow or laggard

---

[1] *Essay in aid of a Grammar of Assent*, 1870, p. 75 (pt. i, chap. iv, § 2). Cf. J. S. Mill, *A System of Logic*, 1843, IV. iv, para. 6.

thing which, not yet having come to full knowledge, has come to see that it lies ahead.

If Nature is what finds expression in Shakespeare's plays, in Gray's 'Elegy', in Wordsworth's 'Idiot Boy' and 'Peele Castle', in *Middlemarch*—and in Pope's poetry—I and my readers need not fear that we shall lack a firm theme. We shall not care very much about the unexceptionable universality of what the theorists claim to be universal. It will be enough that 'every bosom', so far as we care to count them, 'returns an echo'.[1]

2

In the eighteenth century the topic Nature cropped up repeatedly when people were talking together. Witness such a characteristic book as Boswell's *Life of Johnson*. Ready to consider whatever might be advanced by a human being, Johnson participated in whatever discussion was started, whether on bulldogs or Christianity; but the discussion he preferred was one that had Nature for its quarry. As for instance this:

[Burke] 'From the experience which I have had,—and I have had a great deal,—I have learnt to think *better* of mankind.' JOHNSON. 'From my experience I have found them worse in commercial dealings, more disposed to cheat, than I had any notion of; but more disposed to do one another good than I had conceived.' [Gibbon] 'Less just and more beneficent.' JOHNSON. 'And really it is wonderful, considering how much attention is necessary for men to take care of themselves, and ward off immediate evils which press upon them, it is wonderful how much they do for others. As it is said of the greatest liar, that he tells more truth than falsehood; so it may be said of the worst man, that he does more good than evil.' BOSWELL. 'Perhaps from experience men may be found *happier* than we suppose.' JOHNSON. 'No, Sir; the more we enquire, we shall find men the less happy.'[2]

And so on: they draw on their rich experience, having made it rich in the interests of understanding human nature, and in the knowledge that at some serious inquiring hour it would be found worth the drawing on. The matter for such discussions was permanently before you, and if you dozed even on a trivial occasion, you might miss valuable evidence:

---

[1] See Johnson on Gray's 'Elegy', *Lives of the Poets*, iii. 441.   [2] iii. 236 f.

We talked of an evening society for conversation at a house in town, of which we were all members, but of which Johnson said, 'It will never do, Sir. There is nothing served about there, neither tea, nor coffee, nor lemonade, nor any thing whatever; and depend upon it, Sir, a man does not love to go to a place from whence he comes out exactly as he went in.'

This was a matter which every human being might join in discussing; Boswell therefore leapt into it:

I endeavoured for argument's sake, to maintain that men of learning and talents might have very good intellectual society, without the aid of any little gratifications of the senses. Berenger joined with Johnson, and said, that without these any meeting would be dull and insipid. He would therefore have all the slight refreshments; nay, it would not be amiss to have some cold meat, and a bottle of wine upon a side-board. 'Sir, (said Johnson to me, with an air of triumph,) Mr. Berenger knows the world. Every body loves to have good things furnished to them without any trouble. I told Mrs. Thrale once, that as she did not choose to have card-tables, she should have a profusion of the best sweetmeats, and she would be sure to have company enough come to her.' I agreed with my illustrious friend upon this subject; for it has pleased GOD to make man a composite animal, and where there is nothing to refresh the body, the mind will languish.[1]

The course of the talk is clear. Boswell dives into Nature with an instance merely 'for argument's sake', an instance not of man but of small groups of men: 'men of learning and talents'—I shall come to call such men instances of 'second-ary' nature. But this is an argument in which to subdivide man into groups is unnecessary, men of learning and talents being in this matter indistinguishable from every other sort. Mr. Berenger, bringing to bear his knowledge of 'the world', speaks with the better authority. Johnson agrees with him, and Boswell, too.

This was how men talked of Nature in London, and throughout Europe. And their generalizations were the more confident because corroborated by classical literature—litera-ture that was classical because its matter was Natural and its expression unimprovable—and especially by the poems of Homer, Virgil, and Horace. Those ancient poems were beautiful demonstrations that man had long been what he

[1] iv. 90 f.

still was. I have quoted Sterne's remark about the comfort
of having a friend by your side through life. It was not a
new thought—how could it be when its matter was Nature?
Sterne might have called our attention to its ancient expression, as Charles Reade was to, when he made Gerard observe
at a tender point of his friendship with Denys that

> I have found the sayings of the ancients true, that better is a bright
> comrade on the weary road than a horse litter.[1]

The ancient writers helped modern man to recognize as old
the humanity he was experiencing as new.

Differences were noted as well as samenesses. Even in
modern Europe you might be

> A Heretic, or True Believer,
> On this, or t'other Side a River,

and if we 'Turn . . . this Globe' we

> see,
> How diff'rent Nations disagree,
> In what We wear, or eat and drink;
> Nay . . . perhaps in what We think.[2]

Pope himself noted that

> . . . Faith itself has diff'rent dresses worn,

and added

> What wonder modes of Wit should take their turn?[3]

—a state of things that Johnson supplemented with further
instances:

> Ye nymphs of rosy lips and radiant eyes,
> Whom Pleasure keeps too busy to be wise,
> Whom Joys with soft varieties invite,
> By day the frolick, and the dance by night,
> Who frown with vanity, who smile with art,
> And ask the latest fashion of the heart . . .[4]

[1] *The Cloister and the Hearth*, 1861, ii. 219.
[2] Quoted by M. K. Spears, 'The Meaning of Matthew Prior's *Alma*', *ELH. A Journal of English Literary History*, xiii, 1946, 287.
[3] *Essay on Criticism*, ll. 446 f.
[4] *Vanity of Human Wishes*, ll. 323 ff.

And yet in the eighteenth century men refused to be dazzled
by a heterogeneity of illustration, trying to hold fast to the
sameness in the thing being illustrated. Fashions changed,
but not the substance fashioned; though men wore, ate, and
drank different things, they all dressed, ate, and drank;
though their emotions took a changing thing as object, they
remained the same emotions; though they worshipped different gods, they all worshipped.[1] As Johnson put it, invoking
the Laughing Philosopher:

> Once more, Democritus, arise on earth,
> With chearful wisdom and instructive mirth,
> See motley life in modern trappings dress'd,
> And feed with varied fools th' eternal jest.[2]

All told, there was felt to be ample ground for a theory of
Nature when the materials were European, whether here in
the eastern hemisphere, or in the western where an extension
of Europe was flourishing in America.[3] Farther afield, the
evidence was not so clear. Indeed the differences between
ancient Europeans, presented in their barbarity by Homer,
and modern Europeans were insignificant beside the differ-

[1] See A. O. Lovejoy, *Essays in the History of Ideas*, Baltimore, 1948, p. 83.

[2] *Vanity of Human Wishes*, ll. 49 ff. Johnson expresses pointedly what is implicit
in his original, Juvenal's *Satire X*.

[3] The New Englanders of the seventeenth century, being lately Old Englanders,
were recognizably men, though men too zealously given to the discussion of theology,
and of a theology close enough to Calvinism to sharpen the differences between man
and man, and so detract from the bland uniformity of Nature. During the eighteenth
century the prosperity of the colony led to more interest in the secular graces. No
doubt the 'polished and affluent American' of this later time talked about Nature,
or tried to, as Dr. Johnson and his friends did (see *The Literature of the American
People*, ed. A. H. Quinn, pt. i, *The Colonial and Revolutionary Period*, by K. B. Mur-
dock, New York, 1951, p. 88). Reading Pope's *Correspondence*, as now presented by
Professor Sherburn, it is a pleasant shock for an Englishman to find a series of letters
from America. The Rev. Mather Byles, minister of Hollis Street Church in Boston,
sent several letters to Pope in the late 1720's, which present not only 'the image of
a fervent young Bostonian who is all in an ecstacy about the immortal Pope', but
also a 'sketch [of] other readers and admirers: the "several of our principal
Gentlemen both of Church and State" who crowd around eager to see and handle
a letter in Pope's hand; the literati, whose "Genteel Rooms" are embellished with
Pope's portrait in "messotinto"; the "Polite and learned Part" of the American
colonists, who read Pope "with Transport" and talk of him "with Wonder" '. The description is that of Professor Austin Warren, the discoverer of the letters (*Publications of the Modern Language Association of America*, xlviii, 1933, 61 ff.). The same
article draws attention to a fervent poem, *An Epistle to Alexander Pope, Esq; from
South Carolina*, which was printed in London in 1737.

ences between Europeans, whether ancient or modern, and
Eastern and American savages. Much had come to be known
in Europe about these savages; travellers had not been slow
to recount their vivid, indeed their vividly shocking, experiences. Nor were the theorists about Nature slow in drawing
on the evidence to hand. Locke, for instance, appealed to
Mingrelians, Incas, and Tououpinambos as supplementary
proof that 'principles' could not be innate in man, as Europeans might assume, since they were not innate in the
savages of Transcaucasia and South America. This reasoning
diminished the empire of Nature, for if mental possessions
were acquired wholly by experience, they would differ as experience differed. And yet there was some reassurance if,
neglecting Locke's account of the source of knowledge, one
looked at the finished product, at the adult savage and his
behaviour. Acquired one way or another, the principles of
behaviour did not vary so much from European as to remain
wholly outside the European concept of Nature. This view
was put by Voltaire in a brilliant passage:

I . . . understand by Natural Religion, the Principles of Morality
common to human Kind. Sir ISAAC NEWTON admitted in reality no
innate Notions in us, neither Ideas, Sentiments, nor Principles. He
was perswaded with Mr. LOCKE, that all our Ideas come to us by our
Senses, according as our Senses exert themselves. But he believed that
God, having given the same Senses to all Men, there must result therefore the same Wants, the same Sentiments, and consequently the same
general Notions, which are throughout the World the Foundation of
Society. We constantly find that God gives to Bees and Ants, something
to make them live together, which he has not given to Wolves or
Falcons. It is certain, from all Men's living in Society, that there is in
their Nature a secret Tye, whereby God has pleased to attach them to
one another: It is also very certain, that if, at a particular Age, the Ideas,
which come by the same Senses to Men whose Organs are the same,
were not to give them, by Degrees, the same Principles necessary for
every Society, these Societies could not subsist. This then is the Reason
why from *Siam* to *Mexico*, Truth, Gratitude, Friendship, &c. are
esteemed.

I have always been surprized that the great Mr. LOCKE, in the Beginning of his Treatise on *Human Understanding*, where he so well con-
futes the Notion of innate Ideas, should also have advanced that there
is no Notion of Good and Evil common to all Mankind. I believe he

is there fallen into a great mistake, from building his Opinion on the
Accounts of Travellers; who relate, that in certain Countries it is the
Custom to eat Children, and even to eat the Mothers when they become past Child-bearing; that in others, they honour with the Title
of Saints, certain Enthusiasts, who make use of She-Asses instead of
Women. But should not such a Man as Mr. LOCKE have suspected
these Travellers? Nothing is more common amongst them than to see
Things badly, to give a bad Account of what they have seen, to take
that (in a Nation whose Language they do not understand) for a Law
itself, which is only an Abuse of the Law; and lastly, to make a Judgment of the Manners of a whole Péople from some particular Fact,
the Circumstances of which they are unacquainted with.

If a *Persian* was to pass thro' *Lisbon, Madrid,* or *Goa,* on the Day
of an *Auto da Fé,* he would think, not without some Appearance of
Reason, that the Christians sacrifice Men to God: If he reads the
Almanacks which are dispersed among the common People throughout all *Europe,* he would think that we ascribed every Thing to the
Influence of the Moon; whereas at the same Time, so far from believing
so, we laugh at it. Thus, if a Traveller tells me, for Example, that
the Savages eat their own Parents out of Piety: In the first Place he
must give me leave to say that the Fact is very dubious; and secondly,
supposing it is true, far from destroying the Idea of the Respect due
to Parents, it is probably a barbarous Way of shewing a Tenderness
towards them, an horrible Abuse of the Law of Nature. For certainly
the Savage kills his Father and Mother out of Duty only, to deliver
them either from the Troubles of old Age, or the Fury of the Enemy:
And if after that he makes his own Body their Tomb, instead of
leaving them to be devoured by the Conquerors, this Custom, fright-
ful as it is to the Imagination, nevertheless necessarily arises from
the Goodness of his Heart. Natural Religion consists in nothing
more than this Principle, which is known throughout all the World,
'*Do as thou wouldst be done by*'. Now the Barbarian, who slays his
Father to save him from his Enemy, and who entombs him within
himself for Fear his Enemy should become his Tomb, wishes his own
Son may use him so in the like Case. This Law of treating one's
Neighbour. like one's self, Naturally flows from even the grossest
Notions of Things, and sooner or later enters into every Man's Heart:
For all having the same Reason implanted there, it must sooner or
later produce the same Fruits; and it does indeed produce so much the
same, that in every Society, that which is thought useful to that
Society is called by the Name of Virtue.

If there can be found a Nation, or only a Company of ten Persons
on Earth, where what is conducive to the Good of the Community is

not esteemed, I will agree that there is no Natural Rule. Undoubtedly this Rule varies *ad infinitum*, but must we then conclude it does not exist? The Substance of it receives different Forms throughout, but yet throughout retains its Nature.[1]

In this passage Voltaire is working over the first chapters of the *Essay concerning Human Understanding*, and drawing conclusions that struck some men as more acceptable—we infer this because of the use made by Montesquieu and Goldsmith, to name only the great, of the instance of the Persian visiting Europe and drawing his comically false conclusions. In any event what mattered most to the theorists about Nature was the evidence gathered from human nature near home. Occasionally we find cautious expressions like 'human nature in our part of the world'—though that particular instance is the less striking since it comes in what purports to be a travel-book;[2] and Imlac's observation:

> When I compared these men [of 'the northern and western nations of Europe'] with the natives of our own kingdom, and those that surround us, they appeared almost another order of beings.[3]

Usually, however, men were content to think only of their own first-hand evidence from life, and from books about Europe, as we found Johnson, Boswell, and the rest doing. If they called in matter from farther afield, it was usually for the sake of corroborating their own discoveries at home. A modern anthropologist, no doubt, would find in their understanding and use of travellers' tales much that comes under Ker's terms 'sophistry and fallacy'. The eighteenth-century cult of the Noble Savage shows how nicely what was half-known could be made to fit into European thought. When Pope felt the need of an illustration of the way man

> Rests and expatiates in a life to come,

and to encourage only a trembling hope in that direction, he was pleased to draw it from 'the poor [American] Indian':

> . . . simple nature to his hope has giv'n,
> Behind the cloud-topt hill, an humbler heav'n;

[1] *La Métaphysique de Neuton, ou parallèle des sentimens de Neuton et de Leibnitz* (1740), trans. David Eskine Baker as *Metaphysics of Sir Isaac Newton* . . . (1747), pp. 30 ff.
[2] *Gulliver's Travels*, pt. iv, chap. iv.   [3] *Rasselas*, chap. xi.

Some safer world in depth of woods embrac'd,
Some happier island in the watry waste,
Where slaves once more their native land behold,
No fiends torment, no Christians thirst for gold:
To Be, contents his natural desire,
He asks no Angel's wing, no Seraph's fire;
But thinks, admitted to that equal sky,
His faithful dog shall bear him company.[1]

And Gray was pleased to show poetry as an active human thing not only in Greece and Italy but over the world's surface:

In climes beyond the solar road,
Where shaggy forms o'er ice-built mountains roam,
The Muse has broke the twilight-gloom
To chear the shiv'ring Native's dull abode.
And oft, beneath the od'rous shade
Of Chili's boundless forests laid,
She deigns to hear the savage Youth repeat
In loose numbers wildly sweet
Their feather-cinctured Chiefs, and dusky Loves.
Her track, where'er the Goddess roves,
Glory pursue, and generous Shame,
Th' unconquerable Mind, and Freedom's holy flame.[2]

To this Gray appended the note:

Extensive influence of poetic Genius over the remotest and most uncivilized nations: its connection with liberty, and the virtues that Naturally attend on it. [See the Erse, Norwegian, and Welch Fragments, the Lapland and American songs.]

I have taken no pains to test the soundness of Pope and Gray in passages such as this. The thing to note is that in the eighteenth century there was much interest in finding what was common to all men, finding it or creating it. Even though the sceptics, encouraged by Montaigne, were busy showing how greatly men differed even in Europe, let alone farther afield in space and time, the effect for most people was an increased sense of how men tallied.

---

[1] *Essay on Man*, i. 103 ff.
[2] 'The Progress of Poesy', ll. 54 ff.

3

The concept Nature had had a long history in expository prose. Cicero, to go no farther back, referred to it often: he had, for instance, equated *lex naturae* with 'the universally accepted',

and the Roman jurists had similarly identified *jus naturale* with *jus gentium*—with those principles of right *quae apud omnes gentes peraeque servantur, divina quadam providentia constituta, semper firma atque immutabilia permanent*;[1]

in the fifth century it had been invoked by St. Vincent of Lerins as one of the 'notes' distinguishing Catholic truth from heresy: it was he who used the defining words 'quod ubique, quod semper, quod ab omnibus': the word 'Catholic' itself embodied half the concept of Nature, the other half, the *semper*, coming into being as time passed: Dryden's 'milk-white hind' was both 'immortal and unchanged'.[2]

The history of Nature as a concept of literary criticism had also been long. Aristotle's *Art of Poetry* is founded on it, poetry being an imitation, and the love of imitation being general among men. To follow Nature was counselled by Quintilian when dealing with the need of the orator to make his descriptions effective:

we shall secure the vividness we seek, if only our descriptions give the impressions of truth. . . . Fix your eyes on Nature and follow her. All eloquence is concerned with the activities of life, while every man applies to himself what he hears from others, and the mind is always readiest to accept what it recognises to be true to Nature.[3]

Longinus made Nature the test of the sublime:

You may take it that those are beautiful and genuine effects of sublimity which please always, and please all. For when men of different habits, lives, ambitions, ages, all take one and the same view about the

---

[1] See A. O. Lovejoy, *The Great Chain of Being*, 1936, pp. 289 f. For an account of the origin of the sense of Natural law and of the Stoical ideal of living 'according to nature', see H. S. Maine, *Ancient Law*, ed. 1866, pp. 53 ff.

[2] *The Hind and the Panther*, i. 1. It was in the nineteenth century that Catholic dogma was seen to have undergone striking changes, but Newman's explanation of them according to a sort of biological 'development' occupies a book that paid great homage to the idea of static Nature.

[3] *Institutio Oratoria*, VIII. iii. 70 f. (Loeb trans.).

same writings, the verdict and pronouncement of such dissimilar individuals give a powerful assurance, beyond all gainsaying, in favour
of that which they admire.[1]

In English criticism it was invoked by Hamlet when he described the players as 'hold[ing] up as 'twere the mirror to
Nature; [and] show[ing] Virtue her own feature, Scorn her
own image':[2] Virtue and Scorn, being personified, are generalized, and the words 'her own' cut out the accidental. It was
the main prop of Daniel for his noble defence of rime; he
used it first, as Aristotle had, to justify the rhythm of verse;
then to justify rime itself, which is represented as called for
by man, in Europe, when something was found lacking in
the metres of classical Latin:

> *Ill customes are to be left*, I graunt it: but I see not howe that can be
> taken for an ill custome, which Nature hath . . . ratified, all nations
> receiued, time so long confirmed.[3]

The contribution of Dryden and Milton to the debate on
rime I have already referred to.[4] It was on Nature that, half-
way through the seventeenth century, Davenant and Hobbes
grounded the heroic poem—there is a clear echo of Hamlet's
words: the

> Heroick Poem . . . in a perfect glass of Nature gives us a familiar and
> easie view of our selves;[5]

for Davenant, again, 'the noble Quarry' of the Muse 'is men';[6]
for Hobbes

> That which [an epic poet] hath of his own is nothing but experience
> and knowledge of nature, and specially humane Nature . . .[7]

—'hath of his own': that is why Pope called the study of man
by men a study that was 'proper' to them; by that time Le
Bossu had made the same point in his remarks on the epic:

> *Man* being the chief and the most noble of all the Effects which
> God produc'd, and nothing being so proper, nor more useful to *Poets*
> than this Subject . . . .[8]

---

[1] *Longinus on the Sublime*, trans. A. O. Prickard, Oxford, 1906, chap. vii.
[2] III. ii. 26 f.
[3] *Poems and A Defence of Ryme*, ed. A. C. Sprague, ed. 1950, p. 134.
[4] See above, p. 3.   [5] Spingarn, ii. 1.   [6] Id. ii. 3.   [7] Id. ii. 62.
[8] *Monsieur Bossu's Treatise of the Epick Poem*, trans. W. J., 1695, p. 3.

When Milton aspired to write a poem that 'aftertimes' would
'not willingly let . . . die',[1] he was invoking the universal and
the permanent. Reference to Nature is frequent in Dennis's
criticism.

It was the constant praise of Shakespeare that he was, after
Homer, the great poet of Nature. Speaking of Homer, a
minor writer of Pope's day praised him, not without pleo-
nasm, on the ground that readers who

> Search thro' his vast and comprehensive Mind . . .
> Know Nature, and themselves, and all Mankind.[2]

'Comprehensive' had been Dryden's word for the soul of
Shakespeare,[3] as it was to be Wordsworth's of the poet.[4] If
the souls of Homer and Shakespeare were 'comprehensive', it
was because the length and breadth of Nature had met their
match in them. No critic of Shakespeare was more attentive
on this score than Johnson. In the preface to his edition he
rounded up the praise in a paragraph that stands like a
monument:

> *Shakespeare* is above all writers, at least above all modern writers,
> the poet of Nature; the poet that holds up to his readers a faithful
> mirrour of manners and of life. His characters are not modified by the
> customs of particular places, unpractised by the rest of the world; by
> the peculiarities of studies or professions, which can operate but upon
> small numbers; or by the accidents of transient fashions or temporary
> opinions: they are the genuine progeny of common humanity, such as
> the world will always supply, and observation will always find. His
> persons act and speak by the influence of those general passions and
> principles by which all minds are agitated, and the whole system of life
> is continued in motion. In the writings of other poets a character is too
> often an individual: in those of *Shakespeare* it is commonly a species.[5]

And in the notes to that edition he worked it out in particular.
The Natural strokes that he was constantly on the watch for
he found in plenty. So closely does he attend that he can
reconcile as Natural the opposite effects of one passion:

> In *Much Ado about Nothing*, [*Leonato*], the father of *Hero*, depressed
> by her disgrace, declares himself so subdued by grief that *a thread may*

---

[1] *The reason of Church-Government urg'd against Prelaty*, ii, para. 1 *ad fin.*
[2] Bezaleel Morrice, *An Epistle to Mr. Welsted*, 1721, p. 22.
[3] *Essays*, i. 79.   [4] See below, p. 161.   [5] Preface, para. 8.

lead him. How is it that grief in *Leonato* and lady *Constance*, produces effects directly opposite, and yet both agreeable to Nature?

And his explanation, as subtle as it is sound, is that

Sorrow softens the mind while it is yet warmed by hope, but hardens it when it is congealed by despair. Distress, while there remains any prospect of relief, is weak and flexible, but when no succour remains, is fearless and stubborn; angry alike at those that injure, and at those that do not help; careless to please where nothing can be gained, and fearless to offend when there is nothing further to be dreaded.

Triumphantly he adds:

Such was this writer's knowledge of the passions [i.e. emotions].[1]

It was Johnson who used the term 'the common reader',[2] but Pope had already lighted on the term and the distinction it implies. In a letter of 1 November 1729 he spoke of Mallet's play *Eurydice*, which he was trying to get played at Drury Lane:

I think any common Reader judges [poetic drama], of the most material part, as well as the most Learned, that is, of the Moving the Passions.[3]

Pope was denied the pleasure of reading most of the work of Johnson—except for the pleasure of admiring *London* in 1738.

The concept of Nature is a useful one for a critic. It is surely permanently true that a writer cannot dispense with Nature as material, and as guide to its use, since his writing addresses itself to as many readers as can be induced to gather round; and it is surely also true that minor literature is often minor because the Nature in it is weak or shallow or unredeemed from commonplaceness—a distinction I hope to make clearer in a later chapter.[4] The special interest of Nature to students of English literature is that, especially in the eighteenth century, great and lesser literature was produced in conscious relation to it. In other ages, including our own, the relation, though more unconscious, is still, I think, strong. It is never wholly unconscious—in all ages, people who speak of writing that has soundness, use terms of praise that

---

[1] Johnson's *Shakespeare*, note on *King John*, III. i. 7 f.
[2] *Lives of the Poets*, iii. 441.   [3] *Correspondence*, iii. 66.   [4] See below, p. 192.

are either identical with those of the eighteenth century or can be readily translated into them. 'Clever enough but wants Nature' was Tennyson's criticism of much of the dramatic work of his time;[1] and Thackeray exclaimed ironically of the silly plot of Mrs. Trollope's *Vicar of Wrexhill*: 'Here is Nature and reality!'[2] In Arnold's famous Preface of 1853 the term 'poetical' is allowed only for those well-constructed narrative poems which have their action firmly grounded in 'the great primary human affections'. Though little use is made of the term—to take another instance—in the seven volumes of the *George Eliot Letters*,[3] how often is the thing invoked, how often do George Eliot and John Blackwood, her well-judging publisher, say the eighteenth-century thing in their own nineteenth-century terms. In practice, we know when Nature is absent from a piece of literature, or when its claims are flouted. Some authors satisfy its demands as far as their subject-matter goes, and flout it in their expression. Donne's 'Valediction forbidding mourning' takes a Natural matter, lovers saying goodbye before a long separation, and expresses it both Naturally (in the former part of the poem) and un-Naturally (in the latter part, which makes use of the famous or notorious image of the compasses). Johnson laughed at the compasses, which was a pity because they led him to overlook the Nature they are expressing.[4] He did not always see that an idiosyncracy, or even a fashionable wildness, in the expression can be carried, even triumphantly, by a Natural sense—a sense of the sort that readers, innumerable and spread over the centuries, are willing or avid to receive. As we read Donne's poem we become confident that the author is one whose 'touch of Nature' makes us 'kin' to him, and by the time we reach the compasses we know that he will not forget us even though, in the midst of his poem, he is changing the manner of his expression. We do not feel so comfortable when we read a poem of Cleveland's. His idiosyncrasy of expression is wilder than Donne's. It is so wild that we have no patience to search for any Nature the expression may be hiding. Again, some authors have an ex-

---

1 Hallam Tennyson, *Memoir*, 1897, ii. 174.
2 *Stray Papers*, ed. 'Lewis Melville', 1901, p. 284.
3 ed. G. S. Haight, 1954–6.   4 *Lives of the Poets*, i. 34.

pression that may be called Natural, but lack a Natural meaning for it to carry: for instance, Keats's line in the 'Ode to a
Nightingale':

> Now more than ever seems it rich to die.

There is nothing in the wording of this 'death wish' to offend
the 'common reader', who is the repository of Nature; but
he cannot swallow what it is saying. Keats is not there saying something, though about death, that comes home to an
ordinary human being: we feel that his notion of richness at
the point of death slights what is deepest in us, treating
almost as pretty something that is fearful: to him who has
seen death, or has imagined his own, that line can never be
moving; we are not convinced that any man—not even
a poet stricken as we know Keats to have been—could have
felt so. In those same letters, George Eliot is prompted to
a remark by Lytton's last book, finished just before his
death:

> what a blessed lot it is to die on just finishing a book, if it could be a
> good one—I mean, it is blessed only to quit activity when one quits
> life.[1]

Her thought is poorly expressed in the hurry of letter-writing,
but in its general form—when it expands from being about
a book to being about work—it stands in a closer relation to
men than that line of Keats. As does this passage from a late
letter of Charles Reade:

> The time is certainly come when I ought not to write foolish, or
> wicked, or frivolous things for the public; but should I die in the middle
> of a sentence warning the good not to be uncharitable, the wicked not
> to despair, then, methinks, I should die well—better perhaps than if
> I died repeating prayers like a parrot in St. Paul's Church.[2]

Or this from a letter of Pope:

> When a smart fit of sickness tells me this scurvy tenement of my
> body will fall in a little time, I am e'en as unconcern'd as was that
> honest *Hibernian*, who being in bed in a great storm some years ago,
> and told the house would tumble over his head, made answer, What
> care I for the house? I am only a lodger. I fancy 'tis the best time to
> die when one is in the best humour.[3]

---

[1] *The George Eliot Letters*, 1954–6, v. 381.
[2] Malcolm Elwin, *Charles Reade*, 1931, p. 327.   [3] *Correspondence*, i. 148.

When, like Keats, Pope imagined a 'rich' death, he did so only as part of a fantasy:

> The bliss of Man (could Pride that blessing find)
> Is not to act or think beyond mankind;
> No pow'rs of body or of soul to share,
> But what his nature and his state can bear.
> Why has not Man a microscopic eye?
> For this plain reason, Man is not a Fly.
> Say what the use, were finer optics giv'n,
> T' inspect a mite, not comprehend the heav'n?
> Or touch, if tremblingly alive all o'er,
> To smart and agonize at ev'ry pore?
> Or quick effluvia darting thro' the brain,
> Die of a rose in aromatic pain?
> If nature thunder'd in his op'ning ears,
> And stunn'd him with the music of the spheres,
> How would he wish that Heav'n had left him still
> The whisp'ring Zephyr, and the purling rill?
> Who finds not Providence all good and wise,
> Alike in what it gives, and what denies?[1]

One of the things heaven denies us is a 'rich' death, and to 'die of a rose' is the experience only of a hypothetical human being with a physical constitution quite unlike our own. That such a being is an object of ridicule is implied in the very expression: 'die of a rose' is a comic variant of the idiom (so odd when we come to look at it) 'die of a wound', 'die of a fever'.

Standing at the outset of his career as a writer, Pope felt he had overwhelming encouragement to counsel the critic, the poet, the reader, and whoever cared to listen, to 'follow Nature', and to start doing so from the outset:

> First follow Nature, and your judgment frame
> By her just standard, which is still the same:
> Unerring NATURE still divinely bright,
> One clear, unchang'd, and universal light.[2]

And soon after the close of his career came the praise of Voltaire to show how fully he had succeeded in his aim:

---

[1] *Essay on Man,* i. 189 ff.
[2] *Essay on Criticism,* ll. 68 ff.

D'un esprit plus hardi,[1] d'un pas plus assuré,
Il porta le flambeau dans l'abîme de l'être;
Et l'homme avec lui seul apprit à se connaître . . .
L'art de vers est, dans Pope, utile au genre humain.[2]

The poet of Nature 'strikes home, where we all can measure the blow'.[3]

[1] *sc.* than Horace and Boileau.
[2] 'Exorde' to *Poème sur la loi naturelle* (1752).
[3] F. T. Palgrave, *Essays on Art*, 1865, p. 172.

II

MAN AND THE OTHER CREATURES

THE attempt to come to see what was common to all men led in the eighteenth century, as in earlier ages, to the quasi-scientific search for a differentia marking off man from his neighbours inferior and superior on the Scale of Being. These neighbours and the creatures who occupied the rungs stretching in both directions farther and farther away from man did not offer a like solid material for investigation. Accordingly animals and insects, apes and 'the green myriads in the peopled grass',[1] were explored more earnestly than the angelic creatures occupying the rungs higher than man. Some exploration Pope did make in that celestial direction:

> Superior beings, when of late they saw
> A mortal Man unfold all Nature's law,
> Admir'd such wisdom in an earthly shape,
> And shew'd a NEWTON as we shew an Ape.[2]

But when an even more intrepid philosopher went farther along the same lines, 'decid[ing] too easily upon questions out of the reach of human determination', he was in danger of what Soame Jenyns got from Johnson:

He imagines that as we have not only animals for food, but choose some for our diversion, the same privilege may be allowed to some beings above us, *who may deceive, torment, or destroy us for the ends only of their own pleasure or utility.* This he again finds impossible to be conceived, *but that impossibility lessens not the probability of the conjecture, which by analogy is so strongly confirmed.*

I cannot resist the temptation of contemplating this analogy which I think he might have carried further very much to the advantage of his argument. He might have shewn that these *hunters whose game is man* have many sports analogous to our own. As we drown whelps and kittens, they amuse themselves now and then with sinking a ship, and stand round the fields of Blenheim or the walls of Prague, as we encircle

---

[1] *Essay on Man*, i. 210.   [2] Id. ii. 31 ff.

a cock-pit. As we shoot a bird flying, they take a man in the midst of his business or pleasure, and knock him down with an apoplexy. Some of them, perhaps, are virtuosi, and delight in the operations of an asthma, as a human philosopher in the effects of the air pump. To swell a man with a tympany is as good sport as to blow a frog. Many a merry bout have these frolic beings at the vicissitudes of an ague, and good sport it is to see a man tumble with an epilepsy, and revive and tumble again, and all this he knows not why. As they are wiser and more powerful than we, they have more exquisite diversions, for we have no way of procuring any sport so brisk and so lasting as the paroxysms of the gout and stone which undoubtedly must make high mirth, especially if the play be a little diversified with the blunders and puzzles of the blind and deaf. We know not how far their sphere of observation may extend. Perhaps now and then a merry being may place himself in such a situation as to enjoy at once all the varieties of an epidemical disease, or amuse his leisure with the tossings and contortions of every possible pain exhibited together.[1]

And so on, for Johnson is enjoying himself.

There was less of this 'sport[ing] in the wide regions of possibility'[2] when men investigated the creatures as they stretched in the other direction. Indeed by the eighteenth century the evidence that prompted the theory of evolution had already prompted much curiosity and some thought. The process of inquiry, which began at least as early as the sixteenth century when travellers reported of beasts that were strangely like men, reached its most lucid expression much later, in the first of Huxley's three lectures on the *Evidence as to Man's Place in Nature*. Already Pope and his fellows knew enough of the apes to be prepared to receive Huxley's statement:

The question of questions for mankind—the problem which under-lies all others, and is more deeply interesting than any other—is the ascertainment of the place which Man occupies in nature and of his relations to the universe of things.[3]

They were not prepared for the claims Huxley set on his statement, for to Pope and his fellows this question of questions would have faced both ways, to the world of things

---

[1] 'Review of [Soame Jenyns's] "Free Enquiry into the Nature and Origin of Evil",' paras. 1, 57 f. (text of Reynard Library ed., pp. 351, 365 f.).

[2] Johnson's *Lives of the Poets*, i. 177 f.; cf. the quotation from Hobbes below, p. 205.   [3] Op. cit., 1863, p. 57.

(animals, plants, and the rest) and to the world supernatural. But though they were not ready to deny, as Huxley was, the existence of angels, they did not fail to meditate on the beasts, or on descriptions of them, if only to find the decisive fool-proof test determining the difference, which for them was insuperable, between the beasts and man. Here is Boswell, for instance, airing his considerations on this matter in conversation with Burke:

I told [Burke], I had found out a perfect definition of human nature, as distinguished from the animal. An ancient philosopher said, Man was 'a two-legged animal without feathers', upon which his rival Sage had a Cock plucked bare, and set him down in the school before all the disciples, as a 'Philosophick Man'. Dr. Franklin said, Man was a 'tool-making animal', which is very well; for no animal but man makes a thing, by means of which he can make another thing. But this applies to very few of the species. My definition of *Man* is, 'a Cooking Animal'. The beasts have memory, judgment, and all the faculties and passions of our mind, in a certain degree; but no beast is a cook. The trick of the monkey using the cat's paw to roast a chestnut, is only a piece of shrewd malice in that *turpissima bestia*, which humbles us so sadly by its similarity to us. Man alone can dress a good dish; and every man whatever is more or less a cook, in seasoning what he himself eats.— Your definition is good, said Mr. Burke, and I now see the full force of the common proverb, 'There is *reason* in roasting of eggs'.[1]

Burke administers a snub, which perhaps was lost on Boswell in the pounce of the wit (we of the twentieth century have lost the wit, having lost the proverb).[2] To Burke, this was all so much hovering over the unimportant.

[1] Boswell's *Life*, v. 33, n. 3. Boswell is using Johnson's argument against Franklin's definition (see iii. 245). That definition has recently been again challenged: 'Man ... is not the only animal that uses tools. There is for example a bird which uses a cactus thorn to pick insects out of holes, not to mention spiders with their webs' (J. B. S. Haldane, *Everything has a History*, 1951, p. 159). The process of finding a definition is still continuing: 'He is not the only animal which builds. Most birds do so. Many animals store food, and some ants domesticate other insects. But he is the only animal which deliberately shapes tools, and the only one which uses fire' (ibid.). Goethe made the differentia to rest on man's fore-arm and hand, which permit him 'the most perfectly dainty and skillful movement' (Karl Viëtor, *Goethe the Thinker*, Cambridge, Mass., 1950, p. 136: cf. also ibid. p. 141).

[2] Dr. Hilda Hulme informs me that Ray's *Compleat Collection of English Proverbs*, 3rd ed. 1737, p. 150, explains 'reason' as meaning 'art': 'Est modus in rebus.' The art of roasting an egg lies in moving it about among the hot ashes so that it neither bursts nor cooks only on one side. Cf. *As You Like It*, III. ii. 36 f.: 'like an ill roasted egge, all on one side', and Pope's 'The Vulgar boil, the Learned roast an Egg' (*Imitations of Horace*, Ep. II. ii. 85). 'Est modus in rebus' is from Horace.

Usually it seemed so to Pope. But in *An Essay on Man* he committed himself, of necessity, to some of this quasi-scientific scaling: I have already quoted his lines in which angels exhibit Newton as men exhibit an ape. Here are others:

> What would this Man? Now upward will he soar,
> And little less than Angel, would be more;
> Now looking downwards, just as griev'd appears
> To want the strength of bulls, the fur of bears.[1]

or

> Less human genius than God gives an ape;[2]

or

> . . . Since Man from beast by Words is known.[3]

And there is this paragraph from another poem:

> Thou know'st how guiltless first I met thy flame,
> When Love approach'd me under Friendship's name;
> My fancy form'd thee of Angelick kind,
> Some emanation of th' all-beauteous Mind.
> Those smiling eyes, attemp'ring ev'ry ray,
> Shone sweetly lambent with celestial day:
> Guiltless I gaz'd; heav'n listen'd while you sung;
> And truths divine came mended from that tongue.
> From lips like those what precept fail'd to move?
> Too soon they taught me 'twas no sin to love.
> Back thro' the paths of pleasing sense I ran,
> Nor wish'd an Angel whom I lov'd a Man.
> Dim and remote the joys of saints I see,
> Nor envy them, that heav'n I lose for thee.[4]

This semi-scientific interest had one practical advantage in that it helped to collect man into a category, and, by limiting, to animate the inquiry as to his nature. For Pope, the main use of man's neighbours on the Scale lay in their means of comparison:

[1] *Essay on Man*, i. 173 ff.
[2] *Dunciad*, i. 282.
[3] Id. iv. 149.
[4] *Eloisa to Abelard*, ll. 59 ff. Line 69 may be expanded thus: 'At first I thought you an angel, but when you taught me that loving was no sin, I retreated from my misconception and ran back happily through those paths of pleasing sense that I had first traversed in the opposite direction.'

Plac'd on this isthmus of a middle state,
A being darkly wise, and rudely great:
With too much knowledge for the Sceptic side,
With too much weakness for the Stoic's pride,
He hangs between; in doubt to act, or rest,
In doubt to deem himself a God, or Beast;
In doubt his Mind or Body to prefer;
Born but to die, and reas'ning but to err;
Alike in ignorance, his reason such,
Whether he thinks too little, or too much:
Chaos of Thought and Passion, all confus'd;
Still by himself abus'd, or disabus'd;
Created half to rise, and half to fall;
Great lord of all things, yet a prey to all;
Sole judge of Truth, in endless Error hurl'd:
The glory, jest, and riddle of the world![1]

The passage has no rival in the literature of man. Even Hamlet's 'What a piece of work is a man! . . .', that rhapsodical flight that falls to lick the 'quintessence of dust'[2]— even this has not the fullness of Pope's account. Here are more of his attempts to see mankind whole and speak about it whole:

Man never Is, but always To be blest;[3]

To err is human . . .[4]

Virtuous and vicious ev'ry Man must be;[5]

It may be reason, but it is not man;[6]

Man? and *for ever?* Wretch! what wou'dst thou have?
Heir urges Heir, like Wave impelling Wave:
All vast Possessions (just the same the case
Whether you call them Villa, Park, or Chace)
Alas, my BATHURST! what will they avail?[7]

Men must be taught as if you taught them not;[8]

  Oh thoughtless Mortals! ever blind to Fate,
Too soon dejected, and too soon elate![9]

And men must walk at least before they dance.[10]

---

[1] *Essay on Man,* ii. 3 ff.   [2] II. ii. 315 ff.
[3] *Essay on Man,* i. 96 f.   [4] *Essay on Criticism,* l. 525.
[5] *Essay on Man,* ii. 231.
[6] *Moral Essays,* i ('Of the Knowledge and Characters of Men'), 36.
[7] *Imitations of Horace,* Ep. II. ii. 252 ff.   [8] *Essay on Criticism,* l. 574.
[9] *Rape of the Lock,* iii. 101 f.   [10] *Imitations of Horace,* Ep. I. i. 54.

When Pope writes of man he writes of him as an abstraction: he did not attempt to embody his concept in a personage. That course is possible in certain sorts of literature. Narrative, when it is not giving a 'life-like' account of human beings, when for the occasion it is allegory, can display abstract man in the guise of an individual. On these occasions the symbolic individual stands for one of two things—man normal or man 'perfect' (that is, as perfect as possible). Normal man is personified in the Everyman who stands at the centre of the morality play that bears his name, and also in Gulliver.[1] 'Perfect man' was, on one occasion, the subject of a dispute between Boswell and Mrs. Thrale, a dispute

whether Shakespeare or Milton had drawn the most admirable picture of a man. I was for Shakespeare; Mrs. Thrale for Milton; and after a fair hearing, Johnson decided for my opinion.[2]

It may be that Johnson thought Milton's Adam too remote from man as Johnson knew him. According to the chronology worked out by Ussher in the seventeenth century, Adam had existed some 6,000 years ago, utterly remote and sublime. Because of which,

The plan of *Paradise Lost* has this inconvenience, that it comprises neither human actions nor human manners. The man and woman who act and suffer are in a state which no other man or woman can ever know. The reader finds no transaction in which he can be engaged, beholds no condition in which he can by any effort of imagination place himself; he has, therefore, little Natural curiosity or sympathy.[3]

When we read Milton's account of the father of mankind, we do not find ourselves seeking for likenesses between him and ourselves as we do when we read Pope's account of man. The personages that Johnson had in mind when preferring Shakespeare's 'perfect' men were, no doubt, Prospero (what of him was not magician), the elder Hamlet, Duncan, and Horatio. If these are the most perfect men in Shakespeare, one of them exists in a play that is partly symbolic, and the rest at the edge of the play's action. Things are said about the elder

---

[1] Swift introduces Gulliver as at the middle point of society, England, the family, and he goes to a middling college: 'My father had a small estate in Nottinghamshire; I was the third of five sons. He sent me to Emmanuel College in Cambridge . . . .'
[2] Boswell's *Life of Johnson*, iv. 72 f.   [3] Johnson's *Lives of the Poets*, i. 181.

Hamlet, Duncan, and Horatio which would not have been received as wholly true if we had seen more of these personages: Shakespeare would have pared down their perfection if he had shown them more at length. They are perfect only so long as they can furnish matter for rhetoric. In other words, literature abhors the perfect man as anything beyond an object of contemplation.

If Pope had found occasion to show a specimen of man at his best, his letters show that he fancied he knew where the model lay. Of Bolingbroke he speaks with infatuation:

> I have lately seen some writings of Lord B[olingbroke]'s, since he went to France. Nothing can depress his Genius: Whatever befals him, he will still be the greatest man in the world, either in his own time, or with posterity;[1]

on another occasion he describes him to Burlington:

> Mr. Kent could tell you how often I talk'd of you, & wished for you; even at a time when I wish for few or none, when I am almost constantly with the Greatest Man I know, ever knew, or shall know.[2]

Or, finally, to Warburton, who if chance serves will meet 'so great a Genius' at Bath:

> You never saw a *Man*, before (if I know what a Man is).[3]

Altogether, as he said in conversation with Spence:

> Lord Bolingbroke is something superior to any thing I have seen in human nature. You know I don't deal much in hyperboles: I quite think him what I say.[4]

The perfection of Bolingbroke was the more obvious to Pope in contrast to himself. Often it took Pope all his power to remain a specimen of man at his frailest: writing to Swift he notes that

> Infirmities have not quite unmann'd me. . . . When I am sick I lie down, when I am better I rise up;[5]

and towards the end of his life:

> Would to God I were like any other thing they call a Man. . . .[6]

---

[1] *Correspondence,* iv. 6.   [2] Id. iv. 153.   [3] Id. iv. 394.
[4] *Anecdotes,* p. 169.   [5] *Correspondence,* iii. 250.   [6] Id. iv. 293.

Letters and conversation, however, were one thing, and poetry another. Pope was not concerned as a poet with creatures so far beyond the norm as he believed Bolingbroke to be, with

> . . . creature[s] . . . too bright and good
> For human Nature's daily food.[1]

Bolingbroke does figure in the poems, but with head some-what diminished:

> Come then, my Friend, my Genius, come along,
> Oh master of the poet, and the song!
> And while the Muse now stoops, or now ascends,
> To Man's low passions, or their glorious ends,
> Teach me, like thee, in various nature wise,
> To fall with dignity, with temper rise . . .[2]

or here:

> You laugh, half Beau half Sloven if I stand,
> My Wig all powder, and all snuff my Band;
> You laugh, if Coat and Breeches strangely vary,
> White Gloves, and Linnen worthy Lady Mary!
> But when no Prelate's Lawn with Hair-shirt lin'd,
> Is half so incoherent as my Mind,
> When (each Opinion with the next at strife,
> One ebb and flow of follies all my Life)
> I plant, root up, I build, and then confound,
> Turn round to square, and square again to round;
> You never change one muscle of your face,
> You think this Madness but a common case,
> Nor once to Chanc'ry, nor to Hale apply;
> Yet hang your lip, to see a Seam awry!
> Careless how ill I with myself agree;
> Kind to my dress, my figure, not to Me.
> Is this my Guide, Philosopher, and Friend?
> This, He who loves me, and who ought to mend?
> Who ought to make me (what he can, or none,)
> That Man divine whom Wisdom calls her own,
> Great without Title, without Fortune bless'd,
> Rich ev'n when plunder'd, honour'd while oppress'd,
> Lov'd without youth, and follow'd without power,
> At home tho' exil'd, free, tho' in the Tower.

[1] Wordsworth, 'She was a phantom of delight . . .', ll. 17 f.
[2] *Essay on Man*, iv. 373 ff.

In short, that reas'ning, high, immortal Thing,
Just less than Jove, and much above a King,
Nay half in Heav'n—except (what's mighty odd)
A Fit of Vapours clouds this Demi-god.[1]

The superlative here exists only in the comparative of 'what
he can, or none', and Pope sees clearly how easily any greatness his friend will raise him to is at the mercy of physical
discomfort or pain, as at some degree or other it must be in
any man. And if the poems allow Bolingbroke to be 'All-
accomplish'd',[2] they also bring up a charge against '*S*[allu]*st*'
which Bolingbroke seems to have admitted as a charge against
himself:

> How much more safe, dear Countrymen! his State
> Who trades in Frigates of the second Rate?
> And yet some Care of *S*—*st* should be had,
> Nothing so mean for which he can't run mad;
> His Wit confirms him but a Slave the more,
> And makes a Princess whom he found a Whore.
> The Youth might save much Trouble and Expence,
> Were he a Dupe of only common Sense.
> But here's his point; A 'Wench (he cries) for me!
> 'I never touch a Dame of Quality.'[3]

Pope's concern with man led him to write one superb
paragraph and a few lines, some of which have been quoted
ever since by people who have not known them to be his. But
he owed to his thinking about the nature of man more than
the opportunities for these achievements. He owed to it a
standard for judging human character, a standard that he
consulted whatever he was writing.

---

[1] *Imitations of Horace*, Ep. I. i. 161 ff. The Twickenham ed. errs, I think, in
taking the last nine lines of this passage as a description of Bolingbroke: they are
in apposition to 'me', and describe Pope.

[2] *Imitations of Horace*, 'Epilogue to the Satires', dial. ii. 139.

[3] *Imitations of Horace*, Serm. I. ii. 61 ff. See annotations in Twickenham ed.
iv. 81.

III

MAN AND THE CALL TO 'LIVE WELL'

I

SOME of the quotations I have made from Pope show man in action. Pope had represented him as 'in doubt to act, or rest', but usually he acts, and usually rest itself is responsible non-action rather than sleep. 'Being' soon expresses itself in 'doing', and so brings into full light all the considerations of right and wrong.

Pope's concern with morality is constant. Even his translations and his edition of Shakespeare have their passages of it: in a letter of 1720 he is found planning an essay 'on the *Theology* and *Morality* of *Homer*',[1] and in his edition of Shakespeare's plays 'sentences' and moral passages are distinguished by means of a system of stars and commas.[2] This being so, the ten years' 'fate . . . to comment and translate'[3] was not unkindly even for the sort of poetry Pope most delighted in and sought to write. As for the rest of his poetry, it was as much about morals as could be managed.[4]

Scattered all through his poems (and the same can be said of his letters) are those passages studying man as he lives his life, which, despite the persistent currency of some of their phrases, strike each new reader as freshly minted. Here are a few of them. The first, an unusually quiet piece, from *Windsor Forest*:

> Happy the man . . .
> Who wand'ring thoughtful in the silent wood,
> Attends the duties of the wise and good,

---

[1] *Correspondence*, ii. 44.

[2] Pope 'likes sententiousness. He likes Macbeth to give expression to universal truths, to reflect on the worthlessness of life or on what we might hope of old age. . . . In *Hamlet* the only shining passages are sententious speeches, Polonious's advice to Laertes, and Claudius's soliloquy before he prays; of the three passages commended in *Othello*, one is "Who steals my purse steals trash" ' (John Butt, *Pope's Taste in Shakespeare*, The Shakespeare Association, 1936, pp. 9 f.). Cf. T. R. Lounsbury, *The First Editors of Shakespeare*, 1906, pp. 117 f.

[3] *Dunciad*, iii. 331 f.   [4] See Appendix I, pp. 247 ff., below.

> T'observe a mean, be to himself a friend,
> To follow Nature, and regard his end;
> Or looks on heav'n with more than mortal eyes,
> Bids his free soul expatiate in the skies,
> Amid her kindred stars familiar roam,
> Survey the region, and confess her home![1]

Or this brilliant paragraph from a verse letter to his friend
Martha Blount:

> Let the strict Life of graver Mortals be
> A long, exact, and serious Comedy,
> In ev'ry Scene some Moral let it teach,
> And, if it can, at once both Please and Preach:
> Let mine, an innocent gay Farce appear,
> And more Diverting still than Regular,
> Have Humour, Wit, a native Ease and Grace;
> Tho' not too strictly bound to Time and Place:
> Criticks in Wit, or Life, are hard to please,
> Few write to those, and none can live to these.[2]

Or this, the opening of his translation of one of Horace's
epistles:

> St John, whose love indulg'd my labours past,
> Matures my present, and shall bound my last!
> Why will you break the Sabbath of my days?
> Now sick alike of Envy and of Praise.
> Publick too long, ah let me hide my Age!
> See modest Cibber now has left the Stage:
> Our Gen'rals now, retir'd to their Estates,
> Hang their old Trophies o'er the Garden gates,
> In Life's cool evening satiate of applause,
> Nor fond of bleeding, ev'n in BRUNSWICK's cause.[3]

All these typical pieces of Pope's poetry concern themselves with the question of the good life. They differ widely
enough to show that the good life is a subject multifarious
enough for continued investigation. In the first poem,
living is shown as a matter of dying as well as living. Pope,

---

[1] ll. 235 ff. Wordsworth remembered this passage when writing 'To a Skylark':
    Type of the wise who soar, but never roam;
    True to the kindred points of Heaven and Home!
[2] 'Epistle to Miss Blount, with the Works of Voiture', ll. 21 ff.
[3] *Imitations of Horace*, Ep. I. i. 1 ff.

as I have said, seldom forgot the status of death among things Natural: even the *Rape of the Lock* prospectively lays the remaining tresses in the dust. In his letters, on the death of his father, he quotes the line:

> Sic mihi contingat vivere, sicque mori![1]

which becomes the line prompted by the same death in *An Epistle to Dr. Arbuthnot*:

> Oh grant me thus to live, and thus to die![2]

The second and third pieces, however, differ from the first in that they concern a part of the good life rather than the whole of it; they show the sort of holiday which the man who is trying to live well finds himself hankering for over moments more or less long. In the former of the two the twenty-four-year-old Pope, who is sending his friend Martha Blount a copy of a fashionable book of letters translated from the French, assumes a gaiety so beautifully thought out as to suggest the gaiety rather of a philosopher than a philanderer; we discern that Pope's place is inescapably among those 'graver mortals' he pretends to be scandalizing. In the latter he assumes a 'sabbath' seriousness: he is forty-nine (seven times seven),[3] and properly seeking a peace and a privacy to which only a chosen friend may be admitted. If this represents the good life, then it represents a stage of it, not, like the first piece, pretty well the whole of it.

---

[1] *Correspondence*, i. 450. I have not succeeded in discovering the source of this line.

[2] l. 404. Swift, writing to Pope on 29 Sept. 1725, had described Arbuthnot as a 'fit . . . man either to live or die' (*The Correspondence*, ed. F. Elrington Ball, 1910–14, iii. 278). At l. 262 of *An Epistle to Dr. Arbuthnot*, Pope had adapted the similar line of another poet, Denham, for his couplet:

> Oh let me live my own! and die so too!
> ('To live and die is all I have to do').

It is interesting to note that in his edition of Shakespeare he 'emended' the famous lines of *Macbeth* to read:

> And all our yesterdays have lighted fools
> The way to study death.

Cf. Gray's 'Elegy', ll. 83 f.:

> And many a holy text around she strews,
> That teach the rustic moralist to die.

[3] On the climacteric significance of seven in reckoning the years of human life, see Swift, *A Tale of a Tub*, p. 58.

Pope's answer to the question how to live may be stated simply. He saw man as placed by God (whom man could acknowledge but should not 'presume . . . to scan')[1] on the 'isthmus of a middle state',[2] a state of being made serious and, at times, awful by its short duration and its possible continuance in some form after death. On one side of the isthmus is the angel, on the other the beast. The study 'proper' to him is how to make the most of possibilities which, of necessity, are limited to the strictly human: he should seek to avoid the pride of trying to understand or mix with the angels: ·

> In Pride, in reas'ning Pride, our error lies;
> All quit their sphere, and rush into the skies.
> Pride still is aiming at the blest abodes,
> Men would be Angels . . .[3]

and equally he should seek to avoid joining the beasts, or falling lower:

> I am his Highness' Dog at *Kew*;
> Pray tell me Sir, whose Dog are you?[4]

or

> Still to his wench he crawls on knocking knees,
> And envies ev'ry sparrow that he sees.[5]

Man gets the best out of his life on the isthmus when he contrives a human happiness, 'our being's end and aim'.[6] This happiness is 'Virtue's prize',[7] and virtue mainly consists in the appreciation and practice of friendship[8] and benevolence. A man who is happy, and satisfied to be a man proper, chooses always the golden mean, achieving good sense—

> Good Sense, which only is the gift of Heav'n,
> And tho' no science, fairly worth the seven[9]

—and trying to establish its rule in every department of life, personal and social.

---

[1] *Essay on Man*, ii. 1. 'Scan'=pry into.   [2] Id. ii. 3.   [3] Id. i. 123 ff.
[4] 'Epigram. Engraved on the Collar of a *Dog* which I gave to his Royal Highness.'
[5] *Moral Essays*, i ('Of the Knowledge and Characters of Men'), 232 f.
[6] *Essay on Man*, iv. 1.   [7] Id. iv. 169.
[8] He describes his love for his mother as 'a Tye, which tho' it may be more tender, I do not think can be more strong than that of friendship' (*Correspondence*, ii. 166).   [9] See above, p. 6.

Such are the main lines of Pope's morality, and we have the weighty evidence of people as different as Joseph Warton,[1] Dugald Stewart,[2] Kant,[3] Byron,[4] Newman,[5] Ruskin,[6] and Leslie Stephen[7] that it is a sound morality.

[1] '. . . the French can boast of no author who has so much exhausted the science of morals, as POPE has in [the five *Moral Essays*]' (*Essay on the Genius and Writings of Pope*, ed. 1806, ii. 123).

[2] Mark Pattison in his edition of *An Essay on Man*, 1878, p. 11, writes:

'Dugald Stewart, in Lectures delivered in 1792–3, expresses the opinion of that age in speaking of the *Essay* as "the noblest specimen of philosophical poetry which our language affords; and which, with the exception of a very few passages, contains a valuable summary of all that human reason has been able hitherto to advance in justification of the moral government of God". (*Active and Moral Powers; Works*, 7. 133). This might seem a little overstated if it did not stand in close connection with some strictures on particular passages which the same judicious critic condemns as false in sentiment. Pope was also Kant's favourite poet . . . and was habitually quoted by him in his lectures.'

[3] See n. 2 above.

[4] Byron saw Pope as succeeding just where Lucretius failed:

'The depreciation of Pope is partly founded upon a false idea of the dignity of his order of poetry, to which he has partly contributed by the ingenious boast,

"That not in fancy's maze he wandered long,
But *stooped* to Truth, and moralized his song."

He should have written "rose to truth". In my mind, the highest of all poetry is ethical poetry, as the highest of all earthly objects must be moral truth. Religion does not make a part of my subject; it is something beyond human powers, and has failed in all human hands except Milton's and Dante's, and even Dante's powers are involved in his delineation of human passions, though in supernatural circumstances. What made Socrates the greatest of men? His moral truth—his ethics. What proved Jesus Christ the Son of God hardly less than his miracles? His moral precepts. And if ethics have made a philosopher the first of men, and have not been disdained as an adjunct to his Gospel by the Deity himself, are we to be told that ethical poetry, or didactic poetry, or by whatever name you term it, whose object is to make men better and wiser, is not the *very first order* of poetry . . .? It requires more mind, more wisdom, more power, than all the "forests" that were ever "walked for their description", and all the epics that ever were founded upon fields of battle. . . . If Lucretius had not been spoiled by the Epicurean system, we should have had a far superior poem to any now in Existence. As mere poetry, it is the first of Latin poems. What then has ruined it? His ethics. Pope has not this defect; his moral is as pure as his poetry is glorious.'

(*Letter to* [John Murray] . . . *1821* (*Letters and Journals*, v. 554 f.).) The allusion to forests and description refers to one of the questions at issue in the Pope controversy to which this *Letter* contributes, the question whether or not images drawn from external nature are superior for the purposes of poetry to those drawn from art. Byron misses some of the point of 'stooped': see below, p. 251, n. 2.

[5] In the lectures which Newman gave as Rector of the Catholic University of Dublin, he called Pope 'a rival to Shakespeare, if not in genius, at least in copiousness and variety', adding that he was 'a Catholic, though personally an unsatisfactory one'. Speaking to a Catholic audience, his verdict is that 'taking [Pope's] works

2

Two distinct charges have been brought agair
it is not a Christian scheme, and that when it tou
and happiness it ignores the human facts. With
charge goes another—that the poem culminates in a philosophical statement that is insufferably optimistic. The matter
of these charges exists in relation to Nature.

It is clear that if we want a scheme that is specifically Christian, we must go elsewhere: to Pascal's *Pensées* or to the parochial sermons of Newman. Pope was a Christian himself,
but he set out to be a moralist rather than a Christian moralist
—though his own religion was Catholic, it would scarcely
be gathered from the poems. He wished to present a moral
scheme which was acceptable in the eighteenth century, and
which one could imagine as acceptable, say, to Homer and
Virgil. To him a Christian colouring was too much a late
colouring. The Natural man would agree that he did not have
to wait for Christ to get a useful scheme of morality; which
Christ, coming not to destroy but to fulfil, Himself acknowledged in retaining the golden rule—'do as you would be
done by'—a rule which Pope retains in his own version of
the Pater Noster:

> That Mercy I to others show,
> That Mercy show to me.[1]

Where Christianity did improve ordinary human morality
was mainly in its having superior powers for making it
effective: if—to state the case at its lowest—men come to believe in accurate rewards and punishments after death, the
incentive to live well is sharpened. Pope did not avail himself

as a whole, we may surely acquit them of being dangerous to the reader, whether on
the score of morals or of faith' (*Lectures and Essays on University Subjects*, 1859, p. 99).

[6] For Ruskin's several commendations, see index (s.v. 'Pope') to *Works*, ed. Cook
and Wedderburn, 1903–12.

[7] '. . . if we may take Pope's most vigorous expressions as an indication of his
strongest convictions, and check their conclusions by his personal history and by
the general tendency of his writings, we might succeed in putting together something like a satisfactory statement of the moral system which he expressed forcibly
because he believed in it sincerely' ('Pope as a Moralist', in *The Cornhill Magazine*,
xxviii, July–Dec. 1873, p. 591, reprinted in *Hours in a Library* [first series], 1874,
pp. 134 f.). The soundness of that system he accepts without question.

[1] 'The Universal Prayer. Deo Opt. Max.', ll. 39 f. Cf. Voltaire, p. 16, above.

of the Christian means of persuasion. He trusted to the inter-
estingness of his total scheme—no one can fail to be interested in *An Essay on Man*, which, even to ourselves, I think,
is the most gloriously, because as it were most publicly,
exciting of his works: at least, Pope could count on being
read. He also trusted to the reasonableness of the moral
scheme he propounded. Conclusions and statements like the
following commended themselves to men, and still do:

Hope humbly then . . .[1]

All Nature is but Art, unknown to thee;[2]

Love, Hope, and Joy, fair pleasure's smiling train,
Hate, Fear, and Grief, the family of pain;
These mix'd with art, and to due bounds confin'd,
Make and maintain the balance of the mind:
The lights and shades, whose well accorded strife
Gives all the strength and colour of our life.[3]

Lust, thro' some certain strainers well refin'd,
Is gentle love, and charms all womankind:[4]

and so on *ad lib*. However dubious a reader may be over the
logic of certain passages in the poem—or rather over the
choice and reading of the matter from which the logic draws
a conclusion—he can find no fault with most of the statements of the poem or with the moral recommendations which
they state or imply. Pope also trusted in the worth and
quality of the poetry. Poetry has a power over us of some
sort, and while the poetry of the poem as a whole towers in
a splendour that is massive and yet exact and intricate, the
poetry devoted to commending virtue glows with a tenderness that recalls the lights in a picture of Gainsborough's:

What nothing earthly gives, or can destroy,
The soul's calm sun-shine, and the heart-felt joy,
Is Virtue's prize . . .[5]

Let humble ALLEN, with an aukward Shame,
Do good by stealth, and blush to find it Fame.
Virtue may chuse the high or low Degree,
'Tis just alike to Virtue, and to me;
Dwell in a Monk, or light upon a King,
She's still the same, belov'd, contented thing.[6]

[1] i. 91.   [2] ii. 289.   [3] ii. 117 ff.   [4] ii. 189 f.   [5] iv. 167 ff.
[6] *Imitations of Horace*, 'Epilogue to the Satires', dial. i. 135 ff.

Court-virtues bear, like Gems, the highest rate,
Born where Heav'n's influence scarce can penetrate:
In life's low vale, the soil the virtues like,
They please as Beauties, here as Wonders strike.[1]

Ordinary men, and Christians with them, must accept Pope's morality, even if they wish to make additions to it. If they do not wish to make additions, they need not forfeit the chance of being good men, for we have the word of Newman, whom I take as impeccably an authority on these matters, that the goodness of a non-Christian can attain to a highly respectable level. This is one of several statements of a comparison that often interested Newman:

I may say the Church aims at three special virtues, as reconciling and uniting the soul to its Maker:—faith, purity, and charity; for two of which the world cares little or nothing. The world, on the other hand, puts in the foremost place, in some states of society, certain heroic qualities; in others certain virtues of a political or mercantile character. In ruder ages, it is personal courage, strength of purpose, magnanimity; in more civilized, honesty, fairness, honour, truth, and benevolence:— virtues, all of which, of course, the teaching of the Church comprehends, all of which she expects in their degree in all her consistent children, and all of which she enacts in their fulness in her saints; but which, after all, most beautiful as they are, admit of being the fruit of nature as well as of grace; which do not necessarily imply grace at all: which do not reach so far as to sanctify, or unite the soul by any supernatural process to the source of supernatural perfection and supernatural blessedness.[2]

---

[1] *Moral Essays*, i ('Of the Knowledge and Characters of Men'), 93 ff. Stopford A. Brooke wrote as follows (*Theology in the English Poets*, Everyman Library ed., p. 3):
    'The *Essay on Man* is the preservation in exquisite steel-work of the speculations of Leibnitz and Bolingbroke. It is true the devoutness which belonged to Pope's nature modified the coldness of his philosophy, and there are lines in the *Essay on Man* which, in their temperate but lofty speech concerning charity, are healthier than the whole of Cowper's hymns, while the *Universal Prayer* is of that noble tolerance and personal humility which, whether it be called deistical or not, belongs to the best religion all over the world.'
The concluding words invoke Nature. Later Brooke shows that Pope, like several poets dubbed deistical, had 'religious feeling':
    'Now and then, to our surprise, it breaks out, and it does so in the *Universal Prayer*. Beginning with the ordinary and systematic view of God as universal Ruler, but graced with the wider charity of a poet, it passes in the end into personal devotion. No one can read the following lines without hearing in them something of the same melody which afterwards was varied through every key by Cowper.'
And he quotes 'The Universal Prayer', ll. 29–44.
[2] *Certain Difficulties felt by Anglicans in Catholic Teaching*, 1891 ed., i. 246–7.

Is it not clear that so much is here allowed to the good man who has no access to Grace that he can rest sufficiently content, can achieve a virtue ample enough to win the approbation of his fellows, which by definition is the high workaday standard imposed by Nature?

Pope's scheme is purposely non-Christian, but it cannot be called non-religious. Newman—to call on him again—misconceived it in his young days:

> Recalling his state of mind at the age of fourteen, he wrote in a manuscript book of early date:
>
> 'I recollect, in 1815 I believe, thinking that I should like to be virtuous, but not religious . . . I recollect contending . . . in favour of Pope's "Essay on Man". What, I contended, can be more free from objection than it? Does it not expressly inculcate "Virtue alone is happiness below"?'[1]

Even had he wished to, Pope could not have avoided religion, which was a constituent of Nature as surely as the love of one's native land. The instances of his poetry I have already given contain religious references in plenty, and we may note that, in Pope's time, Natural religion was a subject being much investigated. When he described *An Essay on Man* as 'not exclusive of religious regards',[2] he might have phrased the matter more positively. If man must not presume to 'scan' God, that did not mean that man was free to ignore Him. There remained the old reasons for thinking of Him, the obvious reasons that had moved Homer and all later writers and that were writ large in the Universe and in the mind of man. Nature is 'still divinely bright';[3] and 'good sense' (i.e. Nature) is always 'the gift of Heav'n';[4] the 'prize' of virtue is a calm and joyful happiness that 'nothing earthly gives, or can destroy'.[5] I have mentioned already Pope's concern with death, which he shows to be a religious concern. On occasions he prepares in a religious way for his own:

---

[1] *Letters and Correspondence*, ed. Anne Mozley, 1891, i. 22. We might compare Pascal, who left *les honnêtes gens* for the society of Port-Royal.

[2] *Correspondence*, iii. 155.

[3] See above, p. 25. 'Divinely' must be given full weight. It was only in the nineteenth century that it came to mean 'delightfully'.

[4] See above, p. 39.

[5] See above, p. 42.

> Why am I ask'd, what next shall see the light?
> Heav'ns! was I born for nothing but to write?
> Has Life no Joys for me? or (to be grave)
> Have I no Friend to serve, no Soul to save?[1]

Or this sombre prayer opening the last book of the *Dunciad*, the last of the writings he published:

> Yet, yet a moment, one dim Ray of Light
> Indulge, dread Chaos, and eternal Night!
> Of darkness visible so much be lent,
> As half to shew, half veil the deep Intent.
> Ye Pow'rs! whose Mysteries restor'd I sing,
> To whom Time bears me on his rapid wing,
> Suspend a while your Force inertly strong,
> Then take at once the Poet and the Song.[2]

Pope discerned the mighty context of man's 'brief authority' for what it is, but of set purpose he did not dwell on religion, which offered men ways of trying to understand it. The words about saving his soul are introduced by '(to be grave)' which, meaning 'to be very solemnly grave', makes a conscious shift to a plane he did not often frequent. It is indeed a canon of his philosophy that mundane things are the main concern of man, and that things not mundane shed on them only an intermittent light. His criticism of each 'proud scene' is limited as much as possible to the field where man, though he cannot escape the supernatural, can sufficiently get on without a constant sense of it. And that he usually does we have the common complaints of priests to show. 'Learn to live well . . .' is the conclusion advanced by one of the *Imitations of Horace*,[3] and Pope's belief is that you can do so by attending to the daily voice of reason—and on most points does it not speak in the clearest sense?—though knowing full well how terrifyingly that voice will be strengthened for you at the inevitable times and seasons. These terrors the poem I have quoted had already faced:

> 'But why all this of Av'rice? I have none',

his friend had interposed; and the answer comes:

---

[1] *Epistle to Dr. Arbuthnot*, ll. 271 ff.
[2] *Dunciad*, iv. 1 ff.   [3] Ep. II. ii. 322.

I wish you joy, Sir, of a Tyrant gone;
But does no other lord it at this hour,
As wild and mad? the Avarice of Pow'r?
Does neither Rage inflame, nor Fear appall?
Not the black Fear of Death, that saddens all?
With Terrors round can Reason hold her throne,
Despise the known, nor tremble at th' unknown?
Survey both Worlds, intrepid and entire,
In spite of Witches, Devils, Dreams, and Fire?[1]

We are concerned here with an occasion, and an occasion cannot but be brief. Here is that of an hour, 'this' hour perhaps, when death, which saddens all of us, even the grossest, is lording it over the individual in all its blackness. At other more normal times there is a milder discipline, which everyone must acknowledge because it is reasonable, the discipline of what might be called a sense of decency, of what is proper, all things considered, to man.

Pope's hopes from reason are high, but have their scepticism. It was by virtue of intuitive reason that Aristotle had marked off man from the beasts, and in his turn Johnson was to call it 'the great distinction of human nature'.[2] Whether or not the demarcation stood quite firm—Pope allowed even the elephant to be 'half-reasoning'[3]—it stood sufficiently so. Man has the power to criticize the way he wishes to act. Pope often acknowledged man's possession of this intuitive reason:

> A Voice there is, that whispers in my ear,
> ('Tis Reason's voice . . .)[4]

I hold up the couplet at this point because the word 'voice' is worth pausing over. Reason of the other sort—'divine reason', or 'moral reason', or 'moral sense', or 'conscience'— was all but personified by Bishop Butler a year or so before these lines of Pope;[5] and Newman was to support his view of

---

[1] *Imitations of Horace*, Ep. ii. ii. 304 ff.

[2] *Rambler*, No. 162.   [3] *Essay on Man*, i. 222.

[4] *Imitations of Horace*, Ep. i. i. 11 f. Pope is here adding to Horace. Charron had said that 'Nature in every one of us is sufficient . . . if we will hearken unto her' (see L. Whitney, *Primitivism and the Idea of Progress*, Baltimore, 1934, p. 8, and also p. 9).

[5] In his dissertation 'Of the Nature of Virtue', affixed to his *Analogy of Religion*, 1736.

the conscience by appealing to the common view that allowed
it a voice.[1] These writers see the conscience as a live thing,
which is how Pope sees the more general reason in man. But
he cannot agree that it has much practical authority. If reason
sometimes formulates itself for any man into something so
clear as a voice, it is a voice—to complete the couplet—that
only '... sometimes one can hear'. Unfortunately man makes
little use of this instrument lying to hand: for instance, when
Belinda triumphs, the poet interposes the sigh:

> Oh thoughtless Mortals! ever blind to Fate,
> Too soon dejected, and too soon elate![2]

Mortals are blind to Fate, but they could guess what was
coming if they troubled to, and probably guess right. And that
because they would be remembering past experience. Then
they would see that life is ups and downs, which is what the
poets had been saying from the start, with their symbols of
the wheel of fortune and the buckets in the well. Sometimes
man does use his reason, but to no more lasting purpose than
the weaving of Penelope:

> What Reason weaves, by Passion is undone.[3]

Indeed, if pressed, Pope might have agreed with Newman:

> Quarry the granite rock with razors, or moor the vessel with a
> thread of silk; then may you hope with such keen and delicate instru-
> ments as human knowledge and human reason to contend against those
> giants, the passion and the pride of man.[4]

Newman's boyish opinion[5] was a hasty one. Though religion exists in the *Dunciad*, it exists in reserve. It seemed
more proper to leave it so. Let theologians, to whom man
did not much listen, engage in 'scanning' God. Pope's
system of morals, however, is not expressed in poems which
can be placed with the sort of writing that drew the scorn of
Swift, the sort that

are kindly received, because they are levell'd to remove those Terrors
that Religion tells Men will be the Consequence of immoral Lives.[6]

---

[1] *An Essay in Aid of a Grammar of Assent*, 1870, p. 104.
[2] *Rape of the Lock*, iii. 101 f.   [3] *Essay on Man*, ii. 42.
[4] *Discourses on the Scope and Nature of University Education*, Discourse VI (Reynard
Library ed., p. 473).   [5] See above, p. 44.   [6] *A Tale of a Tub*, p. 5.

Indeed, in the last book of the *Dunciad*, a heavy charge is brought against the argumentative Deists for their neglect of religion, and the vision of the return of anarchy to the world includes, among its consequences, that

> *Religion* blushing veils her sacred fires,
> And unawares *Morality* expires.[1]

3

And so to the second objection—that Pope fails in sound sense when relating virtue and happiness. This charge rests on the fourth and last Epistle of *An Essay on Man*, or rather on isolated lines of it, which has been unduly abstracted from its large context. When the Epistle is taken in its place in the poem, the charge must, I think, disappear, for the relation of virtue (by which Pope largely means benevolence) and happiness (by which he does not mean sensual gratification) is the relation of two things always in practice imperfect. Virtue exists in bits and pieces, by fits and starts, and the reward of virtue is a sporadic happiness at the mercy of matters beyond the control of man, and which, moreover, in so far as it exists at all, requires a fine taste for its appreciation:

> Shall burning Ætna, if a sage requires,
> Forget to thunder, and recall her fires?
> On air or sea new motions be imprest,
> Oh blameless Bethel! to relieve thy breast?
> When the loose mountain trembles from on high,
> Shall gravitation cease, if you go by? . . .
>   'But sometimes Virtue starves, while Vice is fed.'
> What then? Is the reward of Virtue bread?
> That, Vice may merit; 'tis the price of toil;
> The knave deserves it, when he tills the soil,·
> The knave deserves it when he tempts the main,
> Where Folly fights for kings, or dives for gain.
> The good man may be weak, be indolent,
> Nor is his claim to plenty, but content. . . .

[1] ll. 649 f. Pope's remarks on religion in his letters come at *Correspondence*, i. 335 ('If the whole religious business of mankind, be included in resignation to our Maker, and charity to our fellow creatures . . . ') and 453 f., at iv. 207 (cf. 199) and 416, which Sherburn's note calls 'Pope's clearest statement as to his religious views'.

Rewards, that either would to Virtue bring
No joy, or be destructive of the thing:
How oft by these at sixty are undone
The virtues of a saint at twenty-one![1]

And so to the summary:

Know then this truth (enough for Man to know)
'Virtue alone is Happiness below.'
The only point where human bliss stands still,
And tastes the good without the fall to ill;
Where only Merit constant pay receives,
Is blest in what it takes, and what it gives;
The joy unequal'd, if its end it gain,
And if it lose, attended with no pain:
Without satiety, tho' e'er so blest,
And but more relish'd as the more distress'd:
The broadest mirth unfeeling Folly wears,
Less pleasing far than Virtue's very tears.
Good, from each object, from each place acquir'd,
For ever exercis'd, yet never tir'd;
Never elated, while one man's oppress'd;
Never dejected, while another's bless'd;
And where no wants, no wishes can remain,
Since but to wish more Virtue, is to gain.
See! the sole bliss Heav'n could on all bestow;
Which who but feels can taste, but thinks can know:
Yet poor with fortune, and with learning blind,
The bad must miss; the good, untaught, will find;
Slave to no sect, who takes no private road,
But looks thro' nature, up to nature's God;
Pursues that Chain which links th' immense design,
Joins heav'n and earth, and mortal and divine;
Sees, that no being any bliss can know,
But touches some above, and some below;
Learns, from this union of the rising Whole,
The first, last purpose of the human soul;
And knows where Faith, Law, Morals, all began,
All end, in LOVE of GOD, and LOVE of MAN.
For him alone, Hope leads from goal to goal,
And opens still, and opens on his soul,
'Till lengthen'd on to Faith, and unconfin'd,
It pours the bliss that fills up all the mind.

[1] iv. 123–8, 149–56, 181–4.

> He sees, why nature plants in Man alone
> Hope of known bliss, and Faith in bliss unknown:
> (Nature, whose dictates to no other kind
> Are giv'n in vain, but what they seek they find)
> Wise is her present; she connects in this
> His greatest Virtue with his greatest Bliss,
> At once his own bright prospect to be blest,
> And strongest motive to assist the rest.[1]

Surely this is a dream for most, indeed all, of us, and is offered as such. For the poem, on which it lies like a crown, has already disqualified us from attaining happiness with the plain fact that

> Virtuous and vicious ev'ry Man must be,
> Few in th' extreme, but all in the degree;
> The rogue and fool by fits is fair and wise,
> And ev'n the best, by fits, what they despise.[2]

Some of the irony of the poem is meant to show that virtue is an unlikely acquirement of man, costing him too much in mental and perhaps also physical comfort:

> Be Virtuous, and be happy for your pains;[3]

and this, amiably rounding on Bolingbroke:

> Is this my Guide, Philosopher, and Friend?
> This, He who loves me, and who ought to mend?
> Who ought to make me (what he can, or none,)
> That Man divine whom Wisdom calls her own.[4]

Taken in its entirety Pope's account of virtue and happiness is that of Johnson. In that early work, the *Life of Savage*, Johnson sees virtue, and so happiness, as within man's grasp:

It were doubtless to be wished that truth and reason were universally prevalent; that every thing were esteemed according to its real value; and that men would secure themselves from being disappointed in their endeavours after happiness, by placing it only in virtue, which is always to be obtained. . . .[5]

Fifteen years later, in *Rasselas*, he mocked the view that man, even when virtuous, has power to command happiness. He

---

[1] *Essay on Man*, iv. 309 ff.   [2] Id., ii. 231 ff.
[3] *Imitations of Horace*, Ep. 1. vi. 62.   [4] Id., Ep. 1. i. 177 ff.
[5] *Lives of the Poets*, ii. 379 f.

gave the specious doctrine to the sage who is all high-flown
eloquence in praise of it until found inconsolable for the
death of the daughter from whom he was expecting comfort
in his old age. Farther on in the same tale, while the 'practice of virtue' is represented as a command laid on man, it is
seen that the command is never in fact complied with:

'Whether perfect happiness would be procured by perfect goodness,'
said Nekayah, 'this world will never afford an opportunity of deciding.
But this, at least, may be maintained, that we do not always find visible
happiness in proportion to visible virtue. All natural and almost all
political evils, are incident alike to the bad and good: they are con-
founded in the misery of a famine, and not much distinguished in the
fury of a faction; they sink together in a tempest, and are driven together from their country by invaders. All that virtue can afford is
quietness of conscience and a steady prospect of a happier state; this
may enable us to endure calamity with patience; but remember that
patience must suppose pain.'[1]

In *Rasselas*, however, Johnson did not deny some degree of
happiness, some 'comparative happiness',[2] to man: what he
denied is any happiness of the sort imagined by the inexpe-
rienced prince as the only acceptable sort:

'Happiness', said [Rasselas], 'must be something solid and permanent,
without fear and without uncertainty.'[3]

Both Pope and Johnson, then, employ the word 'virtue'
comparatively, as all such terms must be employed. I have
already quoted Johnson's remark that

As it is said of the greatest liar, that he tells more truth than falsehood; so it may be said of the worst man, that he does more good than
evil.[4]

The vice of the vicious is not a complete thing, and at the
other end of the brief scale man's virtue is incomplete also.
Virtue that is complete and impossible has therefore to be
called by some distinguishing term. Johnson's term for it is
'romantick' virtue, the sort that is sometimes accredited to
man in story-books. This is his paragraph on Pope's third
Moral Essay, which introduces the virtuous Man of Ross:

[1] Chap. xxvii.   [2] Chap. xi.
[3] Chap. xvii.   [4] See above, p. 11.

Into this poem some incidents are historically thrown, and some known characters are introduced, with others of which it is difficult to say how far they are real or fictitious; but the praise of Kyrl, 'the Man of Ross,' deserves particular examination, who, after a long and pompous enumeration of his publick works and private charities, is said to have diffused all those blessings from 'five hundred a year'. Wonders are willingly told and willingly heard. The truth is that Kyrl was a man of known integrity and active benevolence, by whose solicitation the wealthy were persuaded to pay contributions to his charitable schemes; this influence he obtained by an example of liberality exerted to the utmost extent of his power, and was thus enabled to give more than he had. This account Mr. Victor received from the minister of the place, and I have preserved it, that the praise of a good man, being made more credible, may be more solid. Narrations of romantick and impracticable virtue will be read with wonder, but that which is unattainable is recommended in vain: that good may be endeavoured it must be shewn to be possible.[1]

Pope's use of 'virtuous' must be seen to have the comparative force it was to have for Johnson. When that is allowed, there is nothing wrong with the claim he summed up in the penultimate line of his poem:

> . . . VIRTUE only makes our Bliss below.[2]

4

I have been writing as if we can take Pope's poetry and the prose of *Rasselas* on one level. There is some excuse for this since Johnson's prose is here the medium for a narrative, not for thinking in its stricter form. However that may be, the

---

[1] *Lives of the Poets*, iii. 172 f. It is interesting, now that we have more of Pope's correspondence than Johnson had, to see that he was aware of the matters Johnson raises: he seeks exact particulars about the subject of his portrait, but mainly so as to base his exaggeration on a firm foundation:

'A small exaggeration you must allow me as a poet; yet I was determined the ground work at least should be *Truth*, which made me so scrupulous in my enquiries; and sure, considering that the world is bad enough to be always extenuating and lessening what virtue is among us, it is but reasonable to pay it sometimes a little over measure, to balance that injustice, especially when it is done for example and encouragement to others. If any man shall ever happen to endeavour to emulate the Man of Ross, 'twill be no manner of harm if I make him think he was something more charitable and more beneficent than really he was, for so much more good it would put the imitator upon doing. And farther I am satisfy'd in my conscience (from the strokes in 2 or 3 accounts I have of his character) that it was in his will, and in his heart, to have done every good a poet can imagine' (*Correspondence*, iii. 290).   [2] *Essay on Man*, iv. 397.

thinking that Pope does, being done in poetry, is not to be
wrenched into prosaic daylight and read as if it were a piece
of Hume. Some of the sense conveyed by poetry proceeds
from sources other than its account of the poet's cerebration.
This means that there is what may be called a literary discount from some of Pope's reasoning. The optimism of his
conclusion is shaded for any reader who attends to the poetry
—to the melancholy sounding in it. It sounds over all the
poems as if Pope, like Wordsworth, was hearing 'oftentimes
the still sad music of humanity'. In view of this pervasive
sadness the dubbing of him as a flashy optimist seems an incomplete judgement. Let us understand where Pope stood.
He wrote *An Essay on Man* after Newton had changed men's
conception of the universe:

> Nature, and Nature's Laws lay hid in Night.
> God said, *Let Newton be!* and All was *Light*.

Looking at the earth as part and parcel of the Newtonian
universe, how else could one reasonably see it than as parti-
cipating in the sublime universal order? How could one
escape the logic, as one worked in the medium of logic, that
whatever is on earth must be right, simply because rightness
was written across the whole universe? As one held in one's
hand, as it were, the immense cosmic watch, was it not in-
conceivable to thought that one cog in the fine machinery
failed in its harmonious relation to the whole? Could man
insult the nature of God by imagining that any law of His
could brook an exception? That is how Pope saw it, thinking
out the matter for his Essay. But it was one thing to argue so,
and another to see everything contained in the world as
pleasant to man. The world contained evil, and though, when
one arranged one's thoughts, evil must be allowed to be part
of the general rightness of the universe, it was hideous in its
practical impact on man. When, therefore, we read that
'Whatever is, is RIGHT'[1] we must allow for the content of the
first half of the proposition. The vast matter represented in
the 'Whatever is' is a sorry sight, and is unflinchingly shown
as such in Pope's poems, including *An Essay on Man* itself.
    When Handel came to set the words, he said all this in the

[1] i. 294.

music: the unison phrase to which the singers enunciate 'Whatever is' is a dignified wail, lying across the beat, and though the chords for 'is RIGHT' are loud and quick and sudden, they arrive only after the strings have pursued a melancholy meander, as if aimlessly in 'the *labyrinth* of Life':[1]

and so on, many times repeated in different keys and with the uneasy arpeggio elongated to twice its length on its last appearance: and I may add that the word 'RIGHT' sometimes falls sternly on a minor chord.[2]

But whatever the answer, optimistic or pessimistic, to Pope's long and painful sum, I do not think that man is very much interested in any answer. He knows that conclusions of this immensity are beyond his powers. If there is to be an answer, Pope's is not unlike the answer man is apt to give when he wants an answer to solace him: he will recount the most dreadful sufferings and conclude that all is for the best. But whatever the content of the answer made by Pope, it does not invalidate the description of man as the painful jest

---

[1] Dryden's translation 'Lucretius: against the fear of death', l. 270.

[2] Handel's *Jephtha*, 1751; the chorus 'How dark, O Lord, are thy decrees. . . .' The words of the oratorio are reputed to be by Thomas Morell, and the stanza which borrows from Pope reads, abbreviatedly:

> How dark, O Lord, are thy decrees!
> All hid from mortal sight! . . .
> Yet on this maxim still obey;
> Whatever is, is right.

Handel, by the way, is the musical counterpart of the poet of Nature: cf. Basil Lam, 'Handel and Bach', *The Listener*, 14 Mar. 1957: 'It would be absurd to claim that the Chandos anthems are a document of the deepest religious experience. . . . What they do contain is the expression—whether grave, thoughtful, or jubilant— of ordinary human experience: the quality in Handel which has given to "Messiah" a position denied to all other compositions.'

and riddle, if also the glory, of the world. If we distrust logic.
we do not distrust poetry, and Pope's logic in *An Essay on Man*
coexists with poetry.

One further general point. Being a poet, Pope is not a re-
former. Because he speaks much about practical matters and
even gives practical advice, we cannot hold him altogether
responsible as we do the author of a prose manual of conduct.
Occasionally we get a practical moralist who makes his
counsel a great work of literature—as Pascal and Newman
did. But that literary bonus is over and above the contract
they make with their reader. And the same law inverted
applies to Pope. His practical morality is over and above his
contract to give us poetry. Poetry has little to do with conduct directly. If it exists to profit as well as delight, it is
largely content if its profit consists in a refining of the mind.
Pope did say on occasions that he aimed at the non-literary
end of improving conduct, but he was more true to his first
interest, that of writing poetry, when he subscribed to
Swift's view that 'enemies [are] as necessary for a good
writer, as pen, ink, and paper'.[1] Making his resplendent
poetry out of materials to hand, out of Nature and its trappings, he could not wish them to be otherwise than they
were. 'Whatever is' he had no reason but to take and be
thankful for.

[1] *Correspondence*, i. 358 f.

IV

MAN AND HIS FEELINGS

POPE often refers to 'the heart', and always with the assumption that what it connotes is of supreme, and as it were sacred, importance. It is a department in which the ordinary man has much authority. Johnson remarked that, when it comes to 'questions that relate to the heart of man, the common voice of the multitude, uninstructed by precept, and unprejudiced by authority' is 'more decisive' than, say, the voice of the learned.[1] It was for not being able to join in this 'common voice' that Cloe was damned:

'Yet Cloe sure was form'd without a spot'—
Nature in her then err'd not, but forgot.
'With ev'ry pleasing, ev'ry prudent part,
'Say, what can Cloe want?'—she wants a Heart.
She speaks, behaves, and acts just as she ought;
But never, never, reach'd one gen'rous Thought.
Virtue she finds too painful an endeavour,
Content to dwell in Decencies for ever.
So very reasonable, so unmov'd,
As never yet to love, or to be lov'd.
She, while her Lover pants upon her breast,
Can mark the figures on an Indian chest;
And when she sees her Friend in deep despair,
Observes how much a Chintz exceeds Mohair.
Forbid it Heav'n, a Favour or a Debt
She e'er should cancel—but she may forget.
Safe is your Secret still in Cloe's ear;
But none of Cloe's shall you ever hear.
Of all her Dears she never slander'd one,
But cares not if a thousand are undone.
Would Cloe know if you're alive or dead?
She bids her Footman put it in her head.
Cloe is prudent—would you too be wise?
Then never break your heart when Cloe dies.[2]

[1] *Rambler*, No. 52.
[2] *Moral Essays*, ii ('Of the Characters of Women'), 157 ff.

On several occasions in the letters Pope declared his preference for the 'heart' over the 'head'[1]—hence the great store
he set on friendship, a social condition in which feeling is
uniform because without violence. Accordingly we might
have expected him to be less hard on fools. If we think of
fools as making up for lack of brains by tenderness of feelings, those lines of his—

> take it for a rule,
> No creature smarts so little as a Fool[2]

—will repel us. Some fools, we know, do smart, and perhaps
all the more as they are shown deficient in qualities of the
head. Because of this we admire the pleasant people who can
suffer fools gladly. Pope himself did show some compassion
this way: after saying, in a letter, that '*scoundrels* I hate', he
added 'though *fools* I pardon'.[3] Usually, however, his poems
are almost as hard on fools as on knaves. We shall be more
reconciled to his dislike, I suggest, when we understand the
sort of fool he had in mind: for Pope the fool was the sort of
man he was for Solomon:

Who is that 'fool' of which we hear so much in the Proverbs, who
is always coming in with some short description appended to him—
'whose way is always right in his own eyes;' 'who despiseth his father's
instruction;' who 'hateth reproof;' whose 'lips enter into contention;'
whose 'mouth is his destruction;' who 'returneth to his folly as a dog
returneth to his vomit;' who 'trusteth in his own heart;' 'who uttereth
all his mind;' who 'maketh a mock at sin'? Who is this personage, who
is so self-satisfied, so without all self-control or self-distrust, so confident, such a creature of the present moment, without seriousness, without fear, without foresight, with nothing in him which tells him of
a future which is coming, and warns him of his danger? Is not this a
very common character we meet with in the world? Are we not often
reminded of the 'fool' of Solomon's description?[4]

For Pope a fool was one who had misused, among other
things, his feelings. Part of what he scorned in Sporus was
fool in this sense: his 'Heart' was 'corrupted' and so had lost
its Natural feeling:

> Satire or Sense alas! can *Sporus* feel?[5]

---

[1] See particularly *Correspondence*, iii. 106 and 166.
[2] *Epistle to Dr. Arbuthnot*, ll. 83 f.   [3] *Correspondence*, iii. 116.
[4] J. B. Mozley, *Sermons Parochial and Occasional*, 1882, p. 101.
[5] *Epistle to Dr. Arbuthnot*, ll. 327, 307.

'Fool' in this sense the ordinary man would agree to range with knave.

In Pope's view it is the first requisite of a poem that it should touch 'the heart' of the reader: if it 'gains' that, then it gains 'all its end', and gains it 'at once'.[1] At the appropriate times a poem ought to speak directly 'the language of the heart'. A poet neglected to speak it at his peril: by the 1730's that particular kind of language was all that remained readable of Cowley's:

> Forgot his Epic, nay Pindaric Art,
> But still I love the language of his Heart.[2]

Most of the feeling expressed in Pope's poetry is Natural feeling. Over one long poem it exists in excess—'If you search for passion, where', asked the authoritative Byron, 'is it to be found stronger?'[3] The excess is Eloisa's, and Pope is able to be faithful to it by virtue of the dramatic imagination. But though excessive, Eloisa's feeling is Natural feeling, and at the close of the poem, when the poet himself speaks, the feeling is Natural at a normal pitch:

> And sure if fate some future Bard shall join
> In sad similitude of griefs to mine,
> Condemn'd whole years in absence to deplore,
> And image charms he must behold no more,
> Such if there be, who loves so long, so well;
> Let him our sad, our tender story tell . . . .[4]

As a whole, the poems speak with a man's voice, and that voice sounds in them from the start.[5] Later I shall show that Pope also speaks specifically as a poet; he tells us how he feels about his own poetry and position among his fellow poets.[6] Being statedly the feelings of a poet, they are distinguished from those of a man, but even so lie close to man's. When not speaking as a poet, and when his matter is man's affairs as son, friend, or lover, his feeling is normal feeling, and is welcomed as such.

Much of it, implied and expressly stated, is sad feeling, though the commonplace epithet does not suggest its subtle-

---

[1] *Essay on Criticism*, ll. 154 f.
[2] *Imitations of Horace*, Ep. II. i. 77 f. This phrase occurs again at *Epistle to Dr. Arbuthnot*, l. 399, and at *Correspondence*, iv. 261.   [3] *Letters*, iv. 489.
[4] ll. 359 ff.   [5] See below, pp. 156 ff.   [6] See below, p. 154.

ties. Sad feeling is not inappropriate to his Horatian philosophy, which counsels a mean:

> Aim not at Joy, but rest content with Ease,[1]

and a contented quietness of feeling:

> . . . ease thy heart of all that it admires.[2]

Sad feelings, moreover, are expected of him as a poet, for
we have had more sad-sounding quietness from poets than
otherwise. Johnson, indeed, saw them as finding their happiness in making poetry of that colour:

> To tell of disappointment and misery, to thicken the darkness of
> futurity, and perplex the labyrinth of uncertainty, has been always a
> delicious employment of the poets.[3]

We recall that the last of the Pastorals, which turns the
attention upon age and death, was Pope's favourite. If poets
do find delight in the writing of sad poetry, it is because of
a consent that exists between sadness and poetry. Pope had
more than his share of sadness of the actual sort that was
anything but delicious, and it was noted that his face never
opened beyond a smile.[4] Some of his poetry prompts as full
a laugh as Chaucer's, but otherwise the laughter of poet and
reader is seldom free from a sense of pain, mockery, disgust
and melancholy.

The feeling in his poetry, then, represents Natural feeling
as it is represented in the Wisdom of Solomon: man is only
not a sighing animal because he looks to poetry, and music,
to sigh for him.

Natural feeling, as I shall show, informs the satiric poems.[5]
There remain, however, two related exceptions. In a youthful letter to the young John Caryll about the reception of the
first version of the *Rape of the Lock*, Pope writes:

> Dull fellows that want Witt, (like those very dull fellows that want
> Lechery) may, by well-applyd Stroaks & Scourges, be fetchd up into
> a little of either. I therfore have some reason to hope no man that calls
> himself my Friend (except it be such an obstinate, refractory Person

---

[1] 'Epistle to Miss Blount, with the Works of Voiture', l. 48.
[2] *Imitations of Horace*, Ep. I. i. 76.   [3] *Lives of the Poets*, iii. 224.
[4] See Johnson's *Lives of the Poets*, iii. 202, *n.* 3.
[5] See below, pp. 218 ff.

as yourself) will do me the Injury to hinder these well-meaning Gentle-men from Beating up my Understanding. Whipt wits, like whipt Creams, afford a most sweet & delectable Syllabub to the Taste of the Towne, and often please them better with the Dessert, than all the meal they had before. So, if Sir Plume shoud take the pains to Dress me, I might possibly make the Last Course better than the first. When a stale cold Fool is well heated, and hashed by a Satyrical Cooke, he may be tost up into a Kickshaw not disagreeable.[1]

This cruelty, so nicely worded, is imputed to others with himself as its object. On the later occasion the same nicely worded cruelty is imputed to himself: at the climax of his great apologia he represents himself as overmastered by hatred of the insect-like nastiness of Sporus:

> Yet let me flap this Bug with gilded wings,
> This painted Child of Dirt that stinks and stings. . . .[2]

The mercilessness of this revolts the ordinary man, who can-not forget, as Pope does, that the 'fool' Sporus is a man. Feelings here get the better of Pope, as they do not of Ar-buthnot who, as represented in the poem, interposes the not-able plea that preparations for torture are out of keeping: to Pope's 'Let *Sporus* tremble' he rejoins:

> 'What? that Thing of silk,
> '*Sporus*, that mere white Curd of Ass's milk?
> 'Satire or Sense alas! can *Sporus* feel?
> 'Who breaks a Butterfly upon a Wheel?'[3]

Arbuthnot allows that Sporus is an insect, but is for turning aside in a contempt that has more Nature in it than Pope's calculation of attack.

By and large, however, Pope's feelings are those of Nature.

---

[1] *Correspondence*, i. 163 f.
[2] *Epistle to Dr. Arbuthnot*, ll. 309 f.
[3] ll. 305 ff.

V

'TRUTH', GENERAL AND PARTICULAR

'TRUTH' is one of several terms that recur when Pope speaks of Nature. 'What oft was thought', 'sense', 'common sense', 'good sense', what is 'just', 'truth'—all these terms, which are either synonyms of Nature or closely related to it, recur when Nature is the theme or provides the standard.

There is one use of 'truth' that must be considered at length, the use whereby it takes on a sense at least bordering on the modern sense of 'fact'—'fact', which we define as 'something that has really occurred or is actually the case . . . hence, a particular truth known by actual observation or authentic testimony, as opposed to what is merely inferred, or to a conjecture of fiction'.[1] Pope used 'truth' in something like this humbler sense in the note he attached to the first and second editions of *The Temple of Fame* (it was then entitled *The Temple of Fame: A Vision*).[2] That note is appended to the comparison of the eternal rock of ice, on which the temple stands, to rocks of ice found in the arctic regions:

Tho a strict Verisimilitude be not requir'd in the Descriptions of this visionary and allegorical kind of Poetry, which admits of every wild[3] Object that Fancy may present in a Dream, and where it is sufficient if the moral Meaning atone for the Improbability: Yet Men are Naturally so desirous of Truth, that a Reader is generally pleas'd, in such a Case, with some Excuse or Allusion that seems to reconcile the Description to Probability and Nature. The Simile here is of that sort, and renders it not wholly unlikely that a *Rock* of *Ice* should remain for ever, by mentioning something like it in the Northern Regions, agreeing with the Accounts of our modern Travellers.[4]

---

[1] *O.E.D.*, s.v. 'fact', sense 4.

[2] Cf. the use also where Pope speaks of the '*Truth*' about the Man of Ross, p. 52 above, n. 1.

[3] Pope learned this sort of application of the word from Hobbes, who, in the brilliant passage he has in mind, spoke of the 'train of thoughts' that is 'unguided, without design' (the thoughts of men who are idle or asleep) as a 'wild ranging of the mind' (*Leviathan*, I. iii (*English Works*, iii. 12)). Carrying this or similar connotations, the word plays an important part in later eighteenth- and early nineteenth-century poetry. [4] Twickenham ed., ii. 384.

Here Pope is appealing to what at first sight we should call fact. At that date it would just have been possible for him to use the word in our sense: men were already beginning to mark off 'fact' from 'truth'. Though 'fact' still usually meant 'deed' or 'evil deed', Hobbes, at least on one occasion, had pushed it forward near to its modern sense. In the preface to his translation of the *Odyssey* he wrote:

Justice and Impartiality [belong] as well to History as to Poetry. For both the Poet and the Historian writeth only (or should do) matter of Fact.[1]

Here is something near our modern sense, though not quite at it—Hobbes, who is thinking of the epic poet, has the old sense 'deed' in mind. Pope, according to Abbott's *Concordance*, used the word 'fact' twice in his poems (that concordance does not draw on his poems in their entirety, the biggest omission being the translations of Homer). Once it means 'evil deed'[2] and once, almost but not quite, the colourless 'deed'.[3] Very likely Pope also used the word in his prose, though I have not found him doing so. In his note on the rock of ice, and in a letter to Swift, which I shall quote later,[4] he retained the old word 'truth', and, in so far as he meant what we now call 'fact' by it, sacrificed something of accuracy. But the context of the term suggests that he had his reasons, preferring 'truth' because as a poet of Nature he wanted to claim that he was still moving in general fields.

Man is interested in facts only as and when they can become part of his thoughts, and so qualify to accompany, prompt, or become 'truth'. In this he is like the poet as Wordsworth saw him. (Scientists are interested in facts that they cannot bring home to their minds as their minds are those of ordinary people, but they are seeking constantly to do so.) Pope believed that things like a rock of ice do interest man. And this being so, we cannot take the word 'truth' out

---

[1] Spingarn, ii. 70. The date of this is 1675. We can see the steps by which Hobbes arrived at this modern phrase: in 1629, in the preface to his translation of Thucydides, he spoke of the '*truth*' of history, meaning its faithfulness to facts: and in 1651, in the *Leviathan*, 1. ix (*English Works*, iii. 71), he called history (natural and civil) 'knowledge of fact'. At 1. viii (ed. cit. iii. 58), in a similar context, he had kept the old term '*truth*'.

[2] *Windsor Forest*, l. 321.   [3] *Dunciad*, iv. 433.   [4] See below, p. 209.

of his clause and read, 'Yet men are Naturally so desirous of fact . . . '. Wordsworth meant something like this in his famous lines arraigning Peter Bell for his failure to place the primrose in a human context. Man does not rate the primrose very highly in the scale of Natural interests, though spring flowers of one sort or another mean something cheerful to him, auguring more comfortable temperatures: in so far as he takes an interest in primroses it is not as a botanical fact, but as having practically a 'message' for him. But mankind is more concerned with other ranges of experience, with things more cogent to ordinary life. As it happens there is a record of Pope's having referred to daffodils in a way that would have pained Wordsworth. Spence recorded the following conversation:

[Spence:] 'Pray what is the *Asphodil* of Homer?'
[Pope:] 'Why I believe, if one was to say the truth, 'twas nothing else but that poor yellow flower that grows about our orchards: and if so, the verse might thus be translated in English.

——"the stern Achilles
Stalked through a mead of daffodillies." '[1]

Pope's reference is wholly lacking in Wordsworthian piety, but it would not, I think, shock the Natural man. He was merely referring to the daffodil as a botanical item—and one hit on not so much for its own sake as for making a joke. No doubt, like the Natural man, he would think of daffodils more tenderly as he found them coming before the swallow dares.

A rock of ice is at least as much a truth as a wild flower is. It is of interest to mankind especially when it is part of a country even sparsely inhabited, since temperature affects everyday human life as much as anything can: as Pope was later to point out, riches themselves can do no more than accommodate the rigours of temperature to man's comfort; giving us all we need in giving us 'Meat, Cloaths, and Fire'.[2] Moreover, mankind is interested in rocks of ice when discovered by men against great odds, by such heroic travellers as Pope invokes. For the Natural man a rock of ice is 'something more' than a rock of ice, than a mere fact. It is a fact that rouses primary human interest, at however low a pitch. And so its existence qualifies it for being a 'truth', and that

[1] Spence, p. 285. [2] *Moral Essays*, iii ('Of the Use of Riches', To Bathurst), 80.

sort of a truth which 'Men are Naturally . . . desirous of'.
Pope was no worse off, then, for not anticipating, as Hobbes
did, the modern sense of 'fact'.

Later in his poem comes the temple of Rumour:

Before my View appear'd a Structure fair,
Its Site uncertan, if in Earth or Air;
With rapid Motion turn'd the Mansion round;
With ceaseless Noise the ringing Walls resound:
Not less in Number were the spacious Doors,
Than Leaves on Trees, or Sands upon the Shores;
Which still unfolded stand, by Night, by Day,
Pervious to Winds, and open ev'ry way.
As Flames by nature to the Skies ascend,
As weighty Bodies to the Center tend,
As to the Sea returning Rivers roll,
And the touch'd Needle trembles to the Pole:
Hither, as to their proper Place, arise
All various Sounds from Earth, and Seas, and Skies,
Or spoke aloud, or whisper'd in the Ear;
Nor ever Silence, Rest or Peace is here.
As on the smooth Expanse of Chrystal Lakes,
The sinking Stone at first a Circle makes;
The trembling Surface, by the Motion stir'd,
Spreads in a second Circle, then a third;
Wide, and more wide, the floating Rings advance,
Fill all the wat'ry Plain, and to the Margin dance.
Thus ev'ry Voice and Sound, when first they break,
On neighb'ring Air a soft Impression make;
Another ambient Circle then they move,
That, in its turn, impels the next above;
Thro undulating Air the Sounds are sent,
And spread o'er all the fluid Element.
    There various News I heard, of Love and Strife,
Of Peace and War, Health, Sickness, Death, and Life;
Of Loss and Gain, of Famine and of Store,
Of Storms at Sea, and Travels on the Shore,
Of Prodigies, and Portents seen in Air,
Of Fires and Plagues, and Stars with blazing Hair,
Of Turns of Fortune, Changes in the State,
The Falls of Fav'rites, Projects of the Great,
Of old Mismanagements, Taxations new—
All neither wholly false, nor wholly true.[1]

¹ ll. 420 ff.

If there had been anything in the external world to which
Pope could have referred us, we may be sure he would. In
his poem the temple of Rumour whirls away as Chaucer
created it in the imagination: it was a wonder of the mind,
not a fact of the material world. Was it therefore the less a
truth? This question splits Nature, Natural men, into those
for whom an imaginary wonder is less a 'truth'—by 'truth'
I mean something bound up with the daily interests of man
—than an interesting fact is, and those for whom an imaginary wonder may have as much 'truth' as a fact, or more than a
fact. And in Pope's time the former party—the rationalists,
the scientific men—were growing in number and went on
growing till in the nineteenth century, and our own, they
were and are very numerous indeed. Pope, we may safely say,
would have had nothing to do with the second temple, if it
had not been a temple, and, in the second place, a temple of
something like Rumour; that is, a symbol, and a symbol of
something with which man was much concerned. His poem
was a 'vision poem', 'imitated' from Chaucer. But he imitated
Chaucer's poem for the reason which, at bottom, made
Chaucer invent it; he imitated it because it was about those
human things, fame and rumour. If the poem made use of
some scenic imagery that could not but strike a growing
number of readers as touched with childishness, Pope knew
they would swallow it because of the Natural worth of what
came to be said, partly through the imagery, of something so
Naturally important as rumour.

The 'moral Meaning', as he put it, would 'atone for the
Improbability'. He himself, being a poet, liked pictures,
whether they were strictly related to fact or not. But he
probably preferred the factually authenticated, feeling—as
the great nineteenth-century poets, including Carlyle and
Ruskin, did—that no imagination could improve on fact. I
shall have more to say of this later.[1] But whatever Pope's own
preferences, his note shows him aware that his readers, being
men more undividedly Natural than a poet, would have preferred a temple for rumour which, if the nature of rumour
had allowed it, or if Pope's knowledge of strange foreign
lands had been equal to the occasion, belonged to

[1] See below, pp. 204 ff.

the very world, which is the world
Of all of us,—the place where, in the end,
We find our happiness, or not at all![1]

The closeness of some facts to 'truth' is the more important since items which, at first glance, would be called facts are much drawn on in Pope's poetry. His constant recourse to them was due to his writing of and for mankind, who live in an environment formed of them, and also because he often chose to make his writings satiric. Satire cannot but deal in particulars. That mankind abounds eternally in fool or knave is the rule, but the satirist can only prove it at any given time by pointing to the novelties that foolishness and knavery are producing at the moment. It is the nature of novelties to dazzle, and it is the business of the satirist to remove misconceptions. Fools always hope that foolish novelties are benefits, knaves that knavish novelties go undiscovered. The satirist must catch them red-handed among facts.

Another reason for Pope's concern with particulars, is that, when not a satirist, he is usually an historical poet dealing with the social things of his own time—a poet still concerned with the satirist's material though viewing it without indignation. Whether satiric or historical, Pope is therefore a poet making his poetry 'out of existing materials'.[2]

But the 'particular' and the 'general' seldom exist as unmixed categories. I have argued that the fact of the 'rock of ice' is for Pope, and for man, not without general reference. Facts of this grade are frequently drawn on in his poems. Whenever he is speaking of an individual, that individual cannot but carry with him facts as particular as the rock of ice. When writing of the death of Villiers, he furnishes particulars of the wretched room in which the death took place, with its 'once a flock-bed, but repair'd with straw' and so on: he makes the reader see an individual scene.[3] But in the same way as the rock of ice is interesting because related to the strong human sense of heroism and unusual temperatures, the particulars of Villiers's death are related to such valued

[1] Wordsworth, *The Prelude*, xi. 142 ff.
[2] Newman's phrase in 'Poetry with reference to Aristotle's Poetics' (*Essays Critical and Historical*, ed. 1877, i. 20).
[3] *Moral Essays*, iii ('Of the Use of Riches', To Bathurst), 299 ff.

themes as the fall and death of great men, and the reversal of glory and shame. Men's minds, we know, prefer to relate new particulars to old ones that have already been classified. The particulars about Villiers's death belong to old-established categories: instead of dying like an aristocrat, Villiers dies like a drab. He is an individual, but the particulars attached to him are already generalized, and, because inverted, rank as ironic badges of office. Pope chose particulars which he fore-saw as likely to remain recognizably of that status, because he wished his individuals to rise into permanent types.

Two of his poems provide exceptions to this rule—the two dialogues that Warburton placed together as 'The Epilogue to the Satires', and particularly the second of them. They contain some of the finest poetry Pope ever wrote, but in places its force, which we can infer from its forceful context, is defeated for us by the invincible obscurity of the particulars which should generalize and so keep it warm. Professor Sherburn has written of the second of the poems as follows:

Swift's criticism on the poem is the soundest adverse criticism ever made. Naturally he does not doubt the reality of Pope's pessimism; but he does doubt (as he had earlier) the immortality of a poem so full of journalistic personalities: he assumes that these personal allusions are very well known from Temple Bar to St. James's. This cuts to the heart of the matter. . . Pope's edifice survives as a towering, magni-ficent structure, but the ornaments and gargoyles are so eaten away as to be ruinous and unrecognizable.[1]

Pope's failure here is, by his own standards, a technical one: he failed to make his particulars of the self-generalizing, self-perpetuating sort. Swift raised the same sort of objection to another poem, the *Dunciad* of 1728, and raised them, I think, unjustly. The poem still retains a great general force, which partly results from the surviving force of its particulars. Assuredly it has been as little read by the general reader as any of Pope's poems, but probably because its narrative is difficult through being concentrated rather than because it is crowded with contemporary reference. Despite its direct aim at the literary public of its day—or indeed its several aims at the several publics of 1728, 1729, 1742, 1743, when suc-cessive forms and enlargements of the poem appeared—it

[1] *The Best of Pope*, p. 449.

seems a poem Pope wrote for himself. It is one of his finest achievements, but not in the category in which he most wished to shine, the category of poems about Nature. It struck Swift as even too parochial for the men of the time, unless they happened to be Londoners interested in the scene of writers and booksellers, preachers and city corporation—it offended against the *ubique* and so even more against the *semper*. And yet Pope did his best to give it a general air. He related it to that greatest of public forms, the epic, and it has the grandeur of epic despite its comparative brevity and the meanness that the materials would have had in other hands than his—for the poem is as glorious as *Paradise Lost* to those who see it as Pope and the fit readers of the time saw it. Moreover, he related it to the epic where the epic is of universal interest, especially when his booksellers and authors are set to play games, which no poet could have made more elaborately laughable as wit or farce, and at the same time more grandly sonorous and majestic in the expression. And in the fourth Book, which he added in 1742, there is something like the universality of the scene in the *Temple of Fame*: the Goddess Dulness, as at a royal levee, is being presented with types of fools. Again, as in *An Essay on Criticism*, Pope tried against severe odds to make a limited thing as general as possible.

Here are some instances of his use of particulars that generalize and modernize themselves. In the *Rape of the Lock* he drew on up-to-date particulars by the score. Some of these have survived almost intact. The poem mentions, for instance, four drinks, which were then novel: tea, coffee, chocolate, and citron-waters. Three of these survive today without much change, except that they have spread through all social grades: what were the drinks of the rich of 1714[1] have now become the drinks of everybody—everybody in England, at least, with which, as a practical thing, we are primarily concerned. This change has actually improved the Natural content of the terms. Of the fourth drink, citron-

---

[1] In *A Book of New Epigrams. By the same Hand that Translated Martial* (i.e. Henry Killigrew), 1695, pp. 153 f., there is an epigram 'On Coffee, Tea, and Chocolate', in which the author represents himself as a chocolate-drinker—he hates coffee, and tea is too dear (often £10 a lb.).

waters, we do not know the constituents except after historical research: but as it is mentioned in the line

> ... Citron-Waters Matrons' Cheeks inflame,[1]

it is sufficiently recognizable as alcoholic of the strength preferred by the mature. Modern readers, therefore, are not unduly troubled with the particularity. They are not hopelessly at sea if their editor omits to give them an annotation. They tumble to the import of the particulars because Pope divined that mankind would go on taking cups that inebriate, and so infer correctly the nature and status of citron-waters in 1714.

Then again, on one occasion Pope invited his first readers to see

> A simple Quaker, or a Quaker's Wife,
> Out-do *Landaffe*, in Doctrine—yea, in Life.[2]

The first readers of that couplet were expected to grasp the reference to Mary Drummond, as a few years ago readers of a modern poem would have grasped a reference to, say, Maude Royden. Mary Drummond was the

> Sister of George Drummond, the famous Lord Provost of Edinburgh. She adopted Quaker tenets in the early 1730's and thereafter devoted herself to itinerant preaching throughout Great Britain, collecting funds at the same time for the Royal Infirmary at Edinburgh, which her brother was building. She reached London in 1735, where 'she preached in almost all the Meetings in and about this City, to crowded Audiences, and with great Applause from People of all Seats and Persuasions'.[3]

All this lay behind the phrase 'a Quaker's Wife'. And behind 'Landaffe' lay 'A poor Bishoprick in Wales, as poorly supplied'—that was the posthumously printed note which Pope came to see was called for. The couplet, therefore, was drenched in contemporary matter. But much of its meaning lay safe beyond the contemporary and local, and much of it could be safely guessed by those of Pope's contemporaries who were little better informed about the scraps of the 1730's than a modern reader is. Even if the first readers did not

---

[1] *Rape of the Lock*, iv. 69.
[2] *Imitations of Horace*, 'Epilogue to the Satires', dial. i. 133 f., the poem which came under Swift's stricture—see above, p. 67.   [3] Twickenham ed., iv. 356.

possess all the knowledge Pope hoped for from them, they were happy enough grasping the great deal that was obvious, understanding by the first line any religious person un-fashionably outside the pale of orthodoxy, and by the second any person prominently and fashionably inside it as it was a fashionable thing, and unworthily inside it as it was a thing more honourable. And not merely that: the 'common reader' expanded the couplet into generalities still wider, under-standing that organizations, even the most worthy, decay inevitably till we get the paradox of seeing people outside the organizations who are better specimens according to the standards concerned.

The last of my instances comes from the *Dunciad*. In the fourth Book Pope's satire of 'dull' kinds of men (by 'dull' he meant men, whether stupid or clever, who misdirected such talents as they possessed) includes satire of gardeners fanatic-ally expert. The speech of one such gardener contains this couplet:

> Soft on the paper ruff its leaves I spread,
> Bright with the gilded button tipt its head.[1]

Nobody knows what obsolete detail of the florist's art this gilded button refers to.[2] But before we dismiss it as flying in the face of Nature, we should put the couplet back into its context:

> Then thick as Locusts black'ning all the ground,
> A tribe, with weeds and shells fantastic crown'd,
> Each with some wond'rous gift approached the Pow'r,[3]
> A Nest, a Toad, a Fungus, or a Flow'r.
> But far the foremost, two, with earnest zeal,
> And aspect ardent to the Throne appeal.
> The first thus open'd: 'Hear thy suppliant's call,
> Great Queen, and common Mother of us all!
> Fair from its humble bed I rear'd this Flow'r,
> Suckled, and cheer'd, with air, and sun, and show'r,
> Soft in the paper ruff its leaves I spread,
> Bright with the gilded button tipt its head,
> Then thron'd in glass, and nam'd it CAROLINE:
> Each Maid cry'd, charming! and each Youth, divine!

[1] iv. 407 f.
[2] G. Sherburn, '*The Dunciad*, Book IV', *Studies in English, The University of Texas*, 1944, p. 185.　　　　[3] The Goddess Dulness.

Did Nature's pencil ever blend such rays,
Such vary'd light in one promiscuous blaze?
Now prostrate! dead! behold that Caroline:
No Maid cries, charming! and no Youth, divine!
And lo the wretch! whose vile, whose insect lust
Lay'd this gay daughter of the Spring in dust.
Oh punish him, or to th' Elysian shades
Dismiss my soul, where no Carnation fades.'[1]

The particular of the paper ruff is beautifully cleared up as a detail of early eighteenth-century gardening by the Twickenham edition. But there is no enlightenment forthcoming as to the gilded button. The common reader, however, can see well enough what the passage is getting at. Indeed the force of the particulars is extremely strong even though they are only partly understood. The common reader of today is surprised that what was evidently so pointed a particular passage in 1742 remains so pointed a general passage today. Before we read it, we had not seen or guessed how permanent the florist is, how far back he can trace his ancestry. We may even suspect that it is only the loss of records, or original lack of their existence, that keeps us from tracing it farther back still: Virgil, we know, was a 'curious florist', and in the age prior to Pope's one of his critics wished he had written on the subject 'as he once intended'.[2] 'Flowers are grown for their own sake in the *Georgics* by the old pirate settled near Tarentum.'[3] No doubt the measures Virgil took to prop his blooms were at bottom the same as those of Pope's florists and of ours. Pope's lines, as his note pointed out, are an 'imitation' of a passage in Catullus. They are therefore the more obviously Natural. No human interests seem trivial when they come to be seen as having persisted, and their having persisted helps us to grasp in essentials the forms their trappings took in earlier times. Pope, or it may have been his first editor Warburton, seems to have been aware of the persistance of horticultural tricks. One of them added this note to 'Caroline':

It is a compliment which the Florists usually pay to Princes and great persons, to give their names to the most curious Flowers of their raising . . .

---

[1] iv. 397 ff.   [2] Dryden, *Works*, ed. Scott, 1808, xiii. 331.
[3] W. F. Jackson Knight, *Roman Vergil*, 1944, pp. 166 f.

In that word 'usually' there is a glance at the *quod semper* of
St. Vincent's definition of Nature. That florists point, if indirectly, to primary Nature is clear, as it happens, from the
passage of Edward Young, which Pope must have had in
mind when writing the incident of the carnation. In the
second satire of his *Universal Passion* (the title helps to make
my point) Young wrote:

> Warm in pursuit of Foxes, and Renown,
> *Hippolitus* demands the *Sylvan* crown;
> But *Florio*'s Fame, the product of a shower,
> Grows in his garden, an illustrious flower!
> Why teems the Earth? why melt the vernal Skies?
> Why shines the Sun? to make *Paul Diack*[1] rise.
> From morn to night has *Florio* gazing stood,
> And wonder'd how the Gods could be so good.
> What shape? what hue? was ever nymph so fair?
> He doats! he dies! he too is Rooted there.
> O solid bliss! which nothing can destroy
> Except a cat, bird, snail, or idle boy.
> In Fame's full bloom lyes *Florio* down at night,
> And wakes next day a most inglorious Wight.
> The Tulip's dead! see thy fair Sister's fate,
> O *C——*! and be kind ere 'tis too late.
>   Nor are those enemies I mention'd all;
> Beware, O Florist, thy ambition's fall.
> A friend of mine indulg'd this noble flame,
> A Quaker serv'd him, *Adam* was his name.
> To one lov'd Tulip oft the master went,
> Hung o'er it, and whole days in rapture spent;
> But came, and mist it one ill-fated hour.
> He rag'd! he roar'd! 'what *Dæmon* cropt my flower?'
> Serene, quoth *Adam*, lo! 'twas crusht by me;
> Fall'n is the *Baal* to which thou bow'dst thy knee.

Then comes the question:

> 'But all men want amusement, and what crime
> 'In such a Paradise to fool our time?'

And the answer:

> None; but why proud of this? to Fame they soar;
> We grant *they're Idle*, if they'll ask no more.

[1] Young affixes a note: '*The name of a Tulip.*'

And then this final comment:

> We smile at Florists, we despise their joy,
> And think their hearts enamour'd of a toy;
> But are those wiser whom we most admire,
> Survey with envy, and pursue with fire?
> What's he, who sighs for wealth, or fame, or power?
> Another *Florio* doating on a flower,
> A short-liv'd flower, and which has often sprung
> From sordid arts, as *Florio*'s out of dung.[1]

Pope does not point the general moral, as does the parsonic Young, but because the general moral exists is the reason why he put the florists into his poem. The presence of a general interest in the contemporary particulars keeps them from becoming merely antiquarian lumber.

If in Pope's day they reserved their sharpest meaning for knowing readers, their meaning even when blunter for other readers was still adequately vivid. Scholars labour at understanding Pope as completely as the best-equipped among his first readers understood him. But they do this because of the promise they discerned in Pope even when they were common readers badly equipped to read him well. The scholar of Pope is the common reader who, being sure that there is a more particular sharpness behind, has tried to make himself as much as possible a knowing contemporary of Pope's.

In Pope's poetry there are certain passages where he does what he is seen to like doing, passages that bear his sign manual impressed most clearly. One of these comes in the superb 'On a certain Lady at Court', which I quote in full:

> I know the thing that's most uncommon;
>   (Envy, be silent and attend!)
> I know a Reasonable Woman,
>   Handsome and witty, yet a Friend.
>
> Not warp'd by Passion, aw'd by Rumour,
>   Not grave thro' Pride, or gay thro' Folly,
> An equal Mixture of good Humour,
>   And sensible soft Melancholy.
>
> 'Has she no Faults then (Envy says) Sir?'
>   Yes she has one, I must aver:
> When all the World conspires to praise her,
>   The Woman's deaf, and does not hear.[2]

---

[1] *The Universal Passion*, Sat. ii, 1725, pp. 4 ff.   [2] Twickenham ed., vi. 250.

The lady in question was Mrs. Howard, whom we know to have been deaf. Her deafness was a particular allowed for in the opening line, as well as in the closing one—it was a part of the lady's 'uncommonness', a painful part, which made the rest of her uncommonness, the moral part, the more estimable. No one outside Pope's immediate circle knew this, but no one could have found the compliment at the end of the poem incomprehensible—that compliment is conveyed by a stroke of metaphorical wit beautifully self-sufficient. Another stroke of wit lies behind it—the allusion to actual deafness—but only for those who knew the lady. Physical deafness, if we knew it to be in question, would have been a particular of the self-generalizing sort—those who are not deaf can readily imagine the privation of those who are. But in this poem there is enough wit to subsist even when, for most readers then as now, the particular was not known to exist. It is an extreme instance of Pope's care for the common reader.

VI

MAN AS JUST JUDGE

THE terms *just* and *judgement* are frequent in Pope's poetry. They occur most often in *An Essay on Criticism*, where they stand in obvious relation to 'correctness'[1] as correctness is exact and proper expression by way of words. In this sense *just* receives the following definition in the *Oxford English Dictionary*: 'In accordance with reason, truth, or fact; right; true; correct'; and 'Conformable to the standard of what is fitting or requisite; right in amount, proportion, aesthetic quality, &c.; proper; correct.' The standards concerned—those of accuracy, truthfulness, aesthetic effect —are standards set up by Nature, and the connexion which might strike us as needing explanation—that between correctness and beauty—is explained by the following passage from *The Spectator*, No. 62:

> *Bouhours*, whom I look upon to be the most penetrating of all the *French* Criticks, has taken pains to shew, that it is impossible for any Thought to be beautiful which is not just, and has not its Foundation in the Nature of Things.

'Justness', like 'correctness' itself, is more than a term used in literary criticism, as when Gulliver commended the Houyhnhnms for 'the justness of their similes':[2] it is a term denoting a standard that is applicable to as much of the human matter as possible. The just is a term of measurement: it measures the accuracy of the correspondence between an object and a representation of it. But it is also a term of commendation: it implies that the man who does the measuring is a sound specimen of a human being, who can be trusted to see things as men should. Pope used the words *just* and *judgement* repeatedly in *An Essay on Criticism* because he wished to encourage man to be constantly a good critic of

---

[1] See *On the Poetry of Pope*, pp. 43 ff.
[2] Swift, *Gulliver's Travels*, IV. ix. Cf. Pope's *Correspondence*, i. 276.

literature, and since for him books were the repository of
Nature, a good critic of life. As Reid was to say:

. . . in common language, sense always implies judgment. A man of
sense is a man of judgment. Good sense is good judgment. Nonsense
is what is evidently contrary to right judgment. Common sense is that
degree of judgment which is common to men with whom we can
converse [i.e. carry on social intercourse] and transact business.[1]

The standard for what is just is in the keeping of the judgement, and an examination of the nature and function of the
judgement, as Pope and his contemporaries saw it, must
begin with the passage in which Hobbes gives an account of
fancy, under which term we ourselves would also understand
imagination. Certain of his scattered remarks on the matter
are at variance, but this scarcely concerns the use of those
I am selecting, my object being to be interesting on Pope
rather than to be fair to Hobbes. Hobbes first deals with the
fancy in his account of the intellect of certain classes of men,
an account written about 1640, but not published until 1650
in 'Humane Nature, or the Fundamental Elements of Policy',
the first part of his *Tripos in Three Discourses*. Contrary, he says,
to man's sensual disposition, which induces dulness, wit is

that *quick ranging* of mind . . . which is joined with *curiosity* of comparing the things that come into the mind, one with another: in which
comparison, a man delighteth himself either with finding unexpected
similitude of things, otherwise much unlike, in which men place the
excellency of *fancy*, and from whence proceed those grateful [i.e.
pleasant] similies, metaphors, and other tropes, by which both *poets*
and *orators* have it in their power to make things please or displease,
and shew well or ill to others, as they like themselves; or else in discerning suddenly *dissimilitude* in things that otherwise appear the same.
And this virtue of the mind [i.e. this faculty for finding *dis*similitude]
is that by which men attain to exact and perfect *knowledge*; and the
pleasure thereof consisteth in continual instruction, and in distinction
of places, persons, and seasons, and is commonly termed by the name
of *judgment*: for, to judge is nothing else, but to distinguish or discern:
and both *fancy* and *judgment* are commonly comprehended under the
name of *wit*, which seemeth to be a tenuity and agility of spirits,
contrary to that restiness [i.e. sluggishness] of the spirits supposed in
those that are dull.[2]

---

[1] *The Works*, i. 421.   [2] *English Works*, iv. 55 f.

In this passage Hobbes is taking wit in the old comprehensive sense of 'intellection' as opposed to 'will', and discerning in it the joint work of 'wit' (he uses the same word) and 'curiosity', which collaborate to discover (*a*) similarity between things that are 'otherwise mostly unlike', and (*b*) dissimilarity between things otherwise apparently identical. When they work to the former end they are fancy, when to the latter judgement.

The work that Hobbes allotted fancy and judgement does not exhaust the mind's work. The fancy does its work only in a corner of the mind (even if the mind be that of a poet). Fancy is concerned only with the linking together of objects mainly *dissimilar*, and, as Hobbes saw, there is no reason for this sort of linking to take place very often. Much more work is done by the judgement in discriminating between objects nearly alike—the work, say, of deciding which key to select from a bunch. But the main work of the mind is a grouping of things which are nearly alike, a work with which neither fancy nor judgement has anything to do. This more constant work is implied in the 'imposing of names' other than 'proper' names. It is usually more important to men that they form such groups than that they discriminate between slightly different members of them by calling in judgement. Men derive more benefit from grouping together, say, cups as cups are distinguished from pans than from distinguishing one cup from another, let alone from exercising the fancy to distinguish the common property or properties, whatever those may be, linking cups to, say, primroses.

For the sake of completeness, we may examine what Hobbes says of the fancy. On this occasion at least, he sees it as discovering similitude in things 'otherwise much unlike'. The degree in that word 'much' is to some extent flexible: it allows of different distances in the far-fetching. In similes such as 'her eyes are as bright as candle-flames', 'as dew', 'as fishes', 'as diamonds', 'as suns', 'as lightning', 'as a robin's', there is a considerable range of unlikeness in the minor terms, all of which are 'fetched', and most fetched from far—I am not speaking in terms of feet or miles, though distance in space is sometimes to the point. On this occasion degrees of distance do not count for Hobbes: it is clear from what he says later in the same passage that he is thinking of poets in general rather than of metaphysical poets:

those grateful [i.e. pleasing] similies, metaphors, and other tropes, by which both *poets* and *orators* have it in their power to make things please or displease, and shew well or ill to others, as they like themselves.[1]

In other words, fancy is the means of assembling such a minor term as that in

My way of life
Is fall'n into the sere, the yellow leaf;[2]

and, to leave similes and metaphors, the assembled terms of Otway's line:

Lutes, laurels, seas of milk, and ships of amber;[3]

and of Coleridge's Freudian misquotation of it that better illustrated his point:

Lutes, lobsters, seas of milk and ships of amber.[4]

Though for Hobbes in 1640 wit included fancy, as time went on fancy came to usurp the name of wit completely: it came to be exclusively a name for the faculty for finding similitudes in objects otherwise much unlike. And though Hobbes's instances of wit-fancy were general poetic instances, three years earlier he had shown a preference for metaphors as they were more far-fetched, the metaphors therefore of a certain sort of poet. The evidence depends on an interesting piece of detective work I owe to the authors of 'Wit, "Mixt Wit" and the Bee in Amber'.[5] In his *Briefe of*

---

[1] Cf. Locke: 'This is a way of proceeding quite contrary to metaphor and allusion, wherein for the most part lies that entertainment and pleasantry of wit which strikes so lively on the fancy, and therefore so acceptable to all people; because its beauty appears at first sight, and there is required no labour of thought to examine what truth or reason there is in it. The mind, without looking any farther, rests satisfied with the agreeableness of the picture and the gaiety of the fancy: and it is a kind of an affront to go about to examine it by the severe rules of truth and good reason; whereby it appears that it consists in something that is not perfectly conformable to them' (*Of Human Understanding*, II. xi. 2).   [2] *Macbeth*, v. iii. 22 f.

[3] *Venice Preserved*, v.   [4] *Biographia Literaria*, i. 62.

[5] W. Lee Ustick and Hoyt H. Hudson, *Huntington Library Bulletin*, viii, 1937, 103 ff. I am indebted to this article for several points, though I do not always follow the authors in their interpretation of the materials they use.

the Art of Rhetorique. Containing in substance all that Aristotle hath written in his Three Bookes of that Subject (1635?) Hobbes echoed Aristotle directly in saying that 'A *Metaphor* ought not to be so farre fetcht, as that the Similitude may not easily appeare'.[1] But in adapting III. xi ('Metaphors should be drawn from objects which are proper to the object, but not too obvious'—so the Loeb edition translates) he weighted the sense differently:

> Such *Metaphors* as these [i.e. attributing life to inanimate things, as in saying that a sword 'devours'] come into a Mans mind, by the observation of things that have similitude and proportion one to another. And the more unlike, and unproportional the things be otherwise, the more *grace* hath the *Metaphor*.[2]

The adaptation here is a perversion, and a perversion due to contemporary fashions in poetry. In the seventeenth century generally, metaphysical wit-fancy fetched similitudes very far indeed. This it could only do by reducing the property common to the major and minor terms. Take for instance the property of colour. Colour, on most occasions, is a meagre ground of resemblance between objects, and especially when the colour of the minor term is not 'natural' colour but colour modified by man's artifice. Because of this, the satiric Butler hit on the comparison of the change from night to morning (a process with which man has nothing to do) to the change of colour undergone by a lobster when taken in hand by man and cooked:

> And, like a Lobster boil'd, the Morn
> From black to red began to turn.[3]

According to Hobbes's scale this simile has more to commend it than, say, Shakespeare's

> Night's candles are burnt out, and jocund day
> Stands tiptoe on the misty mountain tops.[4]

Pointing to the distance between dawn and a cooking lobster was Butler's means of reducing a principle of the metaphysicals to the absurd. Wit that went so far afield had the

[1] p. 156.   [2] Hobbes, *Briefe of the Art of Rhetorique*, pp. 173 f.
[3] *Hudibras*, II. ii. 30 f.   [4] *Romeo and Juliet*, III. v. 9 f.

effect of ridiculing the other mental faculty that Hobbes began by including in wit—judgement. Distinguishing between objects which are nearly alike, judgement was outraged when the objects which fancy brought together were unlike in all but one slender particular. Judgement agreed with Aristotle's view that 'objects which are proper [cognate to a fair degree] to the object' form a better source of the minor term of the simile. After the flashing of the metaphysical 'wit' of Cleveland and the rest, man could not but return to a renewed appreciation of the judgement, to agreeing with Boyle's recommendation that a

Man [should] draw his Conceptions from the very Nature of the thing he speaks of, which, among those that can judge of Wit, is held a far greater sign of it, than the saying things more specious, and elaborate.[1]

Boyle's invoking better judges was his means of slighting the metaphysical poets and their Clevelandisms.

I shall show later on that in *An Essay on Criticism* the minor terms of Pope's images were fetched from common life, and so, the subject being reading and criticism, not fetched from far.[2] In the love poems the same principle holds: unlike the metaphysicals, Pope agreed with most poets, ancient and modern, in feeling that remote and startling images were not in keeping, that tenderness made a display of wit-fancy look cheap and insulting. When writing poems other than love poems, however, where feeling did not run so high and he was intent on accuracy of thought, he found in similes a means of sharpening the accuracy: but for this end, he had to be free to choose whatever minor term, near or remote, was most suitable. Even so, he tended to draw his minor terms from near at hand, as for instance in the two similes (one is double-barrelled) of the 'Prologue to the *Three Hours after Marriage*':

> Why on all Authors then should Criticks fall?
> Since some have writ, and shewn no Wit at all.
> Condemn a Play of theirs, and they evade it,
> Cry, damn not us, but damn the *French* who made it,

---

[1] [Robert Boyle], *Occasional Reflections upon Several Subjects*, 1665, p. 37.
[2] pp. 141 f. below.

By running Goods, these graceless Owlers gain,
Theirs are the Rules of *France*, the Plots of *Spain*:
But Wit, like Wine, from happier Climates brought,
Dash'd by these Rogues, turns *English* common Draught: . . .
Poets make Characters, as *Salesmen* Cloaths,
We take no Measure of your Fops and Beaus;
But here all Sizes and all Shapes you meet,
And fit your selves—like Chaps in *Monmouth-Street*.[1]

The main reason why Pope favoured drawing the minor term of a simile from things near at hand was that a minor term could add to the sum of thought as well as make part of it clearer. In the 'Epistle to Mr. Jervas', his painter friend, he used as image what lay at the heart of his theme:

> Smit with the love of Sister-arts we came,
> And met congenial, mingling flame with flame;
> Like friendly colours found them both unite,
> And each from each contract new strength and light . . .
> Oh lasting as those colours may they shine,
> Free as thy stroke, yet faultless as thy line!
> New graces yearly, like thy works, display;
> Soft without weakness, without glaring gay.[2]

Similarly in his 'To Sir Godfrey Kneller *On his painting for me the Statues of* Apollo, Venus *and* Hercules', he used the three pictures concerned as his minor terms:

> What God, what Genius did the Pencil move
>   When KNELLER painted These?
> Twas Friendship—warm as *Phoebus*, kind as Love,
>   And strong as *Hercules*.

This drawing close together of theme and 'decoration' is according to a principle that Pope constantly followed, the principle of making the most of what lay nearest, of encouraging congenial things to cohere, of being jealous of anything centrifugal. He occasionally writes a poem which is self-proclaimed as all simile—the simile poem was a fashionable small 'kind'. But usually he drew on similes only for minor services: they seldom contribute to the structure of a poem, as they may in a poem by a metaphysical poet. The big exception to this is when Pope is writing satire, when

---

[1] Twickenham ed., vi, p. 178, ll. 7 ff.   [2] Id., pp. 156 ff., ll. 13 ff.

similes become a part of the very method of attack. The minor
term here needed to carry as much insult as possible. Pope's
method is well illustrated from his first published essay in
the kind:

> *To the* AUTHOR *of a* POEM, *intitled,* SUCCESSIO.
>
> Begone ye Criticks, and restrain your Spite,
> *Codrus* writes on, and will for ever write;
> The heaviest Muse the swiftest Course has gone,
> As clocks run fastest when most Lead is on.
> What tho' no Bees around your Cradle flew,
> Nor on your Lips distill'd their golden Dew?
> Yet have we oft discover'd in their stead,
> A Swarm of Drones, that buzz'd about your Head.
> When you, like *Orpheus,* strike the warbling Lyre,
> Attentive Blocks stand round you, and admire.
> Wit, past thro' thee, no longer is the same,
> As Meat digested takes a diff'rent Name;
> But Sense must sure thy safest Plunder be,
> Since no Reprizals can be made on thee.
> Thus thou may'st Rise, and in thy daring Flight
> (Tho' ne'er so weighty) reach a wondrous height;
> So, forc'd from Engines, Lead it self can fly,
> And pondrous Slugs move nimbly thro' the Sky.

Here the fetching is from far because from the unexpected:
even 'like *Orpheus*' is unexpected after Pope has made it
clear that Elkanah Settle, the author of the despised poem,
is a bad poet. In the similes, and metaphors, of the satires
Pope stopped at nothing: Sporus is called 'a mere white
Curd of Ass's milk', and there is the protracted nastiness of

> *P[ope].* Faith it imports not much from whom it came⎫
> Whoever borrow'd, could not be to blame,   ⎬
> Since the whole House did afterwards the same: ⎭
> Let Courtly Wits to Wits afford supply,
> As Hog to Hog in Huts of *Westphaly;*
> If one, thro' Nature's Bounty or his Lord's,
> Has what the frugal, dirty soil affords,
> From him the next receives it, thick or thin,
> As pure a Mess almost as it came in;
> The blessed Benefit, not there confin'd,
> Drops to the third who nuzzles close behind;

From tail to mouth, they feed, and they carouse;
The last, full fairly gives it to the *House*.
  Fr[iend]. This filthy Simile, this beastly Line,
Quite turns my Stomach—*P[ope]*. So does Flatt'ry mine;
And all your Courtly Civet-Cats can vent,
Perfume to you, to me is Excrement.[1]

Of fancy and judgement, it is judgement that is more useful
to man in his daily concerns. After the work of that general
faculty of the mind which for the sake of quotidian convenience places objects in categories, it steps in to effect a dis-
association as and when dissociation is more convenient still.
The word 'cup' links all objects which are generally similar
in form and end, and it is judgement that marks off, as
occasion requires, one cup from another. In any one man's
experience most groups will remain undivided by the judgement. I myself know what the word *dog* denotes, and can
appreciate the act of Pope's judgement which subdivided
from dog the 'hound sagacious',[2] but cannot appreciate the
several acts of Macbeth's judgement:

> Ay, in the catalogue ye go for men;
> As hounds, and greyhounds, mongrels, spaniels, curs,
> Shoughs, water-rugs, and demi-wolves, are clept
> All by the name of dogs: the valu'd file
> Distinguishes the swift, the slow, the subtle,
> The housekeeper, the hunter, every one
> According to the gift which bounteous Nature
> Hath in him clos'd; whereby he does receive
> Particular addition, from the bill
> That writes them all alike; and so of men.[3]

Pope himself was content with the bare knowledge that the
judgement might, but usually does not, subdivide mosses
into a great many kinds.[4] Where he did employ judgement
energetically was in making such important divisions as
those between Nature and non-Nature, right and wrong,
good and bad, and so on. Man was seen as 'Sole judge of
Truth', though he remains unfortunately 'in endless Error
hurl'd;[5] and the great men who encouraged Pope as a young

---

[1] *Imitations of Horace*, 'Epilogue to the Satires', dial. ii. 168 ff.
[2] *Essay on Man*, i. 214.   [3] *Macbeth*, III. i. 91 ff.
[4] See above, p. 5.   [5] *Essay on Man*, ii. 17.

poet were lauded as models for a sound judgement of much
of life:

> From these the world will judge of Men and Books,
> Not from the *Burnets, Oldmixons,* and *Cooks.*[1]

Let us, he would say, judge men at least as finely as table
delicacies were judged by Helluo, who,

> The Nose of Hautgout, and the Tip of Taste,
> Critick'd your wine, and analyz'd your meat.[2]

The power to judge rightly was a power he had needed from
the start, but having used it for the establishment of categories, his effort was often engaged in the other direction—in
seeing that 'wit' did not bring together things that were
mainly dissimilar, in pondering the quantity and quality of
the likeness that made for coherence among the things
assembled by the judgement, all of which activity was in the
interests of forming opinions about human matters which
were as valid as possible.

[1] *Epistle to Dr. Arbuthnot,* ll. 145 f.
[2] *Moral Essays,* ii ('Of the Characters of Women'), 80 f.

VII

MAN AND THE BEAUTIFUL,
THE UGLY, THE GROTESQUE, AND
THE INDECENT

I

THE relation of the beautiful to Nature stood firm for
Pope, and it is the more important to examine it because
between him and ourselves stands Keats.

As it happened, the relation received explicit statement
only in those lines the first of which, detached from their
context, I have already quoted as a *locus classicus* of the idea
of Nature in all its generality:

> First follow Nature, and your judgement frame
> By her just standard, which is still the same:
> Unerring NATURE, still divinely bright,
> One clear, unchang'd, and universal light,[1]

on which immediately follow:

> Life, force, and beauty, must to all impart,
> At once the source, and end, and test of Art.

Literature, which is included in what Pope calls 'art', finds its
materials in Nature and presents itself to mankind, who value
the life, force, and beauty that literature draws from its
Natural materials, and test the worth of the whole by standards set up by Nature, or, in other words, by the standards
of the common reader. This places in Nature the source and
credentials of beauty.

The questions raised directly and indirectly by the status
he accorded to beauty in this passage are crucial in a discussion of Pope's poetry. When a poet speaks of beauty, however vaguely, it behoves his critic to pay attention, since what
he thinks of beauty must lie near to what he thinks of poetry.
His views on the matter are only his views: as Mallarme

---

1 *Essay on Criticism*, ll. 68 ff.

would say, it is not by virtue of theories, ideas, or opinions that he is a poet. The status of his poetry will depend not on the worth of his views on beauty, but on the beauty he creates as a thing put on paper and transferred thence to the minds of his readers. Nevertheless the beauty he creates is likely to bear some relation to his views.

In the field of human affairs beauty, as Pope saw, does not occupy a prominent place. He therefore used the word rarely. He knew that even those few exceptional people whose aesthetic tastes are strong and durable cannot possibly give beauty more than a certain prominence in their lives: the cult of the aesthetic is doomed to break down. Any prominence that beauty achieves in the life of ordinary people it achieves at certain seasons and under certain conditions. Then they are very much concerned with it. But just because this pertinent beauty is attached to human beings, they are least able to attend to it for what it is in itself. To one human being— unless for the moment he is being a painter, in *esse* or *posse*— no other human being can exist picture-like as a surface arrangement of colours. The sensuous display coexists in vital relationship with things like love, lust, morality, social usage, money, domesticity, jealousy, envy, comfort, friendship, parenthood. Indeed, where human beauty is concerned, it is because so many cognate interests are aroused, and in conflict, that stories by the hundreds have taken their rise from the complex. The *Rape of the Lock* is a primary example of a complex of interests of which human beauty is one. In that complex, beauty may occupy the centre on occasions:

> . . . Beauty draws us with a single Hair.[1]

On occasions, it may even blind us:

> If to her share some Female Errors fall,
> Look on her Face, and you'll forget 'em all.[2]

But on other and longer occasions it has a rival and a superior: however effectively 'awful Beauty' has 'put . . . on all its Arms',[3] it is in the end powerless—

---

[1] *Rape of the Lock*, ii. 28.   [2] Id. ii. 17 f.   [3] Id. i. 139.

Unless good Sense preserve what Beauty gains . . .
Beauties in vain their pretty Eyes may roll;
Charms strike the Sight, but Merit wins the Soul.[1]

But whether beneficial or harmful, momentarily supreme or
usually subsidiary, human beauty, human ugliness, and the
innumerable compounds of them are close concerns of mankind. Nor does it matter that tastes in beauty differ. What
alone matters is that for mankind human beauty has a taste,
that, whether pleasantly or not, it attacks man's palate. Man
has achieved a working philosophy for dealing with the many
attacks made on him from that quarter, and it is to the
pattern of this philosophy that all great stories are shaped.
To revert to the *Rape of the Lock*. Its sexual morality is
readily approved as Natural. That morality is made most explicit in the speech of Clarissa from which I have just quoted,
and it won from Johnson a paragraph lively with Natural
approval:

> The purpose of the Poet is, as he tells us, to laugh at 'the little un-
> guarded follies of the female sex'. It is therefore without justice that
> Dennis charges *The Rape of the Lock* with the want of a moral, and for
> that reason sets it below *The Lutrin*, which exposes the pride and dis-
> cord of the clergy. Perhaps neither Pope nor Boileau has made the
> world much better than he found it; but if they had both succeeded, it
> were easy to tell who would have deserved most from publick gratitude.
> The freaks, and humours, and spleen, and vanity of women, as they
> embroil families in discord and fill houses with disquiet, do more to
> obstruct the happiness of life in a year than the ambition of the clergy
> in many centuries. It has been well observed that the misery of man
> proceeds not from any single crush of overwhelming evil, but from
> small vexations continually repeated.[2]

The moral of the exquisite poem stands as firm as a kitchen
table. But the poem is Natural in its narrative and picture as
well as in its moral—though its narrative and picture are
primary Nature acting through secondary (again I point forward to a later discussion):[3] we can imagine that the heroes
and heroines of the world's literature—from Paris and Helen
to, say, the personages in Mr. Nigel Dennis's *Boys and Girls
Come out to Play*—would accord the story their ready or en-

[1] Id. v. 16 ff.   [2] *Lives of the Poets*, iii. 234.   [3] See below, pp. 118 ff.

forced assent. And accord their assent also to this outburst of
Pope's Eloisa, however much some of them might feel the
need to modify it in the interests of society:

> How oft', when press'd to marriage, have I said,
> Curse on all laws but those which love has made!
> Love, free as air, at sight of human ties,
> Spreads his light wings, and in a moment flies.
> Let wealth, let honour, wait the wedded dame,
> August her deed, and sacred be her fame;
> Before true passion all those views remove,
> Fame, wealth, and honour! what are you to Love?
> The jealous God, when we profane his fires,
> Those restless passions in revenge inspires;
> And bids them make mistaken mortals groan,
> Who seek in love for ought but love alone.
> Should at my feet the world's great master fall,
> Himself, his throne, his world, I'd scorn 'em all:
> Not *Caesar*'s empress wou'd I deign to prove;
> No, make me mistress to the man I love;
> If there be yet another name more free,
> More fond than mistress, make me that to thee!
> Oh happy state! when souls each other draw,
> When love is liberty, and nature, law;
> All then is full, possessing, and possest,
> No craving Void left aking in the breast:
> Ev'n thought meets thought ere from the lips it part,
> And each warm wish springs mutual from the heart.
> This sure is bliss (if bliss on earth there be)
> And once the lot of *Abelard* and me.[1]

The cruelty of the 'character' of Sporus, as I have said, shows
Pope, by the measure of Nature, to be too intensely angry,
but the beauty he ascribes to his victim shocks mankind as it
shocked Pope:

> . . . this Bug with gilded wings,
> This painted Child of Dirt that stinks and stings . . .
> Fop at the Toilet, Flatt'rer at the Board,
> Now trips a Lady, and now struts a Lord.
> *Eve*'s Tempter thus the Rabbins have exprest,
> A Cherub's face, a Reptile all the rest;
> Beauty that shocks you . . . .[2]

---

[1] *Eloisa to Abelard*, ll. 73 ff.   [2] *Epistle to Dr. Arbuthnot*, ll. 309 ff.

The working philosophy as to sexual beauty is well established, and it is in accord with it that Pope presented human
beauty. As a poet of Nature he used the word 'beauty' more
often as a concise synonym for beautiful women than as an
abstract noun. But, also as a poet of Nature, he used it to
imply a limitation. When 'beauties' are mentioned, the
suggestion is that the synonym is limitingly exact, that the
women in question lack all other womanly virtues:

> Beauties in vain their pretty Eyes may roll:
> Charms strike the Sight, but Merit wins the Soul.[1]

On the basis of this we can generalize as to the place of
beauty in Pope's philosophy. It did not exist for him in a
category to itself, a category high enough to place it, as
Shaftesbury placed it, beside goodness and truth. It was, at
best, an embellisher. And so the crucial question for Pope
was the worth of the thing embellished. Beauty depended
for its value on the company it kept. He valued it most as it
adorned Nature.

His attitude is declared when he turns to consider architecture, an art in which he had some practical concern. In
buildings beauty was ridiculous unless it embellished useful-
ness. Like splendour, which at its best is beauty with
grandeur added, beauty

> . . . borrows all her rays from Sense.[2]

That was why the splendours of Timon's gardens were
offensive—I shall come to quote the passage on another
occasion.[3] One of the grandest of recently built show-places
was Vanbrugh's Blenheim, but for Pope the aesthetic was
partly defeated by the architect's disregard for what was
fundamental to everything else, the convenience of the
human beings who were to live in it:

> Upon the Duke of MARLBOROUGH's
> House at Woodstock.
>
> *Atria longe patent; sed nec cœnantibus usquam,*
> *Nec somno locus est; quàm bene non habites?*
>   Mart. Epig.

[1] *Rape of the Lock,* v. 33 f.
[2] *Moral Essays,* iv ('Of the Use of Riches', To Burlington), 180.
[3] See below, pp. 100 f.

See, Sir, here's the grand Approach,
This Way for his Grace's Coach;
There lies the Bridge, and here's the Clock,
Observe the Lyon and the Cock,
The spacious Court, the Colonnade,
And mark how wide the Hall is made?
The Chimneys are so well design'd,
They never smoke in any Wind.
This gallery's contriv'd for walking,
The Windows to retire and talk in;
The Council-Chamber for Debate,
And all the rest are Rooms of State.
  Thanks, Sir, cry'd I, 'tis very fine.
 But where d' ye sleep, or where d' ye dine?
 I find by all you have been telling,
 That 'tis a House, but not a Dwelling.[1]

At Blenheim the dining-room exists, but is draughtily distant from the kitchens. When Gulliver was pinned between the bones on a Brobdingnagian dinner-plate, Swift noted in explanation of his escape that 'Princes seldom get their meat hot'.[2] Mankind likes its meat hot: fire, along with clothes and meat, are things that even riches exist to provide first of all. But the riches sunk in Blenheim could not show fire as having been applied to meat recently enough to justify the useless beauty of the arrangements—the diners missed 'the beauty of it hot'.[3] Something like the same questions were prompted by Timon's villa. Many might count it aesthetically inept that

  Two Cupids squirt before . . .

but nobody could approve that

  a Lake behind
Improves the keenness of the Northern wind.[4]

Finally, as for the house and its entertainment, the visitor would find himself asking:

---

[1] *Original Poems and Translations by Mr. Hill, Mr. Eusden, Mr. Broome, Dr. King, &c.,* 1714, p. 33. In the Twickenham ed., vi. 412, this poem is placed among 'Poems of Doubtful Authorship'. If not written by Pope, it may be taken to represent his views, since one of his letters gives virtually a prose version of it (*Correspondence,* i. 431 f.).

[2] *Gulliver's Travels,* II. iii. The coolness of hot dishes was a notable deficiency at Versailles.

[3] A popular phrase introduced into T. S. Eliot's *Waste Land,* l. 167.

[4] *Moral Essays,* iv ('Of the Use of Riches', To Burlington), 111 f. 'Improves' hits at the landscape-designers.

Is this a dinner? this a Genial room?
No, 'tis a Temple, and a Hecatomb.[1]

If the beauty of Timon's villa did not exist, that of Blenheim did, but was begrudged. Art should not begin as 'fine' till art as practical had seen that all the simple necessaries were assured. Nature did not approve what though beautiful slighted her. One of the items in Pope's praise of Burlington is that

You show us Rome was glorious, not profuse,
And pompous buildings once were things of Use.[2]

Before looking at Pope's concern with the beautiful in external nature, there is something more to say. Touched for once with Platonic philosophy, mankind has become accustomed to use the term 'beauty' not only of concrete objects but of abstractions. In general usage 'beauty' is applied to abstract things like character, disposition, 'sentiments' (in the old meaning of sincere opinions). No doubt something more than a Platonic spirituality is expressed when such abstractions are called 'beautiful': moral character may be invisible but it inhabits a physical body that smiles the more sweetly because of the beauty of the character—given our face by our parents, we partly remake it as our character persists in wearing it for frontispiece.

It is an indication of the strength of Pope's attachment to Nature that he often honoured this usage. He honoured it constantly in his criticism of Homer. It tells the more strongly there because he advertised his criticism as aesthetic in the literary sense: 'The chief Design' of his criticism was to 'comment upon *Homer* as a Poet'.[3] In the course of that criticism Pope often called Homer's story and persons 'beautiful'. That is expected, story and persons being for the imagination concrete. But as often as not, he applied the term to Homer's morality. Perhaps Horace had something like this in mind when he declared that Homer exhibited clear and intelligible distinctions between the beautiful, the base,

---

[1] Id., ll. 155 f.
[2] Id., ll. 23 f.
[3] *Iliad*, 'Observations on the First Book', p. 5. And cf. the instructions to Broome, whom Pope employed to translate excerpts from the commentary of Eustathius (*Correspondence*, i. 270).

the useful, and their opposites.[1] Pope would not have called
'beautiful' what was not founded on Nature: when beauty
existed without that foundation it was tinsel. That is why he
could not approve many of the 'metaphysical' poems of the
seventeenth century—when speaking of one group of incomplete critics, he alleged that they

> . . . to *Conceit* alone their taste confine,
> And glitt'ring thoughts struck out at ev'ry line;
> Pleas'd with a work where nothing's just or fit;
> One glaring Chaos and wild heap of wit.
> Poets like painters, thus, unskill'd to trace
> The naked nature and the living grace,
> With gold and jewels cover ev'ry part,
> And hide with ornaments their want of art.[2]

2

With this as preparation we can turn to study Pope's 'description'.

That term is used in the famous paragraph that summa-
rizes his career as a poet:

> Soft were my Numbers, who could take offence
> While pure Description held the place of Sense?
> Like gentle *Fanny*'s was my flow'ry Theme,
> A painted Mistress, or a purling Stream . . .
> . . . not in Fancy's Maze [I] wander'd long,
> But stoop'd to Truth, and moraliz'd [my] song.[3]

Description implies description at length: of a series of sense-
impressions described in numerous words. I shall use it also
to denote description in few words, whether of few or more
sense-impressions. Description implies, as any words do, a
voice, a voice a man, and a man thought and feeling. When
seeking to write 'pure' description, a poet can hope to do no
more than cut out as many traces of thought and feeling as
possible—'purity', or limitation to sense-impressions, will
never be absolute. In discussing the charge that Pope

---

[1] *Epistles*, II. ii. 1 ff. The usage survives in Newman's 'Poetry with reference to
Aristotle's Poetics': see *Essays Critical and Historical*, ed. 1877, i. 16: 'Romeo
and Juliet are too good for the termination to which the plot leads: so are Ophelia
and the Bride of Lammermoor. In these cases there is something inconsistent with
correct beauty, and therefore unpoetical.'   [2] *Essay in Criticism*, ll. 289 ff.
[3] *Epistle to Dr. Arbuthnot*, ll. 147 ff., 340 f.

brought against the descriptions in his early poems I shall be concerned, therefore, not only with the qualities of the sense-impressions they embody, but with the degree to which they are mixed with thought and feeling, as also with the nature of that thought and feeling.

Sense-impressions contribute so incessantly and so variously to our waking life that we have a right to expect a poet to honour them with a due place in his object. We have a right to expect him to show that he has found the world a vivid thing, daedal, tintinnabulant, bleeding with colours, burning with scents and flavours. Accordingly, when Pope dismissed his earlier poems as poems that described in favour of his later ones as poems that presented 'sense' or Nature, we might feel uneasy as to the poetry of the later poems, unless we happened to know them in advance. To know the later poems is to know them as poetry complete. Indeed, anyone coming on the lines I have just quoted in their place in *An Epistle to Dr. Arbuthnot* sees that he must take Pope's account of the contents of these later poems as a rhetorical account, having just enough to truth to stand on, and no more.

In the first place we do not need to divide Pope's early poems from his later with incisiveness: his work is remarkably of a piece since it was mature at so early a stage.[1] There is description in numerous words in the early work—numerous, that is, by the rigorous standards of economy already set up by the young Pope—and also in the later, where the descriptions, when long, cover a vast ground and are crowded with sense-impressions from various sources, descriptions that are long only because they are made up of many small descriptions.[2] Economy can coexist with spread and richness if you are economical about each of a great number of things. There is also, in both early and late work, description in few words. But the descriptions in words comparatively numerous are rarer in the late work than in the earlier. So hedged about, Pope's remark about description can stand. But not as it applies to description dubbed as 'pure'. Even in the early work his description is remarkably 'impure', being not only picture but the medium for Nature:

[1] See Appendix I, pp. 247 ff. below.   [2] See below, pp. 197 f.

On her white Breast a sparkling *Cross* she wore,
Which *Jews* might kiss, and Infidels adore.
Her lively Looks a sprightly Mind disclose,
Quick as her Eyes, and as unfix'd as those:
Favours to none, to all she Smiles extends,
Oft she rejects, but never once offends.
Bright as the Sun, her Eyes the Gazers strike,
And, like the Sun, they shine on all alike.
Yet graceful Ease, and Sweetness void of Pride,
Might hide her Faults, if *Belles* had Faults to hide:
If to her share some Female Errors fall,
Look on her Face, and you'll forget 'em all.[1]

Like an unhurried shepherd, Pope is folding his Natural thoughts, even if he allows them to browse a little on the way in. And after what I have said of his liking to have beauty useful, this is what we should expect.

Pope, then, does allot a due place in his subject-matter to pleasant sense-impressions. But there are varieties and grades of them. What, then, is the nature of Pope's, and the powers of the senses with which he received them? On the evidence of Donne's poems, for instance, their author's senses were vigorous, keen, free, and manly; and, to take another instance, the senses of Dryden were those of a lumbering, burly, even brutish giant, occasionally touched to a big downy softness. On the same evidence, that of the poems, the senses of Pope were at once warm, 'snail-horn', and voracious. To speak generally, they were the senses of Keats.

As shown in his poetry, Keats's senses exercised themselves almost wholly on the beautiful, if sometimes on the austerely beautiful: they were senses on a diet. And the external world offers enough of the beautiful to keep even such tireless fastidious senses fully employed. In reading his poetry, so strenuous is the play of the senses, we almost forget that the object is chosen by a thorough-going specialist: he can make his limits seem wide ones. But readers of much poetry know that finer pleasures are offered by poets who see the world steadily, with whatever passionate vision, and see it whole. Keats knew the hard truth of this with the added pain of knowing that the powers to reach to it—powers he

---

[1] *Rape of the Lock*, ii. 7 ff.

prayed to possess—might never be his, or not early enough. He was under no delusion as to ·the supremacy of Shake-speare, Chaucer, Milton, Spenser, and Wordsworth. He did not allow the right of Pope to join these poets, but that delu-sion was coincident on the respective places he and Pope occupied in time: Keats had to despise his 'father' in order to have the chance to be himself, had to despise the poet of a line like

> To Isles of fragrance, lilly-silver'd vales,[1]

because he was also the poet of lines like

> How Henley lay inspir'd beside a sink,[2]

and

> Who shall decide, when Doctors disagree?[3]

But readers of Keats have not always allowed him the benefit of those completer ideals of his, ideals which lay beyond such poetry as he attained to writing. They have taken his poetry not as the marvellous work of one who saw the cruel dis-parity between itself and *Venus and Adonis*—to make the fairest comparison—but as an ideal in itself. With all his wonderfully sure hold on certain sorts of things, Keats, un-like the young Shakespeare, had no sure hold on mankind. I may remark in passing that readers who drench themselves in Keats's poetry, as he drenched himself in the beautiful, spoil themselves for reading other poetry. They spoil them-selves for reading the poetry of Pope, having forgone the power to experience poetry that allots a merely due place to the Keatsian and a due place to everything else. And because Pope does not give them the Keatsian beautiful by itself, they sometimes fail to see that he gives them it at all.

Evidence of the Keats in Pope exists plentifully in the re-cords of his life, especially in Spence's *Anecdotes* and Pope's letters. In *On the Poetry of Pope* I quoted several instances.[4] Of the more purely biographical evidence, the brightest in-stance is that decisive moment in 1718 when Pope chose a place to live in. His choice was the narrower in that pro-fessional reasons required him to live near London but not

---

[1] *Dunciad*, iv. 303.   [2] Id. ii. 425.
[3] *Moral Essays*, iii ('Of the Use of Riches', To Bathurst), 1.   [4] pp. 24 ff.

in it. To a poet of Nature who depended for the fulness of his material on men as well as on books about men, London with all its hum of news and 'music of humanity' must needs be audible. And, more entirely practical still, publishers had to be accessible constantly—in 1735, to cite the bumper year, the great business man among the poets saw sixty-eight books and pamphlets through the press.[1] For practical reasons, then, Pope needed a place to and from which his

[1] In between the earlier and the later writing come Pope's translations of Homer and the edition of Shakespeare's plays. The interval was deemed necessary for financial reasons. Pope's Catholic religion ruled out party writing, and he did not care to accept bribe and pension. The only way left, therefore, was that of making money by writing 'pure' literature; and, against hard conditions, which were of recent growth and so all the harder, he gained a competence on the scale that allowed him to live the life he wanted to. Professor R. H. Griffith has made his historic achievement clear:

'Pope was the first man in English Literature to accumulate an independent fortune from the sale of books that were written as works of art. As well as poet, he was a man of business. He meant to see that his published books 'succeeded'. Taking environment by the throat, he compelled it to serve his own ends: he ameliorated risk into a reasonable certainty. In his youth, he meditated upon patronage, and dismissed it as a system for his own aggrandizement. It was an obsolescent system. As other customs inheriting from the feudal organization of society decayed after the Rebellion, so patronage disintegrated through stages of a sort of stock-company patronage, which was publishing by subscription, and political-party patronage, which was the shifting of the burden of support in the reign of good Queen Anne from individual shoulders to the shoulders of the government. In his manhood, Pope watched the disintegration through. On the other hand, with education spreading out and downwards, the writing class had developed proportionally more rapidly than the class of reading purchasers of books. Hardship, poverty, a fierce struggle to survive had ensued among writers, often a losing struggle. Prose and verse from 1670 to 1740 are replete with whimpers, moans, sardonic laughter, anathemas upon the Muses' arid breasts. A dependable patron was gone, a sustaining public was not yet come. With such a recalcitrant condition Pope wrestled; from it he wrested success. He resorted at times to subterfuges we think undignified, but he lost no contemporary prestige by them; we pronounce them base, he thought them fire with which to whip the devil. And, as we have seen, he knew his devils pretty intimately. The subterfuges of the Letters were the worst. Yet see what he did with them. The letters as part of the *Works* of Wycherley fell utterly flat in 1729, in spite of two famous names associated with them. He took the very same letters, the sheets indeed of the identical book that had failed, and, by manipulation and managed publicity, forced them in 1735 to become the literary sensation of a decade. If Pope is not the greatest among English poets, he is the greatest advertiser and publisher among them. The conclusion of the whole matter is, that by right ways and by wrong ways Pope was a very powerful influence in developing by the beginning of the second half of the eighteenth century that "reading public" in which, ever since, men of letters have moved and had their being, and by which they have lived.'

(Griffith, I. ii, pp. xlvi f.)

waterman could carry Pope and manuscript and print. But
for reasons equally cogent he could not live inside London,
though he might love to visit it. That a poet needs a quiet
place had been discovered at least as long ago as by Horace,
and confirmed as recently as by Cowley:

Poetry was born among the Shepherds. . . . The truth is, no other
place is proper for [the] Work [of the Muses]; one might as well
undertake to dance in a Crowd, as to make good Verses in the midst
of Noise and Tumult.[1]

As for Horace's views, Pope found occasion to endorse as
well as to 'imitate' them with exuberant vivacity:

But grant I may relapse, for want of Grace,
Again to rhime, can *London* be the Place?
Who there his Muse, or Self, or Soul attends?
In Crouds and Courts, Law, Business, Feasts and Friends?
My Counsel sends to execute a Deed:
A Poet begs me, I will hear him read:
In Palace-Yard at Nine you'll find me there—
At Ten for certain, Sir, in Bloomsb'ry-Square—
Before the Lords at Twelve my Cause comes on—
There's a Rehearsal, Sir, exact at One.—
'Oh but a Wit can study in the Streets,
'And raise his Mind above the Mob he meets.'
Not quite so well however as one ought;
A Hackney-Coach may chance to spoil a Thought,
And then a nodding Beam, or Pig[2] of Lead,
God knows, may hurt the very ablest Head.
Have you not seen at Guild-hall's narrow Pass,
Two Aldermen dispute it with an Ass?
And Peers give way, exalted as they are,
Ev'n to their own S-r-v--nce[3] in a Carr?
Go, lofty Poet! and in such a Croud,
Sing thy sonorous Verse—but not aloud.
Alas! to Grotto's and to Groves we run,
To Ease and Silence, ev'ry Muse's Son:[4]
Blackmore himself, for any grand Effort,
Would drink and doze at *Tooting* or *Earl's-Court.*
How shall I rhime in this eternal Roar?
How match the Bards whom none e'er match'd before?[5]

---

[1] 'Of Agriculture.'   [2] An oblong mass, an ingot.
[3] 'Sir-reverence', human excrement.   [4] Cf. the phrase 'every mother's son'.
[5] *Imitations of Horace,* Ep. ii. ii. 88 ff.

Pope, who had been lucky while he had no choice but to live with his parents in Binfield and Chiswick ('this deep desert solitude four miles from London'),[1] chose with exquisite discrimination when choice was open to him. The villa he settled on was one that commanded, from the point of an angle, two reaches of broad and wooded Thames—the place still commands as lovely and wide a prospect of wood and water as, roughly speaking, exists in England: Gray was soon to say that 'I do not know a more *laughing* [i.e. *riant*] Scene, than that about Twickenham & Richmond'.[2] When Pope was not staying at home, or not paying one of his several business or holiday visits to London, he was still in the country—'rambling' from seat to seat of his aristocratic friends. All told, he spent as large a proportion of his life in the country as Wordsworth did.

And outside the letters here are some pieces of contemporary evidence: the first that of a poet, the author-to-be of *The Shepherd's Week*, and also of *Trivia*. Gay saw Pope as a countryman, let alone as a country poet:

> You, who the Sweets of Rural Life have known,
> Despise th' ungrateful[3] Hurry of the Town . . .[4]

This was in 1713, when Gay had before him not only the *Pastorals* but *An Essay on Criticism* and the first version of the *Rape of the Lock*. And nothing cropped up later either in Pope's life or in his poetry to make his description obsolete. Secondly the evidence of a philosopher. Pope sent Berkeley a copy of the *Rape of the Lock* and received in reply from Leghorn advice as to a country poet, though a country poet whose field could be expanded:

Green fields and groves, flow'ry meadows and purling streams are no where in such perfection as in *England*: but if you wou'd know lightsome days, warm suns, and blue skies, you must come to *Italy*: and to enable a man to describe rocks and precipices, it is absolutely necessary that he pass the *Alps*.[5]

---

[1] *Correspondence*, i. 463.
[2] *Correspondence*, ed. Toynbee and Whibley, 1935, i. 407.
[3] unpleasant.
[4] *Rural Sports*, 1713, ll. 1 f. And cf. 'To Bernard Lintott', 1712, ll. 80 ff.
[5] *Correspondence*, i. 222.

As a last instance, take the evidence of Lord Orrery, in the letter purporting to be that of a county candidate's wife:

Dear Lady Charlotte,

I have been plagued, pestered, teased to death, and hurried out of my wits, ever since I have been in this odious country. O my dear, how I long to be in town again! Pope and the poets may say what they like of their purling streams, shady groves and flowery meads; but I had rather live all my days among the cheesemongers' shops in Thames-street, than pass such another spring in this filthy country.[1]

I have noted our right as readers to expect evidence from a poet that he has responded vividly to the assaults on his senses. This expectation has been particularly high in Eng-land where a poet has always been expected to show his re-sponse to sense-impressions of beautiful things in the country as opposed to the town. That Pope shows this response to the rural beautiful means that he can satisfy the demands of the English reader as they have declared themselves throughout the history of English poetry, from medieval to modern. And this despite his international ambition to be a poet of Nature. Sense impressions of the beautiful, beautiful descrip-tions—such things, whether urban or rural, are not of first concern to the poet of man. Nature, however, is subject to interference by cross-interests coming, so to speak, from within her family. Among the disturbers of her universality are interests local and national, cross-interests which she can-not but cherish as Natural while she deplores them as national —all men love their land, though all lands differ. English-men, like men of all nations, have loved the poetry of Nature, but as Englishmen they have also loved the poetry of field and hill, stream and sea, as Frenchmen, say, as a rule, have not. It is therefore to be reckoned a hard fate for an English poet to be dubbed a 'town poet'. And in Pope's case it is harder because he only deserves the nickname on the score of certain of his poems. The word 'poet', which is included in both titles, is in the last event the only word that matters, but meanwhile a love of fair play—to appeal to another character-istic of the Englishman—must clear him of the charge in so

[1] Contributed to *The Connoisseur*, 13 June 1754, and reprinted in *England in Johnson's Day*, by M. Dorothy George, 1928, pp. 99 f.

far as he is innocent. He is not a poet whose senses fed most
happily among houses and streets. They fed happily wherever they found themselves, but they preferred to be in the
country.[1]

To put this matter of Pope's country poetry in perspective.
It was not because he was a country poet that he gained his
great reputation at home and abroad. In England, however,
because he was something of a country poet, he was liked the
more: Englishmen prefer an English poet to put rocks and
stones and trees among his objects.

From the poetry I can best demonstrate what I am claiming for it by quoting two passages where he allowed the
Keatsian, though much mixed with other things, to play
longest: first the description of Timon's garden:

> At Timon's Villa let us pass a day,
> Where all cry out, 'What sums are thrown away!'
> So proud, so grand, of that stupendous air,
> Soft and Agreeable come never there.
> Greatness, with Timon, dwells in such a draught
> As brings all Brobdi[n]gnag before your thought.
> To compass this, his building is a Town,
> His pond an Ocean, his parterre a Down:
> Who but must laugh, the Master when he sees,
> A puny insect, shiv'ring at a breeze!
> Lo, what huge heaps of littleness around!
> The whole, a labour'd Quarry above ground.[2]
> Two Cupids squirt before: a Lake behind
> Improves the keenness of the Northern wind.
> His Gardens next your admiration call,
> On ev'ry side you look, behold the Wall!

[1] Readers may be surprised to find Wordsworth taking up the same position
(if so, the moral would seem to be that they should not take their idea of him from
textbooks):

'Mamma spoke of the beauty of Rydal, and asked [Wordsworth] whether it
did not rather spoil him for common scenery. 'Oh no,' he said, 'it rather opens
my eyes to see the beauty there is in all; God is everywhere, and thus nothing is
common or devoid of beauty. No, ma'am, it is the *feeling* that instructs the
seeing. Wherever there is a heart to feel, there is also an eye to see: even in a city
you have light and shade, reflections, probably views of the water and trees,
and a blue sky above you, and can you want for beauty with all these? People
often pity me while residing in a city, but they need not, for I can enjoy its
characteristic beauties as well as any.'
(Caroline Fox, *Memories of Old Friends*, ed. Horace N. Pym, 1882, pp. 158 f.)
[2] Cf. *Correspondence*, i. 432.

No pleasing Intricacies intervene,
No artful wildness to perplex the scene;
Grove nods at grove, each Alley has a brother,
And half the platform just reflects the other.
The suff'ring eye inverted nature sees,
Trees cut to Statues, Statues thick as trees,
With here a Fountain, never to be play'd,
And there a Summer-house, that knows no shade;
Here Amphitrite sails thro' myrtle bowers;
There Gladiators fight, or die, in flow'rs;
Un-water'd see the drooping sea-horse mourn,
And swallows roost in Nilus' dusty Urn.[1]

And the description of the grand tour:

Intrepid then, o'er seas and lands he flew:
Europe he saw, and Europe saw him too.
There all thy[2] gifts and graces we display,
Thou, only thou, directing all our way!
To where the Seine, obsequious as she runs,
Pours at great Bourbon's feet her silken sons;
Or Tyber, now no longer Roman, rolls,
Vain of Italian Arts, Italian Souls:
To happy Convents, bosom'd deep in vines,
Where slumber Abbots, purple as their wines:
To Isles of fragrance, lilly-silver'd vales,
Diffusing languor in the panting gales:
To lands of singing, or of dancing slaves,
Love-whisp'ring woods, and lute-resounding waves.
But chief her shrine where naked Venus keeps,
And Cupids ride the Lyon of the Deeps;
Where, eas'd of Fleets, the Adriatic main
Wafts the smooth Eunuch and enamour'd swain.
Led by my hand, he saunter'd Europe round,
And gather'd ev'ry Vice on Christian ground;
Saw ev'ry Court, heard ev'ry King declare
His royal Sense, of Op'ra's or the Fair;
The Stews and Palace equally explor'd,
Intrigu'd with glory, and with spirit whor'd;
Try'd all *hors-d'œuvres*, all *liqueurs* defin'd,
Judicious drank, and greatly-daring din'd;
Dropt the dull lumber of the Latin store,
Spoil'd his own language, and acquir'd no more;

---

[1] *Moral Essays*, iv ('Of the Use of Riches', To Burlington), 99 ff.
[2] Dulness's.

All Classic learning lost on Classic ground;
And last turn'd *Air*, the Echo of a Sound!
See now, half-cur'd, and perfectly well-bred,
With nothing but a Solo in his head. . . .[1]

The Keatsian beautiful shines full-orbed in those two passages, whatever else they include. It is never absent for long from his work, however brief its stay on any occasion. The two samples are supreme, but samples are not scarce. They are plentiful, though not at that length. By ordinary standards Pope draws on his sense-impressions amply. If he did not overdo the account of his response to external nature or to the beautiful in it, that was not because of any deficiency of response.

3

The similarity of Pope to Keats may be pursued further. As country poets they are nearer together because they prefer similar country. Readers of Keats's poetry do not always notice how near he came to being a country poet as Pope, Thomson, Cowper, and Crabbe were country poets. He failed only in that he did not like country men. He did like, however, to enter into the results of their labours. He liked the country as it was tamed, near to towns or houses without being near enough for them to show. There is nothing unusual in that liking on the part of an English poet—except that Keats was unaware of it. Few of our poets have liked country in all its wildness. Even Wordsworth seldom left sheeptrack and shepherd. Keats stood tip-toe upon a little hill: no countryman would lift his heels in such a place, but Keats was only able to do so because heavy-footed farmers have cleared little hills of forest trees and brushwood. Keats was at his happiest in such a garden as that at Hampstead where in springtime he heard the nightingale. In his ode, even when the bird flew to wilder places, they were places not uncivilized: they had their mossy ways that in the fashion beloved in English gardens were 'winding'. It was 'Ossian' and Emily Brontë who felt that country did not begin till heather began. And it was Shelley who was 'tameless' like the west wind—his flight from man was even farther than that of

[1] *Dunciad,* iv. 293 ff.

'Ossian' and Emily Brontë's because like a meteorologist and marine naturalist he was happiest among the elements. So that, although Keats will not thoroughly acknowledge the civilization, he and Pope were alike in preferring country that had been claimed and tamed by man. By Keats's time a great deal of the countryside had been taken over: much that we all admire to this day in rural England is a garden made by the 'improvers', whom Pope encouraged. As country poets Keats and Pope differ in the number of the interests at stake rather than in their choice of field. In the country Pope still had his eye on man, or on man's work. That was the first reason for his admiration of the matter of *Cooper's Hill*:

throughout which, the Descriptions of Places, and Images rais'd by the Poet, are still tending to some Hint, or leading into some Reflection, upon moral Life or political Institution: Much in the same manner as the real Sight of such Scenes and Prospects is apt to give the Mind a compos'd Turn, and incline it to Thoughts and Contemplations that have a Relation to the Object;[1]

which passage could also stand as motto for his own *Windsor Forest*.

And when he saw beautiful country, there was for Pope another human enrichment. He saw it with the eye of a painter. As early as 1713 he had started to take lessons in painting from his friend Charles Jervas, and there is evidence in his letters and conversation that his training made him conscious of nice effects of lights and shade.[2] There are two obvious instances in the poetry. First, the description of Windsor Forest which is sophisticated by the artist and also more warmly humanized by the poet of Nature:

> Here hills and vales, the woodland and the plain,
> Here earth and water seem to strive again;
> Not Chaos-like together crush'd and bruis'd,
> But, as the world, harmoniously confus'd:
> Where order in variety we see,
> And where, tho' all things differ, all agree.
> Here waving groves a chequer'd scene display,
> And part admit, and part exclude the day;
> As some coy nymph her lover's warm address
> Not quite indulges, nor can quite repress.

[1] *Iliad*, xvi, n. on l. 466.   [2] See *On the Poetry of Pope*, pp. 23 ff.

There, interspers'd in lawns and op'ning glades,
Thin trees arise that shun each other's shades.
Here in full light the russet plains extend:
There wrapt in clouds the blueish hills ascend.
Ev'n the wild heath displays her purple dyes,
And 'midst the desert fruitful fields arise,
That crown'd with tufted trees and springing corn,
Like verdant isles the sable waste adorn.[1]

Then the instance of the pheasant from the same poem:

See! from the brake the whirring pheasant springs,
And mounts exulting on triumphant wings:
Short is his joy; he feels the fiery wound,
Flutters in blood, and panting beats the ground.
Ah! what avail his glossy, varying dyes,
His purple crest, and scarlet-circled eyes,
The vivid green his shining plumes unfold,
His painted wings, and breast that flames with gold?[2]

Pope discovered this beauty for himself. The description was made with the eye on the object, though the eye transfers to the object some of its own bright light.[3] But he was aware that Dutch painters had been before him. The powers of painters to move men is usually not so strong as the power of poets. It was men that the pheasant had been shot by, and it was to men the excited 'See!' is addressed. The poet, as distinct from the Natural man, does get a look in, but only after forcing his way through the crowd of mankind. It is the poet, rather than the shooters, who feels the shot as the bird felt it, and who grieves for its unavailing splendours. Otherwise the pheasant exists in a crowd of mankind.

Pope's sophistication of nature reached its fullest point in his garden, and the triumph of the garden was its begemmed grotto. He said he designed the garden variously, so as to encourage a variety of moods[4] (a remark which makes nonsense of tracts of literary history as found in textbooks),[5] and the author of *Endymion* and of the odes on the nightingale

---

[1] *Windsor Forest*, ll. 11 ff.   [2] Id., ll. 111 f.

[3] Cf. Pope's description of Clifton, *Correspondence*, iv. 201, for similar 'exaggeration'.   [4] I regret that I have mislaid the reference for this remark.

[5] Pope is here seen to be conscious of the sort of material Wordsworth used for that batch of poems in the 1807 *Poems* called 'Moods of my own Mind', and which encouraged later poets to follow his example—see, e.g., Tennyson's 'Palace of Art'.

and Grecian urn would have lingered in it with pleasure. But
it was designed for company as well as solitude:

> Thou who shalt stop, where *Thames'* translucent Wave
> Shines a broad Mirrour thro' the shadowy[1] Cave;
> Where lingering Drops from Mineral Roofs distill,
> And pointed Crystals break the sparkling Rill,
> Unpolish'd Gemms no Ray on Pride bestow,
> And latent Metals innocently glow:
> Approach. Great NATURE studiously behold!
> And eye the Mine without a Wish for Gold.
> Approach: But aweful! Lo th' *Ægerian* Grott,
> Where, nobly-pensive, ST. JOHN sate and thought;
> Where *British* Sighs from dying WYNDHAM stole,
> And the bright Flame was shot thro' MARCHMONT's Soul.
> Let such, such only, tread this sacred Floor,
> Who dare to love their Country, and be poor.[2]

4

For all his exaggeration Pope persuades us that he described the pheasant 'with his eye on the object'. That was
because it fell from the local sky. Berkeley had counselled
Pope to see other countries besides England. The advice had
its attractions,[3] but in the event it was shelved: he did not
cross the channel, let alone the Alps. One reason was that his
bodily health was always precarious, so that he could not even
face a journey to Ireland to see Swift.[4] Another reason par-
took of Newman's when he refused to be drawn to Rome for
the sake of a fashionable audience: 'Birmingham people have
souls.'[5] Pope's interest in souls, and in minds, hearts, characters, personal natures, was served well enough in England.
He needed nothing beyond what lay to hand—if not always
in men and scene, then in books describing other men and
other places. Scenes, however grand, must come second to

[1] 'abounding in shade' (*O.E.D.*, sense 2a). In poems of the nineteenth century, and
in the 'Georgian' poetry of the twentieth, the word is so common as to be an item
in a poetic diction. Its meaning in these poems, however, is usually not the literal
one, but the meaning 'indefinite', 'faintly perceptible'.

[2] 'Verses on a Grotto by the River Thames at Twickenham, composed of Marbles,
Spars, and Minerals.'

[3] *Correspondence*, i. 232, and cf. Spence's *Anecdotes*, p. 8.

[4] *Correspondence*, iii. 383.

[5] *Life of . . . Newman*, Wilfred Ward, 1912, ii. 539.

man. If Italy had had a different brand of human nature to offer, he would have been sharply interested. That it had not was sufficiently indicated in the 'Italian souls' encountered, admittedly at their worst, by English fools doing the grand tour.[1] But he would not have visited Italy for edification merely ocular. Half a century had still to run before Blake announced that

> Great things are done when Men & Mountains meet;
> This is not done by jostling in the street.[2]

And though Blake did say that, he did not act on it: like Pope he was interested first of all in men, and scarcely left London. Great things were done when Wordsworth and mountains met, but at a price: mountains did not really strengthen his hold on mankind. Johnson knew mankind as well as anyone ever did, and that because he swam in 'the full tide of human existence . . . at Charing-cross'.[3] All the same, Johnson and Pope did not despise wild country when readily accessible. The *Journey to the Western Islands of Scotland* shows the attraction of such distant grandeur as exists in Britain, and, as I have said, it was only Pope's frailty that forbade his taking an excursion far afield. Nor did they close the eye of the mind to sights they could experience only in imagination. Pope had already written his Alpine simile when Berkeley urged ocular verification:

> A *little learning* is a dang'rous thing;
> Drink deep, or taste not the Pierian spring:
> There shallow draughts intoxicate the brain,
> And drinking largely sobers us again.
> Fir'd at first sight with what the Muse imparts,
> In fearless youth we tempt the heights of Arts,
> While from the bounded level of our mind
> Short views we take, nor see the lengths behind;
> But more advanc'd, behold with strange surprise
> New distant scenes of endless science[4] rise!
> So pleas'd at first the tow'ring Alps we try,
> Mount o'er the vales, and seem to tread the sky,

---

[1] See above, p. 101.
[2] *Poetical Works*, ed. John Sampson, 1905, p. 228.
[3] Boswell's *Life of Johnson*, ii. 337.   [4] knowledge.

Th' eternal snows appear already past,
And the first clouds and mountains seem the last;
But, those attain'd, we tremble to survey
The growing labours of the lengthen'd way,
Th' increasing prospects tire our wand'ring eyes,
Hills peep o'er hills, and Alps on Alps arise![1]

and for Johnson that foreign simile was 'perhaps the best
that English poetry can shew'.[2] Moreover, having read the
accounts of 'our modern Travellers', Pope was soon to write
the description of the rock of Arctic ice, a description I have
already discussed, but not quoted:

So *Zembla*'s Rocks (the beauteous Work of Frost)
Rise white in Air, and glitter o'er the Coast;
Pale Suns, unfelt, at distance roll away,
And on th' impassive Ice the Lightnings play:
Eternal Snows the growing Mass supply,
Till the bright Mountains prop th' incumbent Sky:
As *Atlas* fix'd, each hoary Pile appears,
The gather'd Winter of a thousand Years.[3]

They did not despise such things. Of course we do not know
how much grander Pope's descriptions of Alpine and Arctic
sublimity would have been if he had written them with the
eye on the objects themselves instead of on the objects created
in the imagination by the accounts in black and white by men
whose first job was to be sailors and travellers. But what, after
all, are rocks and stones, when placed in the balance against
man, and what, however vivid the description of them, when
balanced against 'sense' as Pope understood it?

5

When the beautiful achieved a place in Pope's poetry he
not only showed it as demanded in the interests of mankind,
but also tried to give it the interpretation mankind puts on it.
When in the *Pastorals* he spoke of winter, he saw it as a
season not without its Keatsian beauty: the 'groves . . . shine
with silver frost',[4] and the rock of ice in the *Temple of Fame* is

---

[1] *Essay on Criticism*, ll. 215 ff.   [2] *Lives*, iii. 229.
[3] *Temple of Fame*, ll. 53 ff.   [4] 'Winter', l. 9.

'the beauteous Work of Frost'.[1] Nevertheless, the shining groves are said to show

> Their beauty wither'd, and their verdure lost.[2]

And their beauty is withered *because* their verdure is lost. Pope stated the beauty in the word 'silver', a beauty which at this time Ambrose Philips stated at length in his delightful 'Winter Piece', a poem Pope admired.[3] But he withdrew it, and withdrew it according to a Natural aesthetic scale. Some painters and poets had already discovered beauty in winter, and they did not withdraw it. Mankind may perhaps be slowly catching up with their vision: Nature may be changing, be growing more conscious of beauty that is inhuman. If so, it is still a very small return for all the aesthetic labours of the nineteenth century; and, so far as winter beauty goes, any improvement in man's liking for it is no doubt due to an improved command over the hardships of winter, for James Russell Lowell saw that winter was enjoyable, aesthetically as well as otherwise, when man was prepared against its rigours. If man is now better prepared, he will be more ready to see in it what the nineteenth-century poets and painters—I should also name Thomson from the preceding century—came to see in it. In Pope's day, and perhaps still in ours, mankind was willing to see late spring and summer and part of autumn as beautiful, but not any other season. For mankind, in England at least, the country is beautiful in proportion as it is green, and further in proportion as its green is bright green. Dryden had spoken for mankind when he said that the eye

looks with pain on craggy rocks and barren mountains, and continues not intent on any object, which is wanting in shades of greens to entertain it.[4]

---

[1] l. 53. In a note in the *Iliad*, Pope admires a 'very fine' simile in Spenser, 'where he represents the Person of *Contemplation* in the Figure of a venerable old Man almost consum'd with Study.

> *His snowy Locks adown his Shoulders spread,*
> *As hoary Frost with Spangles doth attire*
> *The mossy Branches of an Oak half dead.'*

(*Iliad*, xiii, n. on l. 948.)

[2] 'Winter', l. 10.

[3] *Correspondence*, i. 101.

[4] Dedication to *The Indian Emperor*.

Isaac Watts noted that green, and blue, were 'the sweetest colours in nature',[1] and Mason that

> green is to the eye, what to the ear
> Is harmony, or to the smell the rose.[2]

Of which Hartley ventured an explanation on scientific grounds:

Green . . . the middle Colour of the Seven primary ones, and consequently the most agreeable to the Organ of Sight, is also the general Colour of The Vegetable Kingdom, *i.e.* of external Nature.[3]

When Pope sees the enormities of architecture and garden at Timon's villa, his eye, like that of mankind, is a 'suff'ring eye'.[4] Again, when in his dream he sees the unfolding splendours of the Temple of Fame it is with 'aking Sight'.[5] The scale of measurement applied by Pope is that of the normal human eye, to which everything is presented.

As man enters into poetry, he takes the highest place, and the beautiful as such leaves it. What is advanced pertains to him, in all its variety, and whether the pertinent matter is beautiful, ugly, or indifferent is neither here nor there. Pope brought man into his poems, and the Keatsian beautiful fended for itself. The remarkable thing is that it kept as many niches as it did. Taking his readings from the scale of Nature, he did not always do so without protest. He remarked to Spence that

A tree is a nobler object than a prince in his coronation robes.— Education leads us from the admiration of beauty in natural objects, to the admiration of artificial (or customary) excellence.—I don't doubt but that a thorough-bred lady might admire the stars, *because* they twinkle like so many candles at a birth-night.[6]

As if he were Wordsworth, Pope deplored the application of a scale of aesthetic values constructed by education and constructed all awry. Aesthetically considered, stars and trees

---

[1] *Reliquiae Iuvenales*, ed. 1742, p. 37.

[2] *The English Garden: A Poem. Book the First*, 1772, p. 20; cf. A. D. McKillop, *The Background of Thomson's 'Seasons'*, Minneapolis, 1942, pp. 57 f.

[3] *Observations on Man*, 1749, i. 420. Cf. also i. 194.

[4] *Moral Essays*, iv ('Of the Use of Riches', To Burlington), 119.   [5] l. 246.

[6] *Anecdotes*, p. 11. With the lady's hypothetical preference compare the actual preference of the 'very fashionable baronet in the brilliant world', Boswell's *Life*, i. 461.

are of more account than fine clothes and brilliant indoor lighting. And yet the scale Pope cannot but accept is another scale altogether. The fine lady was typical of mankind in her preferences, which were not wholly aesthetic: mankind, as I have said, is never concerned with the aesthetic pure and simple. Her preferences were for splendour made by man for his own contemplation and use against splendour he cannot touch (when it is that of stars) and can do no more than touch (when it is that of trees). What man can do to trees—plant, trim, fell, and now at last shift, even when full grown, from place to place—he does. As a poet of Nature he cannot but take mankind as it is, with all its so-called education on its head.

Pope did not overlook the practical end of certain beautiful items in external nature. He looked at them as Defoe did —in other words, as ordinary men do. Ordinary men look at trees, but cannot fail to think of their use as timber or fuel. If they see that an apple-tree in bloom is 'fair', they also see that the blossoms, in Herrick's words, are 'pledges of a fruitful tree'. If the 'golden Ear Imbrown[s] the Slope', loaves are made from wheat. If the pheasant is a bird of glistening beauty, it gives men pleasure, alas, to shoot it and to eat it when shot.

And the same practical eye assesses the ugly and indifferent things also. Pope was faithful to all this mingling of motives and values. He found a due place in his poems for all the human uses of country things. The most downright statement on this head comes in the first essay 'Of the Use of Riches', which I have already quoted:

> What Riches give us let us then enquire[:]
> Meat, Fire, and Cloaths. What more? Meat, Cloaths, and Fire.[1]

In other words all men, whether rich or poor, look to external nature for the fulfilment of those elementary needs that make the 'aesthete' impossible in actuality. And so with this recognition as centre stand all those dozens of descriptions of foods. In addition to the shot pheasant, there is the lamb:

> The lamb thy riot dooms to bleed to-day,
> Had he thy Reason, would he skip and play?
> Pleas'd to the last, he crops the flow'ry food,
> And licks the hand just rais'd to shed his blood;[2]

[1] *Moral Essays,* iii ('Of the Use of Riches', To Bathurst), 81 f.
[2] *Essay on Man,* i. 81 ff.

and the fare of a country table:

> Content with little, I can piddle here
> On Broccoli and mutton, round the year;
> But ancient friends, (tho' poor, or out of play[1])
> That touch my Bell, I cannot turn away.
> 'Tis true, no Turbots dignify my boards,
> But gudgeons, flounders, what my Thames affords.
> To Hounslow-heath I point, and Bansted-down,
> Thence comes your mutton, and these chicks my own:
> From yon old wallnut-tree a show'r shall fall;
> And grapes, long-lingring on my only wall,
> And figs, from standard and Espalier join:
> The dev'l is in you if you cannot dine;[2]

and the wine:

> 'Annual for me, the grape, the rose renew
> 'The juice nectareous, and the balmy dew;'[3]

and the eggs:

> The Vulgar boil, the Learned roast an Egg.[4]

Fish may flash and be all 'bedropp'd with gold',[5] but, more important, fish are man's food. Deprived of sight of the rose and of the aromatic pain of smelling it,[6] man's physical existence as a whole goes on much the same. Pope's poetry takes us into the kitchen and round the table as much as into the fields, where *mutatis mutandis* the heroes of Homer often found themselves, and the characters of many a comedy. The Anglo-Saxon riddle that I have already referred to honoured food as it honoured one's native land. We are among the *semper*, the *ubique*, and the *ab omnibus*.

When Pope, the describer 'following Nature', described those places and things in and among which men found themselves, he described them as an ordinary man would if, retaining his ordinariness, he were gifted with power to descry and describe. He described them with senses that did not work eclectically, but 'like the Sun . . . sh[o]ne on all

---

[1] 'out of play' = out of place (*O.E.D.*, sense iv *b*).
[2] *Imitations of Horace*, Sat. ii. ii. 137 ff.   [3] *Essay on Man*, i. 135 ff.
[4] *Imitations of Horace*, Ep. ii. ii. 85. For the roasting of eggs see above, p. 29, n. 2.
[5] *Windsor Forest*, l. 144.   [6] *Essay on Man*, i. 200.

alike'.[1] And so entered his poetry all those pell-mell sense-impressions of objects which, beautiful, ugly, grotesque, or indifferent, came home to men's business and bosoms. Here are samples, and in the random order that best accords with their variety. First, the gardens of 'Sabinus':

> Thro' his young Woods how pleas'd Sabinus stray'd,
> Or sat delighted in the thick'ning shade,
> With annual joy the red'ning shoots to greet,
> Or see the stretching branches long to meet!
> His Son's fine Taste an op'ner Vista loves,
> Foe to the Dryads of his Father's groves,
> One boundless Green, or flourish'd Carpet views,
> With all the mournful family of Yews;
> The thriving plants ignoble broomsticks made,
> Now sweep those Alleys they were born to shade.[2]

Or the tapestry the Goddess of Dulness presented to Curll:

> A shaggy Tap'stry, worthy to be spread
> On Codrus' old, or Dunton's modern bed;
> Instructive work! whose wry-mouth'd portraiture
> Display'd the fates her confessors endure.
> Earless on high, stood unabash'd De Foe,
> And Tutchin flagrant from the scourge below.
> There Ridpath, Roper, cudgell'd might ye view,
> The very worsted still look'd black and blue.[3]

Or this of unwilling country solitude:

> She went, to plain-work, and to purling brooks,
> Old-fashion'd halls, dull aunts, and croaking rooks,
> She went from Op'ra, park, assembly, play,
> To morning walks, and pray'rs three hours a day;
> To pass her time 'twixt reading and Bohea,
> To muse, and spill her solitary Tea,
> Or o'er cold coffee trifle with the spoon,
> Count the slow clock, and dine exact at noon;
> Divert her eyes with pictures in the fire,
> Hum half a tune, tell stories to the squire;
> Up to her godly garret after sev'n,
> There starve and pray, for that's the way to heav'n.[4]

---

[1] *Rape of the Lock*, ii. 14.
[2] *Moral Essays*, iv ('Of the Use of Riches', To Burlington), 89 ff.
[3] *Dunciad*, ii. 143 ff.
[4] 'Epistle to Miss Blount, on her leaving the Town, after the Coronation', ll. 11 ff.

Or this, describing a Thames-side street, in the manner of Spenser:

And on the broken Pavement here and there,
Doth many a stinking Sprat and Herring lie;
A Brandy and Tobacco Shop is near,
And Hens, and Dogs, and Hogs are feeding by;
And here a Sailor's Jacket hangs to dry:
At ev'ry Door are Sun-burnt Matrons seen,
Mending old Nets to catch the scaly Fry;
Now singing shrill, and scolding eft between,
Scolds answer foul-mouth'd Scolds; bad Neighbourhood I ween.[1]

Or this, a Lord Mayor's day:

'Twas on the day, when [Thorold,] rich and grave,
Like Cimon, triumph'd both on land and wave:
(Pomps without guilt, of bloodless swords and maces,
Glad chains, warm furs, broad banners, and broad faces) . . .[2]

Or those couplets describing beautiful outdoor things, also in the *Dunciad*.[3]

6

Some of the material that I have been collecting as beautiful bordered on or occupied the category of the useful as it has been determined according to man's need for food, clothing, warmth, sport, horticulture. I also spoke of the beautiful as it exists to be loved in the naked human body. At some point in the process of loving, beauty itself becomes indecent as a public thing, and to this sort of indecency we can add others that are unpleasant from start to finish. There has been, and is, some variation, as times and places vary, in what is counted indecent in love-making, but little variation in the indecency of the merely unpleasant. Pope himself witnessed to variation when he trimmed Chaucer to the taste of 1709 and 1714.[4] I suggest that we define the indecent, which is a constant part of Nature, as, roughly speaking, the matter that man in his social capacity—as a man dressed and standing among his fellows of both sexes and of all ages—has

---

[1] 'Imitations of English Poets. . . . II. Spenser. The Alley', ll. 10 ff.
[2] *Dunciad*, i. 85 ff.
[3] See *On the Poetry of Pope*, p. 22.   [4] See Twickenham ed., ii. 8 ff.

thought greatly 'unbecoming' at any time from Homer's day to Pope's, and—to recall the geography of the definition with which we started—at any place, during that time, in Europe or the eastern fringe of America. For us in England in the twentieth century the glaring exception to the limits I am calling Natural came in the sixties of the last century when the indecent spread its proscriptions as never before: and if we add the eastern fringe of America, we can enlarge the sixties into several decades. In Pope's time—partly as a protest against the practices of the Restoration period— the extension of the forbidden field was already beginning. For instance, the Duke of Buckingham, referring to a manuscript poem of his, notes in a letter to Pope that

> I think I have altered it to be less faulty by changing the word Lust: for however fancy overrules me, it has always been my opinion that no word should be in Poetry, especially in this little kind [the lyric], which a woman cannot decently pronounce.[1]

During the seventeenth century it had come to be felt strongly that poems were written for women equally with men— which pointed to a change, or at least to an official change, in the composition of the reading public. This meant that the freedom Donne had enjoyed, writing for men rather than for men and women, was no longer so amply available. A new literary category was established, the category of what was regarded as indecent for women, or rather 'ladies', to read or hear. Later on, in the eighteenth century, the reading public was spreading to include children, who were coming to occupy a more prominent place on the hearth, where reading aloud was favoured. This meant that by 1773 even Spenser was being bowdlerized (as we have come to word it).[2] Thereafter, until into the twentieth century, indecent and unpleasant bodily matters had to rest content with innuendo, the adults filling in the gaps to suit themselves. Obviously this account of changes in manners is too sweeping, and that there are exceptions and qualifications will be clear as I proceed.

[1] [Pope's] *Correspondence*, i. 386.
[2] See Dorothy Marshall, 'Manners, Meals, and Domestic Pastimes', in *Johnson's England*, ed. A. S. Turberville, Oxford, 1933, i. 338.

Inside the geographical limits I have defined, the indecent has been clearly enough marked out during historic time; and where variation has existed, it has been conscious variation, and so of less account—even in the 1860's English people's response to the indecent and 'unpleasant' must have been as ready as ever, though it had to be kept more private. This being so, we can raise no objection when a poet of Nature includes indecent and 'unpleasant' things in his object. Indeed we congratulate him that his object includes what is so markedly accessible in everybody's self-knowledge. Sir Robert Walpole, whose guests sometimes included Pope, 'always talked bawdy at his table, because', he said, 'in that all can join'[1]—his very expression, we note, invoked the criteria of Nature in its 'always' and 'all'. Perhaps Sir Robert was trying to keep alive manners that were already fast dying out: by the mid-eighteenth century, one would have thought, bawdy provoked too conscious a response. If, however, we are readers reading in private—and that is how most of us read our literature—that vividness of response is all to the good. Pope knew as well as Swift did that a reader's response to literature is never sharper than when the words speak of the naked human body, to laugh at it, despise it, or honour it. On that subject we cannot escape having an emotional response, which, if the provocation is strong, may almost be as intense as emotional response to deeds of sublime heroism, say, or to a public execution, or to Blondin's walking by tightrope over Niagara Falls. And this being so, it is a pity for a poet when, because of personal choice or the demands of his time, he cannot, as Wordsworth and Tennyson could not, write of Nature whole. In the words of Hartley Coleridge, adapting words of Pope, 'Human nature, and entire human nature, is the poet's proper study'.[2] Being human creatures, Wordsworth and Tennyson studied Nature complete, but kept some of the results private. Pope was as free as Chaucer and Swift, and he was even freer than Shakespeare because he wrote not for public recital, though in a theatre, but for private reading. Pope's vocabulary is as complete as Chaucer's, and it is in vocabulary that we find our keenest test on this particular count—indirection and periphrasis may be

---

[1] Boswell, iii. 57.   [2] *Essays and Marginalia*, 1851, i. 17.

keen as mustard but only the Saxon words themselves can, as it were, draw blood. Pope's use of the indecent varies from poem to poem. *Eloisa to Abelard* honours the naked human body, and, the facts of the story being what they are, inevitably requires from us some degree of visualization. The degree is rightly kept as low as possible without being false to one of the constituents of Eloisa's nature, her sensuality. In the first edition it was higher than in the third—the last revised text—which excised one couplet, whether or not because it had been pilloried by one of Pope's dunces as an instance of what was alleged to be his pruriency.[1] The indecencies of the *Rape of the Lock* were also pilloried for the same retaliatory purpose, but Pope left them untouched, after they had been heightened in the 1714 version. They were proper to a poem as sophisticated as this, a poem written as by a member of the well-bred section of society, according to whose regulations strong innuendo was permissible.[2] The degree to which it was permissible at the time may be gathered from Pope's remarks on Addison:

> . . . (excuse some Courtly stains)
> No whiter page than Addison remains;[3]

and yet *The Spectator* makes innuendo in plenty. That is only part of his business, for, like everything else in the poem, the innuendos are each a nucleus of several other things, of which wit, epic 'mockery', and tenderness are some. (Because of these complications some readers never notice them.) The 'Verses to be prefix'd before Bernard Lintot's new Miscellany' run an argument with elegance only to end it with the crudest possible appeal to Nature—a trick that Swift was to use in that pastoral-to-end-all-pastorals, 'A Pastoral Dialogue'.

In the *Imitations of Horace* the indecent exists of necessity as part of the charge: being satires, they concern vice, which either takes the indecent as its sole object or is accompanied by excursions into it that are socially or morally reprehen-

---

[1] See Twickenham ed., ii. 319.

[2] In some of his letters to Teresa and Martha Blount and other young ladies Pope goes beyond innuendo into a sort of mildly Swiftian indecency.

[3] *Imitations of Horace*, Ep. ii. i. 215 f. By 'Courtly stains' Pope means flattery of a royal personage.

sible. In the *Dunciad* the literary principle of its sometimes fulsome inclusion is that the satire is the stronger the farther its matter departs from that of the *Aeneid* or *Paradise Lost*.

All told, Pope is nowhere more masterly than in his treatment of the indecent, which varies from the brilliantly witty to the gloriously comic—as instances of the latter take the description of bashful Jenny in 'Sober Advice from Horace' or of the diving-match in the second book of the *Dunciad*.

I have noted that in the *Rape of the Lock* the indecent is always co-expressed with other matters, some of which we associate, when separate, with the Keatsian beautiful. An almost constant concomitant, owing to the sort of theme Pope chose, is a moral reference. His matter and speech are often free because the indignities of man make nonsense of his proud pretensions. To a detached view, he insists, man is more ludicrous than he always allows. I need not quote from the scores of passages where he confounds man with his proximity to the beast. I have already quoted passages that show how certain men and types have lost their footing on the Scale of Being, and fallen lower than the beasts. For Pope filth, sex, bodily grotesqueness, ugliness—as also the beautiful[1]—are usually instruments of moral correction.

Pope's attitude to the indecencies he made use of carries the approval of the common reader. It is Natural matter and Pope's attitude to it is Natural, being as sound as his general feelings are sound. Reading his poems, we side with him as with what we sometimes call a normal man, as we do not when we read the writings of, say, Swinburne or D. H. Lawrence. A proof of this is that, unless Pope refers to it, we never think of his own 'crazy carcase'.

---

[1] The beautiful, as it exists in this and that man's gardening, is an index to moral character—see *Moral Essays*, iv.

VIII

SECONDARY NATURE

I

UP to this point I have limited the content of the term Nature to the Nature that every human being discovers he possesses in his own right in mind and heart. This Nature is Nature in its purest and completest sense, and we may call it primary, borrowing the term from the author of *Sohrab and Rustum*, who, in an eloquent and desperate plea, distinguished 'the great primary human affections' as the right material for narrative poetry.[1] But primary Nature, though the most reliable and perhaps the profoundest thing men find in their possession, is not a thing they are called on to be gazing at continually. A writer interested in talking of it as it is in itself—the writer interested in recording imaginary actions prompted by it falls into a different category—cannot talk of it for long. And because of this restriction, he has recourse to secondary Nature. To drop from primary to secondary is to produce a shrinkage of the sublime, to fall nearer to the sophisticated. Whereas primary Nature speaks to us in our nakedness, secondary speaks to us as we are clothed in worldly wisdom. We leave 'bosom' for 'business', or at least we mix those two interests.

If primary Nature is what mankind 'knows', then secondary is what one section of mankind 'knows' and the rest 'knows of'.

To take instances. All mankind, at every level of the conscious and the sub-conscious, knows that blood is thicker than water, both in its literal and applied sense; on the other hand, only a certain portion of mankind knows at all those levels that power corrupts—not all have themselves been corrupted through holding power, but those who have not 'know of' it. Men respond to primary Nature in all their nakedness. There is no escape possible: primary Nature has Man trans-

---

[1] Matthew Arnold, the Preface to *Poems*, 1853.

fixed. When we hear that power corrupts we do not respond as a race; we respond as a party, mankind being divided; if . we are powerful we look in our hearts and see we are corrupted, and either glory in the discovery or feel ashamed; if we are powerless we look at the powerful, and either sigh or groan or shrug our shoulders. But though secondary Nature does not achieve a response that is one and the same, it does achieve a universal response. Everybody is still interested, though more diversely.

We can observe the drop from primary to secondary Nature even in *An Essay on Man*. That grand title engages Pope to give us primary Nature, and the poem roundly fulfils the promise: no other English poem has directly provided so much of it. And yet its thirteen hundred lines—we only think of them as few by ignoring the magnitude they achieve through their gnomic conciseness—are always sliding into secondary. At one moment we get such primary Nature as the lines on vice:

> Vice is a monster of so frightful mien,
> As, to be hated, needs but to be seen;
> Yet seen too oft, familiar with her face,
> We first endure, then pity, then embrace;[1]

and the next a passage like that on the four ages of man, a passage promising nothing but primary Nature, but at one point giving us that under cover of secondary—'scarfs, garters, gold' and 'baubles'[2] are associated only with people who are rich:

> Whate'er the Passion, knowledge, fame, or pelf,
> Not one will change his neighbour with himself.
> The learn'd is happy nature to explore,
> The fool is happy that he knows no more;
> The rich is happy in the plenty giv'n,
> The poor contents him with the care of Heaven.
> See the blind beggar dance, the cripple sing,
> The sot a hero, lunatic a king;
> The starving chemist in his golden views
> Supremely blest, the poet in his muse.
> See some strange comfort ev'ry state attend,
> And Pride bestow'd on all, a common friend;

---

[1] ii. 217 ff.   [2] 'A child's plaything' (*O.E.D.*, sense 2).

See some fit Passion ev'ry age supply,
Hope travels thro', nor quits us when we die.
    Behold the child, by nature's kindly law,
Pleas'd with a rattle, tickled with a straw:
Some livelier play-thing gives his youth delight,
A little louder, but as empty quite:
Scarfs, garters, gold, amuse his riper stage;
And beads and pray'r-books are the toys of age:
Pleas'd with this bauble still, as that before;
'Till tir'd he sleeps, and Life's poor play is o'er![1]

Those who hold power and those who are held by it divide
mankind. The proportions of the fractions may not be greatly
discrepant, since, as Swift has told us, 'great fleas have little
fleas . . .'. It is well when there is something like an even
balance between the parties. Terence's proverbial line, 'Homo
sum: humani nihil a me alienum puto', loses some of its force
if we insist on a too liberal interpretation: in practice the alien
soon reasserts itself. We cannot be expected to be much interested, for example, in a novel of Wilkie Collins that takes
for main characters a deaf-mute person and a blind person.
If such unfortunate people are not alien to men, they are
almost so. Wordsworth's 'Idiot Boy' is a triumph of Nature
expressed in narrative form because poor Johnny was not put
at the centre of the story: that honoured position was reserved for his mother and her sympathetic neighbour. We
know that Wordsworth himself saw an idiot sublimely as one
whose life was hidden with God,[2] but this unusual notion
would not be gathered from the poem, any more than we
should gather from Pope's poems that his religion was the
Roman Catholic. The poem avoids idiosyncratic views and
centres in Betty, who is motherhood and nothing else—and
all the more intensely so because her son being an idiot needs
her the more. Its groups of secondary Nature are kept big—
mothers and women (represented by Susan Gale) placed
quietly against the rest of mankind. It was usually into size-
able groups that Pope divided mankind—fools, knaves, good
men, rich and poor, civilized and primitive, Englishmen and

---

[1] ii. 261 ff.
[2] *Early Letters of William and Dorothy Wordsworth* (1787–1805), ed. E. de Selin-
court, Oxford, 1935, p. 297.

Frenchmen, ancients and moderns, friends, enemies, and the indifferent, the proud and the modest, patriots and time-servers, professionals and the rest. Instances can be taken at random:

> An honest Man's the noblest work of God;[1]
>
> 'Tis strange, the Miser should his Cares employ,
> To gain those Riches he can ne'er enjoy;[2]
>
> 'The RIGHT DIVINE of Kings to govern wrong';[3]
>
> Thus unlamented pass the proud away,
> The gaze of fools, and pageant of a day![4]
>
> Who shall decide, when Doctors disagree . . .?[5]
>
> 'Twas all for fear the Knaves should call him Fool;[6]
>
> No creature smarts so little as a Fool;[7]
>
> But touch me, and no Minister so sore;[8]
>
> Such Tears, as Patriots shed for dying Laws;[9]
>
> Love seldom haunts the Breast where Learning lies,
> And *Venus* sets ere *Mercury* can rise.[10]

In inquiries and verdicts such as some of these the proportion borne by the groups to the rest of mankind runs lower. A fair number of us may be knaves and fools, but few of us are doctors (learned men) or ministers, and fewer still kings. Yet the groups are large or prominent enough for all men who do not belong to them to 'know of' them with a closeness and authority lacking from their knowledge of, say, furriers, lepers, Maoris, fullers, bone-articulators, deaf-mutes, biochemists, serenos, paviours. Reading those lines, all men assent to Pope's opinion, or dissent from it, with a full mind. Often Pope divides mankind proportionally into halves—into male and female, young and old, married and single, parents and the childless. In practice, he found that the groups existed in scores, not hundreds. Sometimes a

[1] *Essay on Man*, i. 248.
[2] *Moral Essays*, iv ('Of the Use of Riches', To Burlington), 1 f.
[3] *Dunciad*, iv. 188.
[4] 'Elegy to the Memory of an Unfortunate Lady', ll. 43 f.
[5] *Moral Essays*, iii ('Of the Use of Riches', To Bathurst), 1.
[6] *Moral Essays*, i ('Of the Knowledge and Characters of Men'), 207.
[7] *An Epistle to Dr. Arbuthnot*, l. 84.
[8] *Imitations of Horace*, Sat. II. i. 76.
[9] 'Prologue to Mr. Addison's Tragedy of Cato', l. 14.
[10] 'The Wife of Bath her Prologue', ll. 369 f.

group, whether large or smaller, will be divided into two, sometimes shown as divided into two under certain conditions:

> 'Most Women have no Characters at all;'[1]
> Love seldom haunts the Breast where Learning lies;[2]
> Old Politicians chew on wisdom past;[3]

'Most', 'seldom', and 'old' impose limitations; still, though secondary Nature suffers division, it remains.

Usually, if he subdivides mankind, Pope gives us groups. If he gives us an individual, it is usually as a member of his group. Even in the satires, where there is sometimes close resemblance to an actual historical man in 'Timon' or 'Atticus', Pope does not necessarily identify the two. And even when he names an individual by his actual name—Wharton, Villiers, or, with a difference, the Man of Ross—the picture transcends the sitter and takes on some generality. He is seldom speaking of an individual merely as an individual, however hard such a line as the second of these—

> Does not one Table *Bavius* still admit?
> Still to one Bishop *Philips* seem a Wit?[4]

—must have come home, and been seen to come home, to Ambrose Philips. The principle of the avoidance of the merely individual is of importance in literature, and Coleridge has this comment on it:

I adopt with full faith the principle of Aristotle, that poetry as poetry is essentially *ideal*, that it avoids and excludes all *accident*; that its apparent individualities of rank, character, or occupation must be representative of a class; and that the *persons* of poetry must be clothed with *generic* attributes, with the *common* attributes of the class: not with such as one gifted individual might *possibly* possess, but such as from his situation it is most probable before-hand that he *would* possess;

to which he adds:

Say not that I am recommending abstractions; for these class-characteristics which constitute the instructiveness of a character, are so modified and particularized in each person of the Shakespearean Drama,

---

[1] *Moral Essays*, ii ('Of the Characters of Women'), 2.
[2] 'The Wife of Bath her Prologue', l. 369.
[3] *Moral Essays*, i ('Of the Knowledge and Characters of Men'), 248.
[4] *Epistle to Dr. Arbuthnot*, ll. 99 f.

that life itself does not excite more distinctly that sense of individuality which belongs to real existence. Paradoxical as it may sound, one of the essential properties of Geometry is not less essential to dramatic excellence; and Aristotle has accordingly required of the poet an involution of the universal in the individual. The chief differences are, that in Geometry it is the universal truth, which is uppermost in the consciousness; in poetry the individual form, in which the truth is clothed.[1]

2

The most obvious instance of Pope's division of mankind is that into men and women, a division showing the complexity, and sometimes the elusiveness, of the categories of primary and secondary Nature.

Any knowledge that male human beings have of Nature as it exists in female is (as I have already said in this sentence) 'knowledge of'. When Pope writes:

> Woman's at best a Contradiction still;[2]
> . . . she who scorns a Man, must die a Maid;[3]
> . . . ev'ry Woman is at heart a Rake;[4]

—to these propositions there are two responses: women respond to them as to primary Nature, giving them the hearty response they give to such a proposition as 'To err is human'; but a part is not the whole, and the rest of mankind are concerned only as observers, though as observers very much interested. The degree of heartiness in the response, by the way, has nothing to do with the truth of the statement: any statement about the sexes meets with the same degree of response whether it is accepted as true, kept for scrutiny as possibly true, or rejected as untrue. On other occasions, Pope speaks of the other half of mankind:

> With hairy Sprindges we the Birds betray,
> Slight Lines of Hair surprize the Finny Prey,
> Fair Tresses Man's Imperial Race insnare,
> And Beauty draws us with a single Hair.[5]

[1] *Biographia Literaria*, ii. 33 f.
[2] *Moral Essays*, ii ('Of the Characters of Women'), 270.
[3] *Rape of the Lock*, v. 28.
[4] *Moral Essays*, ii ('Of the Characters of Women'), 216.
[5] *Rape of the Lock*, ii. 25 ff.

> Lust, thro' some certain strainers well refin'd,
> Is gentle love, and charms all womankind.[1]
> [Men] dream in Courtship, but in Wedlock wake.[2]

To such propositions women respond as men do to those about women.

So far so good. But not all Pope's divisions into male and female are rigid divisions. Sometimes the literal subject is one sex, though the real subject is mankind. The first Moral Essay, 'Of the Knowledge and Characters of Men', includes the line:

> When Flatt'ry glares, all hate it in a Queen;[3]

and the passage:

> Search then the Ruling Passion: There, alone,
> The Wild are constant, and the Cunning known;
> The Fool consistent, and the False sincere;
> Priests, Princes, Women, no dissemblers here.[4]

It also contains two 'characters' of women:

> The frugal Crone, whom praying priests attend,
> Still tries to save the hallow'd taper's end,
> Collects her breath, as ebbing life retires,
> For one puff more, and in that puff expires.
> 'Odious! in woollen! 'twould a Saint provoke,
> (Were the last words that poor Narcissa spoke)
> 'No, let a charming Chintz, and Brussels lace
> 'Wrap my cold limbs, and shade my lifeless face:
> 'One would not, sure, be frightful when one's dead—
> 'And—Betty—give this Cheek a little Red.'[5]

The question to ask here is, Are these two characters merely of women? If so, they have no right to a place in an essay calling itself 'Of the Knowledge and Characters of Men', even when 'Men' is taken, as in part it must be taken, to mean mankind. The crone and Narcissa figure in scenes of miserliness and foppishness, and these are scenes of primary Nature, their function in the poem being that of illustrating the maxim that mankind

> Shall feel [their] ruling passion strong in death.[6]

---

[1] *Essay on Man*, ii. 189 f.   [2] 'The Wife of Bath her Prologue', l. 103.
[3] l. 120.   [4] ll. 174 ff.   [5] ll. 238 ff.   [6] l. 263.

It is still primary Nature that we are being shown in opera-
tion, though in a person that at first sight looks wholly
secondary, being a woman and, as instances of secondary
Nature invite, vividly hung round with particulars.

In the companion essay, 'Of the Characters of Women', the
word 'women' precludes any double meaning: unlike 'men'
it cannot enlarge into 'mankind': the theme as stated offers
us secondary Nature and that alone. Pope's plan, as stated in
his 'Argument', was to consider 'the Characters of *Women*
. . . only as contradistinguished from the other Sex', and to
show, in the first place, that their '*Particular Characters* . . .
are more various than those of Men'—in other words to ex-
pand that famous epitaph on women that Virgil put into the
mouth of the god Mercury when he charged Aeneas to leave
Dido quickly: 'varium et mutabile semper femina'[1]—and
in the second place to show that 'the *General Characteristick*
[of women], as to the *Ruling Passion*, is more uniform and
confin'd'. Whether his instances of women's particular characters—he enumerates them as those of the affected, the soft-
natured, the cunning, the whimsical, the witty and the refined,
the stupid and the silly—show more variety than those of
males, in the sense of showing greater range of difference
between instances, it would be hard to decide. Where they
are obviously more various is *within* each instance, though
perhaps a better word than 'various' would have been 'subtle'
or 'complex': Pope never produced anything more subtle
than his characters of Narcissa (the former essay shows a
Narcissa at the point of death, this a Narcissa very much
alive) and of Flavia:

> Narcissa's nature, tolerably mild,
> To make a wash, would hardly stew a child;
> Has ev'n been prov'd to grant a Lover's pray'r,
> And paid a Tradesman once to make him stare,
> Gave alms at Easter, in a Christian trim,
> And made a Widow happy, for a whim.
> Why then declare Good-nature is her scorn,
> When 'tis by that alone she can be born?
> Why pique all mortals, yet affect a name?
> A fool to Pleasure, yet a slave to Fame:

[1] *Æneid*, iv. 569 f.

Now deep in Taylor and the Book of Martyrs,
Now drinking citron with his Grace and Chartres.
Now Conscience chills her, and now Passion burns:
And Atheism and Religion take their turns;
A very Heathen in the carnal part,
Yet still a sad, good Christian at her heart.[1]

Then this of Flavia:

Flavia's a Wit, has too much sense to Pray,
To Toast our wants and wishes, is her way;
Nor asks of God, but of her Stars to give
The mighty blessing, 'while we live, to live'.
Then all for Death, that Opiate of the soul!
Lucretia's dagger, Rosamonda's bowl.
Say, what can cause such impotence of mind?
A Spark too fickle, or a Spouse too kind.
Wise Wretch! with Pleasures too refin'd to please,
With too much Spirit to be e'er at ease,
With too much Quickness ever to be taught,
With too much Thinking to have common Thought:
You purchase Pain with all that Joy can give,
And die of nothing but a Rage to live.[2]

The second part of Pope's plan, that designed to distinguish
women from males and so to supplement the physiological
distinction, gave us this:

In Men, we various Ruling Passions find,
In Women, two almost divide the kind;
Those, only fix'd, they first or last obey,
The Love of Pleasure, and the Love of Sway.
    That, nature gives; and when the lesson taught
Is but to please, can Pleasure seem a fault?
Experience, this; by Man's Oppression curst,
They seek the second not to lose the first.
    Men, some to Bus'ness, some to Pleasure take;
But ev'ry Woman is at heart a Rake;
Men, some to Quiet, some to public Strife;
But ev'ry Lady would be Queen for life.
    Yet mark the fate of a whole Sex of Queens!
Pow'r all their end, but Beauty all the means.
In Youth they conquer with so wild a rage,
As leaves them scarce a Subject in their Age:

[1] ll. 53 ff.   [2] ll. 87 ff.

> For foreign glory, foreign joy, they roam;
> No thought of Peace or Happiness at home.
> But Wisdom's Triumph is well-tim'd Retreat,
> As hard a science to the Fair as Great!
> Beauties, like Tyrants, old and friendless grown,
> Yet hate Repose, and dread to be alone,
> Worn out in public, weary ev'ry eye,
> Nor leave one sigh behind them when they die.
> Pleasures the sex, as children Birds, pursue,
> Still out of reach, yet never out of view,
> Sure, if they catch, to spoil the Toy at most,
> To covet flying, and regret when lost:
> At last, to follies Youth could scarce defend,
> It grows their Age's prudence to pretend;
> Asham'd to own they gave delight before,
> Reduc'd to feign it, when they give no more:
> As Hags hold Sabbaths, less for joy than spight,
> So these their merry, miserable Night;
> Still round and round the Ghosts of Beauty glide,
> And haunt the places where their Honour dy'd.
> See how the World its Veterans rewards!
> A Youth of frolicks, an old Age of Cards,
> Fair to no purpose, artful to no end,
> Young without Lovers, old without a Friend,
> A Fop their Passion, but their Prize a Sot,
> Alive, ridiculous, and dead, forgot![1]

This is what Pope can do towards a generalization on the female half of mankind, though there are other attempts elsewhere, for instance in the 'Epilogue to *Jane Shore*':

> Our sex are still forgiving at their heart.[2]

Even so little is a substantial achievement—Pope has certainly improved, for instance, on Rapin's discovery that the 'character' of woman is modesty;[3] he has got at least as far as Virgil with his 'various' and 'fickle'. But in the former portion of the essay, the first two hundred lines, we are given characters of women which, at bottom and apart from their silken texture, are perhaps equally characters of males. Since the title of this second essay is inelastically what it is, we must

---

[1] ll. 207 ff.   [2] l. 12.
[3] *Reflections on Aristotle's Treatise of Poesie. . . . By R. Rapin* [trans. T. Rymer], 1674, p. 37.

see these characters as technical failures—failures, that is, as instances of the categories set up; seeking to be instances of one field of secondary Nature, and that alone, they end by being instances both of that and of secondary Nature in another field, the field of males. Here are, for instance, the characters of Rufa and Sappho:

> Rufa, whose eye quick-glancing o'er the Park,
> Attracts each light gay meteor of a Spark,
> Agrees as ill with Rufa studying Locke,
> As Sappho's diamonds with her dirty smock,
> Or Sappho at her toilet's greasy task,
> With Sappho fragrant at an evening Mask.[1]

What is here said of women is as true of males, if I retain my proviso that we discount the finesse and surface detail; Pope had indeed said as much of males in his former Essay:

> See the same man, in vigour, in the gout;
> Alone, in company; in place, or out;
> Early at Bus'ness, and at Hazard late;
> Mad at a Fox-chace, wise at a Debate;
> Drunk at a Borough, civil at a Ball;
> Friendly at Hackney, faithless at Whitehall.[2]

And the powerful character of Atossa, being that of a termagant, is partly that of a male:

> But what are these to great Atossa's mind?
> Scarce once herself, by turns all Womankind!
> Who, with herself, or others, from her birth
> Finds all her life one warfare upon earth:
> Shines, in exposing Knaves, and painting Fools,
> Yet is, what'er she hates and ridicules.
> No Thought advances, but her Eddy Brain
> Whisks it about, and down it goes again.
> Full sixty years the World has been her Trade,
> The wisest Fool much Time has ever made.
> From loveless youth to unrespected age,
> No Passion gratify'd except her Rage.
> So much the Fury still out-ran the Wit,
> The Pleasure miss'd her, and the Scandal hit.
> Who breaks with her, provokes Revenge from Hell,
> But he's a bolder man who dares be well:

---

[1] *Moral Essays,* ii ('Of the Characters of Women), 21 ff.   [2] ll. 130 ff.

Her ev'ry turn with Violence pursu'd,⁻
Nor more a storm her Hate than Gratitude.
To that each Passion turns, or soon or late;
Love, if it makes her yield, must make her hate:
Superiors? death! and Equals? what a curse!
But an Inferior not dependant? worse.
Offend her, and she knows not to forgive;
Oblige her, and she'll hate you while you live:
But die, and she'll adore you—Then the Bust
And Temple rise—then fall again to dust.
Last night, her Lord was all that's good and great,
A·Knave this morning, and his Will a Cheat.
Strange! by the Means defeated of the Ends,
By Spirit robb'd of Pow'r, by Warmth of Friends,
By Wealth of Follow'rs! without one distress
Sick of herself thro' very selfishness!
Atossa, curs'd with ev'ry granted pray'r,
Childless with all her Children, wants an Heir,
To Heirs unknown descends th' unguarded store
Or wanders, Heav'n-directed, to the Poor.[1]

In his argument Pope seems to confess the material too difficult for him:

Of the Characters of *Women* (consider'd only as contradistinguished
from the other sex.) That these are yet more inconsistent and incomprehensible than those of Men, of which Instances are given even
from such Characters as are plainest, and most strongly mark'd. . . .
How Contrarieties run thro' them all.

But tho' the *Particular Characters* of this Sex are more various than
those of Men, the *General Characteristick*, as to the *Ruling Passion,* is
more uniform and confin'd.

It is only in the rest of the Argument that the differences between the characters of women and men come out clearly:

Men are best known in publick Life, Women in private, 199. What
are the *Aims*, and the *Fate* of the Sex, both as to *Power* and *Pleasure*?
219, 231. &c. Advice for their true Interest, 249. The Picture of an
esteemable Woman, made up of the best kind of Contrarieties, 269, &c.[2]

Towards the end of the second Essay, Pope seems to revert to the view he started with. On its first appearance, we
took it as casual and cynical:

---

[1] *Moral Essays*, ii ('Of the Characters of Women'), 115 ff.
[2] The numerals refer to lines of the poem.

> Nothing so true as what you once let fall,
> 'Most Women have no Characters at all'.
> Matter too soft a lasting mark to bear,
> And best distinguish'd by black, brown, or fair.[1]

At the close, he again seems to be taking refuge in the physical:

> Heav'n, when it strives to polish all it can
> Its last best work, but forms a softer Man.[2]

At any rate, having done what he could to divide mankind down the middle, he ends by merging the halves back again into one. Mankind appears as androgynous, and the principle of 'the all in each' is reasserted. In the first, then, of his two Essays it is mankind that is concerned, though his instances of Nature primary and secondary are on the whole instances tricked out with male particulars. The title of his second, 'Of the Characters of Women', announces the drop from primary to secondary Nature, but since the secondary that it discovers exists in both women and males, climbs back to primary. Perhaps a subject so subtle is best left confused, or complicated. But Pope is a poet, and the poetry supplements, or in some ways gets the better of, the thinking. The contrasted colouring of the two essays, to use Pope's image, tells us as much as his argument. The former essay is trenchant and terse; we might think of it as Dryden tightened up. But the second shimmers:

> How many Pictures of one Nymph we view,
> All how unlike each other, all how true!
> Arcadia's Countess, here, in ermin'd pride,
> Is there, Pastora by a fountain side.
> Here Fannia, leering on her own good man,
> And there, a naked Leda with a Swan.
> Let then the Fair one beautifully cry,
> In Magdalen's loose hair and lifted eye,
> Or drest in smiles of sweet Cecilia shine,
> With sim'pring Angels, Palms, and Harps divine;
> Whether the Charmer sinner it, or saint it,
> If Folly grows romantic, I must paint it.

[1] ll. 1 ff.

[2] ll. 271 f. Note the limitation in 'all it can': human beings cannot be completely 'polished'. 'It's last best work': God created woman after he had created man (Genesis, ii. 22).

Come then, the colours and the ground prepare!
Dip in the Rainbow, trick her off in Air,
Chuse a firm Cloud, before it fall, and in it
Catch, ere she change, the Cynthia of this minute.[1]

The profoundest sense of the argument is expressed in the
elusiveness of its verbal colouring. It suggests that the mind
of women is, as Feste would say, 'a very opal'.

3

In the argument to 'Of the Characters of Women' Pope,
as I have said, frankly confessed that the characters of women
seemed to him more 'incomprehensible' than those of men.
Aware of the complexity of the human mind, character, and
personality, the simplicity of Nature, which was an important object in his searching into individuals, lay for him at the
farther end of much subtle inquiry and observation. He enlarged on the conditions in the opening part of 'Of the
Characters of Man', a piece that he was helped to write by
his favourite essay of Montaigne, 'De l'Inconstance de nos
Actions',[2] and by Swift's account of madness in *A Tale of a
Tub*. The poem begins with:

Yes, you despise the man to Books confin'd,
Who from his study rails at human kind;
Tho' what he learns, he speaks and may advance
Some gen'ral maxims, or be right by chance.
The coxcomb bird, so talkative and grave,
That from his cage cries Cuckold, Whore, and Knave,
Tho' many a passenger he rightly call,
You hold him no Philosopher at all.
And yet the fate of all extremes is such,
Men may be read, as well as Books too much.
To Observations which ourselves we make,
We grow more partial for th' observer's sake;
To written Wisdom, as another's, less:
Maxims are drawn from Notions, these from Guess.[3]

And the truth is that there is little to choose between the

---

[1] ll. 5 ff.
[2] *Essaies*, II. i. See Sherburn, in *Essays on the Eighteenth Century presented to
D. Nichol Smith*, Oxford, 1945, p. 50.   [3] ll. 1 ff.

results of learning about man from books and from direct observation—merely the difference between a notion (the written account of what, according to Locke, exists 'more in the thoughts of men than in the reality of things')[1] and one's own guesswork. The material under observation is unique in each instance:

> There's some Peculiar in each leaf and grain,
> Some unmark'd fibre, or some varying vein:
> Shall only Man be taken in the gross?
> Grant but as many sorts of Mind as Moss.[2]

Then each instance differs within itself:

> That each from other differs, first confess;
> Next, that he varies from himself no less:[3]
> Add Nature's, Custom's, Reason's, Passion's strife,
> And all Opinion's colours cast on life.[4]

'Yet more', Pope continues:

> Yet more; the diff'rence is as great between
> The optics seeing, as the objects seen.
> All Manners take a tincture from our own,
> Or come discolour'd thro' our Passions shown.
> Or Fancy's beam enlarges, multiplies,
> Contracts, inverts, and gives ten thousand dyes.
>   Our depths who fathoms, or our shallows finds,
> Quick whirls, and shifting eddies, of our minds?
> Life's stream for Observation will not stay,
> It hurries all too fast to mark their way.
> In vain sedate reflections[5] we wou'd make,
> When half our knowledge we must snatch, not take.
> On human actions reason tho' you can,
> It may be reason, but it is not man:
> His Principle of action once explore,
> That instant 'tis his Principle no more.
> Like following life thro' creatures you dissect,
> You lose it in the moment you detect.[6]

---

[1] Twickenham ed., III. ii. 16.   [2] ll. 15 ff.
  [3] See the enlargement on this idea, quoting Locke, Addison, Gray, and Southey, in I. Todhunter's *William Whewell*, 1876, i. 344 ff.   [4] ll. 19 ff.
  [5] The phrase 'sedate reflexions' also occurs at *Correspondence*, ii. 429.
  [6] ll. 23 ff.

And so to more of this psychology:

> Oft in the Passions' wild rotation tost,
> Our spring of action to ourselves is lost:
> Tir'd, not determin'd, to the last we yield,
> And what comes then is master of the field.
> As the last image of that troubled heap,
> When Sense subsides, and Fancy sports in sleep,
> (Tho' past the recollection of the thought)
> Becomes the stuff of which our dream is wrought:
> Something as dim to our internal view,
> Is thus, perhaps, the cause of most we do.
>
> In vain the Sage, with retrospective eye,
> Would from th' apparent What conclude the Why,
> Infer the Motive from the Deed, and shew,
> That what we chanc'd was what we meant to do.
> Behold! If Fortune or a Mistress frowns,
> Some plunge in bus'ness, others shave their crowns:
> To ease the Soul of one oppressive weight,
> This quits an Empire, that embroils a State:
> The same adust[1] complexion has impell'd
> Charles to the Convent, Philip to the Field.
>
> Not always Actions shew the man: we find
> Who does a kindness, is not therefore kind,
> Perhaps Prosperity becalm'd his breast,
> Perhaps the Wind just shifted from the east:
> Not therefore humble he who seeks retreat,
> Pride guides his steps, and bids him shun the great:
> Who combats bravely is not therefore brave,
> He dreads a death-bed like the meanest slave:
> Who reasons wisely is not therefore wise,
> His pride in Reas'ning, not in Acting lies.
>
> But grant that Actions best discover man;
> Take the most strong, and sort them as you can,
> The few that glare each character must mark,
> You balance not the many in the dark.
> What will you do with such as disagree?
> Suppress them, or miscall them Policy?
> Must then at once (the character to save)
> The plain rough Hero turn a crafty Knave?
> Alas! in truth the man but chang'd his mind,
> Perhaps was sick, in love, or had not din'd.

1 burnt up.

> Ask why from Britain Cæsar would retreat?
> Cæsar himself might whisper he was beat.
> Why risk the world's great empire for a Punk?
> Cæsar perhaps might answer he was drunk.
> But, sage historians! 'tis your task to prove
> One action Conduct; one, heroic Love.[1]

Pope is here speaking of individuals, but he is dealing with them not for their own sake, but for the sake of coming to generalize, if possible on the wide scale of Nature. Man was a riddle, and Pope aimed at guessing at solutions. That he did not think he had got very far, even after writing *An Essay on Man*, may be gathered from the modesty of his calling it an essay—a trial account, or, as Johnson was to define the form, or its content, 'a loose sally of the mind'; and also from that line concluding one of the last poems he wrote:

> Yes, the last Pen for Freedom let me draw,
> When Truth stands trembling on the edge of Law:
> Here, Last of *Britons!* let your Names be read;
> Are none, none living? let me praise the Dead,
> And for that Cause which made your Fathers shine,
> Fall, by the Votes of their degen'rate Line!
>   *Fr[iend]*. Alas! Alas! pray end what you began,
> And write next winter more *Essays on Man*.[2]

It is even possible that the investigation of secondary Nature called for more experience than the investigation of primary. Consider, for instance, the experience behind this line of Pope's:

> Old Politicians chew on wisdom past.[3]

Perhaps Pope did not need to meet many old politicians before he could guess that, as a class, they lingered on in a sapience gone stale on them. But before he put his guess into print he had met several. The list of his early friends is mainly a list of statesmen,[4] and one of the closest of his early friends was Sir William Trumbull, who had been Secretary

---

[1] ll. 41 ff.

[2] *Imitations of Horace*, 'Epilogue to the Satires', dial. ii. 248 ff. See Twickenham ed., v. xxx, where in 1736 Pope is shown planning to write four epistles 'which naturally follow the Essay on Man'.

[3] *Moral Essays*, i ('Of the Knowledge and Characters of Men'), 248.

[4] See below, p. 147 n.

of State to William III. Already by 1714 he knew enough on this topic to appreciate a harmless affectation in Swift, noting that

He talked of Politicks over Coffee, with the Air & Stile of an old Statesman, who had known something formerly, but was shamefully ignorant of the Three last weeks.[1]

Such experiences, we know, were treasured up—Atterbury noted that 'you forget nothing'[2]—and tested by more experience against the time when a poem might need to generalize with solid authority. His experience at the death-bed of Wycherley contributed, we can see, to his idea that ruling passions ruled most powerfully on such occasions.[3] The death of Fenton helped to confirm it.[4] Lacking the actual experience of the future death-bed of his old friend and enemy Lady Mary Wortley Montagu, he could anticipate it in the question he put to Hugh Bethel:

You mention the Fame of my old Acquaintance Lady Mary as spread over Italy. Neither you delight in telling, nor I in hearing, the Particulars which acquire such a Reputation; yet I wish you had just told me, if the Character be more *Avaricious*, or *Amatory*? and which Passion has got the better at last?[5]

On another occasion, writing to Jervas, he noted his renewed conviction of 'the Truth of a Maxim we once agreed in'.[6] In these examples we can see Pope at his work of collecting and confirming particulars about other human beings, as individuals and members of classes. Always seeking to arrange and organize into the simplicity of Nature primary or secondary, he looked as long and closely as any of our dramatists and novelists, as long and closely as Chaucer or Browning among the poets, at the 'glaring chaos and wild heap' of men, 'the field full of folk'.

[1] *Correspondence,* i. 234. [2] Id. i. 84. [3] Id. i. 329.
[4] Id. iii. 128. [5] Id. iv. 377. [6] Id. i. 243.

IX

NATURE AND 'MR. POPE'

I

WHEN it comes to Pope's protracted account of himself and his affairs, the contact with Nature, primary and secondary, is kept surprisingly firm. It is indeed a prolonged subtle generalization occasionally dropping into the individual pure and simple.[1]

Pope often makes himself, as an individual man, an instance of Nature primary, and as a poet, an instance of Nature both secondary and primary. The poet is at least as good a sample of secondary Nature as a king is: everybody 'knows of' the creature. Even so, Pope constantly reduces his status so as to bring himself closer to man.

In *An Essay on Criticism* and elsewhere, he referred to the writing of poetry as a craft, as a professional and technical matter, clear of hieratic mystery. In his poetry as a whole he did not speak of inspiration but of words and lines: not of poetry but of 'song', 'sing-song', 'verse', 'numbers', 'rhyme', the product of 'that unweary'd mill'.[2] He is a poet speaking as if he were Anthony Trollope, and we might infer from it all that Pope was the excellent man of business we know him to have been.[3] On one occasion he refers to himself as

Composing Songs, for Fools to get by heart[4]

(a line which, since readers were already eagerly committing his couplets to memory, cut both ways). On another, he describes his 'song' as 'idle'.[5] When he did suggest that poetry took its rise in quarters more mysterious than the fingers, it was often to mock at the poet whose inspiration was bogus:

> Here she[6] beholds the Chaos dark and deep,
> Where nameless Somethings in their causes sleep,
> 'Till genial Jacob, or a warm Third day,
> Call forth each mass, a Poem, or a Play:

---

[1] See below, pp. 142 ff.   [2] See below, p. 139.   [3] See above, pp. 96 f.
[4] *Imitations of Horace*, Ep. II. ii. 126.   [5] *Epistle to Dr. Arbuthnot*, l. 28.
[6] The Goddess of Dulness.

How hints, like spawn, scarce quick in embryo lie,
How new-born nonsense first is taught to cry,
Maggots half-form'd in rhyme exactly meet,
And learn to crawl upon poetic feet . . .
Swearing and supperless the Hero[1] sate,
Blasphem'd his God, the Dice, and damn'd his Fate.
Then gnaw'd his pen, then dash'd it to the ground,
Sinking from thought to thought, a vast profound!
Plung'd for his sense, but found no bottom there,
Yet wrote and flounder'd on, in mere despair.
Round him much Embryo, much Abortion lay,
Much future Ode, and abdicated Play;
Nonsense precipitate, like running Lead,
That slip'd thro' Cracks and Zig-zags of the Head;
All that on Folly Frenzy could beget,
Fruits of dull Heat, and Sooterkins of Wit. . . .[2]

And when Horace had presented the poet in the role of public
benefactor, Pope improved on the occasion till his paragraph
towered with humble utilities:

Now Times are chang'd, and one Poetick Itch
Has seiz'd the Court and City, Poor and Rich:
Sons, Sires, and Grandsires, all will wear the Bays,
Our Wives read Milton, and our Daughters Plays,
To Theatres, and to Rehearsals throng,
And all our Grace at Table is a Song.
I, who so oft renounce the Muses, lye,
Not ——'s self e'er tells more *Fibs* than I;
When, sick of Muse, our follies we deplore,
And promise our best Friends to ryme no more;
We wake next morning in a raging Fit,
And call for Pen and Ink to show our Wit.
    He serv'd a 'Prenticeship, who sets up shop;
Ward try'd on Puppies, and the Poor, his Drop;
Ev'n Radcliff's Doctors travel first to France,
Nor dare to practise till they've learn'd to dance.
Who builds a Bridge that never drove a pyle?
(Should Ripley venture, all the World would smile)
But those who cannot write, and those who can,
All ryme, and scrawl, and scribble, to a man.

---

[1] Colley Cibber in this version of 1742, Theobald in that of 1728.
[2] *Dunciad*, i. 55 ff., 115 f.

Yet Sir, reflect, the mischief is not great;
These Madmen never hurt the Church or State:
Sometimes the Folly benefits mankind;
And rarely Av'rice taints the tuneful mind.
Allow him but his Play-thing of a Pen,
He ne'er rebels, or plots, like other men:
Flight of Cashiers, or Mobs, he'll never mind;
And knows no losses while the Muse is kind.
To cheat a Friend, or Ward, he leaves to Peter;
The good man heaps up nothing but mere metre,
Enjoys his Garden and his Book in quiet;
And then—a perfect Hermit in his Diet.
Of little use the Man you may suppose,
Who says in verse what others say in prose;
Yet let me show, a Poet's of some weight,
And (tho' no Soldier) useful to the State.
What will a Child learn sooner than a song?
What better teach a Foreigner the tongue?
What's long or short, each accent where to place,
And speak in publick with some sort of grace.
I scarce can think him such a worthless thing,
Unless he praise some monster of a King,
Or Virtue, or Religion turn to sport,
To please a lewd, or un-believing Court.
Unhappy Dryden!—In all Charles's days,
Roscommon only boasts unspotted Bays;
And in our own (excuse some Courtly stains)
No whiter page than Addison remains.
He, from the taste obscene reclaims our Youth,
And sets the Passions on the side of Truth;
Forms the soft bosom with the gentlest art,
And pours each human Virtue in the heart.
Let Ireland tell, how Wit upheld her cause,
Her Trade supported, and supply'd her Laws;
And leave on SWIFT this grateful verse ingrav'd,
The Rights a Court attack'd, a Poet sav'd.
Behold the hand that wrought a Nation's cure,
Stretch'd to relieve the Idiot and the Poor,
Proud Vice to brand, or injur'd Worth adorn,
And stretch the Ray to Ages yet unborn.
Not but there are, who merit other palms;
Hopkins and Sternhold glad the heart with Psalms;
The Boys and Girls whom Charity maintains,
Implore your help in these pathetic strains:

How could Devotion touch the country pews,
Unless the Gods bestow'd a proper Muse?
Verse chears their leisure, Verse assists their work,
Verse prays for Peace, or sings down Pope and Turk.
The silenc'd Preacher yields to potent strain,
And feels that grace his pray'r besought in vain,
The blessing thrills thro' all the lab'ring throng,
And Heav'n is won by violence of Song.[1]

Men's debt to poets has been stated often but never placed
so low as in passages like this. And though Pope meant to
shame the reader into making handsomer admissions on his
own, the least poetical of readers could not but be reassured.

It was as the manipulation of writing materials that he
usually presented the work of poetic composition. I have just
quoted his disarming phrase 'his Play-thing of a Pen'. Or
there is this:

Why did I write? What sin to me unknown
Dipt me in Ink, my Parents', or my own?[2]

And if pen and ink are not to hand, poets seize on what is:

Is there . . .
A Clerk, foredoom'd his Father's soul to cross,
Who pens a Stanza[3] when he should *engross*?
Is there, who lock'd from Ink and Paper, scrawls
With desp'rate Charcoal round his darken'd walls?[4]

Or even a skewer.[5] The poet used the same instrument as a
clerk did. He was a technician as a gardener was ('Prune the
luxuriant'[6]) or as a schoolmaster ('the uncouth refine'[7]), or
as a miller ('ev'ry Wheel of that unweary'd Mill'[8]), or as a
sailor:

Who-e'er offends, at some unlucky Time
Slides into Verse, and hitches in a Rhyme.[9]

[1] *Imitations of Horace*, Ep. II. i. 169 ff.
[2] *Epistle to Dr. Arbuthnot*, ll. 125 f.
[3] 'stanza' rather than 'couplet': he is penning a love-song.
[4] *Epistle to Dr. Arbuthnot*, ll. 15 ff.
[5] *Imitations of Horace*, Sat. II. i. 98:

Or whiten'd Wall provoke the Skew'r to write.

[6] Id., Ep. II. ii. 174.   [7] Id.
[8] Id., Ep. II. ii. 78.   [9] Id., Sat. II. i. 77 f.

He was a versifier with 'a knack'.[1] It was true that poets
were few in number, but that merely meant that they were a
small group within a large one, the large group of what we
now call skilled workers. 'I left no Calling', he says in self-
justification, 'for this idle trade.'[2] Of course, as I shall note
later, he did not always represent skill as the be-all and end-
all of poetry.[3] No poet, indeed, has shown a more religious
sense of the devotedness poetry requires of its poets. But that
sense was mainly expressed in the prose of letters to friends.
In his public verse he usually claimed little more than skill.
And the charges that Cowper and Newman brought against
him on some occasions—that he was a mechanical poet—
may have been weighted by their having taken such passages
as I have quoted too much on their face value. Pope, however, meant, up to a point, what he said, and he said it often
because, seeing and valuing himself as a member of the
human race and of society, he wished to be employed as far
as possible in the way other men were employed, and to be
credited with being so employed. We accept his account of
how poems are written in the same familiar way as we accept
his account of the rest of his everyday affairs: those affairs
are not identical with the affairs of ourselves—how could
they be?—but they exist in an identical relationship with
them as our own with the affairs of any third party. We
accept Pope as a poet, then, as we accept him as a man concerned with his friends, enemies, writing, publishing, his
health, hobbies, garden, and grotto. Unlike the romantic
poet, he keeps the poet close to his fellow men. We do not
find him writing a line like

> And leaves the world to darkness and to me,

or saying that he wanders lonely as a cloud.
    Of one of his poems about writing, *An Essay on Criticism*,
he had feared that the matter might be found too remote to
interest the general reader. He told a friend that he did not
expect a second edition after the thousand copies of the first
were sold because 'not one gentleman in three score even of
a liberal education can understand [it]'.[4] And yet a couplet

---

[1] See below, p. 214.   [2] *Epistle to Dr. Arbuthnot*, l. 129.
[3] See below, pp. 154, 194.   [4] *Correspondence*, i. 128.

in the envoy-like conclusion of the poem showed that he
hoped, at the lowest, for a much larger public than the best-
equipped: he would be content, he had said,

> Content, if hence th' unlearn'd their wants may view,
> The learn'd reflect on what before they knew.[1]

His humble aim was the double one of reminding his better-
prepared readers of knowledge they already possessed, and
of acquainting other readers with what it would be to their
everyday advantage to start knowing. And to this end he had
tried to be as helpful as possible by treating the whole technical subject of criticism as a human matter, and so relating
secondary to primary Nature. He had followed his own
advice:

> Nor in the Critic let the Man be lost.[2]

He remembered, when writing his *Essay*, that few of his
readers would themselves be authors, but that all of them,
being readers caught in the act, were critics willy-nilly.
Critics, but untrained ones. To reach them, it behoved him
to make his argument clear. Johnson, even John Dennis,
could have made passages of it clearer, but neither Johnson
nor Swift could have improved the clarity of those scores of
clear passages and hundreds of clear couplets where Pope
was the happy master of his matter. His method for speaking
clearly was not only that of using terms scrupulously—as
scrupulously as he could on a subtle subject; in addition, it
was the method dear to all philosophers, that of using the
sort of imagery that has made its hearth and home in the
memory of any reader. The clarity of Pope's remarks becomes
more 'shining' by means of images which are common-
places of everyday experience: weather, watches, apothe-
caries, doctors, horsemanship, mules, tops spinning, weapons
disposed in an armoury, wives, mistresses. Pope may not
always have been clear what he meant by the complex word
'wit', and so his readers may not always have been accurately
edified, but in couplets like the following the image was so

---

[1] *Essay on Criticism*, ll. 739 f.
[2] Id., l. 523. Cf. the 'Epistle to *James Craggs*, Esq.', ll. 12 f.:

> But candid, free, sincere, as you began,
> Proceed—a Minister, but still a Man.

full of interest as to endow its major term with a firm sense,
a sense as much a matter of picture as of thought. We guess
the sort of the 'wit' that is in question when we are told that
it coexists with judgement in a particular way:

> . . . wit and judgment often are at strife,
> Tho' meant each other's aid, like man and wife.[1]

This Natural sort of imagery helped 'the learn'd' and 'th'
unlearn'd' together. And readers, of whatever status, were
also helped by Pope's method of conducting the argument
on the edge of satire, making free use of terms like 'fool'
and 'knave', terms to which everybody listens attentively—
Samuel Rogers excused his own satiric conversation on the
ground that, having a weak voice, sharp sayings were the only
ones that carried.

Pope's fear that the readers of *An Essay on Criticism* would
be few was not justified by the event. If he was right in his
figure of three hundred, he underrated the number of
readers who, when faced with the topics discussed, found,
perhaps to their surprise, that their interest in them sufficed.
The first edition of the poem consisted of a thousand copies,[2]
and in the first three years of its published life the poem was
reprinted four times in London and once in Dublin.

2

When Pope represents himself as a man, rather than as a
poet, it is as an individual completely himself, with the result
that the interest in Nature sometimes looks like a stalking-
horse from behind which springs his egotism. His unfolding
of a poet's personality is a new thing in English poetry, being
completer than that of Donne, who from this point of view is
his strongest predecessor. We have come to see the need to
draw a distinction between the 'I' of a poem and the 'I' of
daily speech. Any poet, any author, may use the first person
with the implication that it is identical with himself as a man.
Sometimes the two are identical absolutely, as when Milton
speaks of himself in his later poems; sometimes there is a
discrepancy that does not matter one way or the other, as
when Dorothy Wordsworth's diary tells us facts about the

---

[1] *Essay on Criticism*, ll. 82 f.   [2] *Correspondence*, i. 128.

content of a poem of William's which the 'facts' given in the poem contradict; sometimes so much is at stake that we have to be cautious, as when Donne uses 'I' in his erotic poems; and there are other degrees of relationship. Where Pope is concerned, the Miltonic conditions come as near to being satisfied as Pope had it in his nature to satisfy them. In other words the 'I' in the poem is as faithful to the actual self as the 'I' in the letters. The faithfulness may vary to some extent, but remains fairly firm on the whole.

I propose to consider it by way of a distinction drawn by Coleridge after his examination of *Venus and Adonis*:

> While [Shakespeare] darts himself forth, and passes into all the forms of human character and passion, the one Proteus of the fire and the flood; [Milton] attracts all forms and things to himself, into the unity of his own IDEAL. All things and modes of action shape themselves anew in the being of MILTON; while SHAKESPEARE becomes all things, yet forever remaining himself.[1]

The words 'the one Proteus' and 'remaining himself' mean that Shakespeare produced his poetry (the poetry in his plays and poems) as any other poet produces his; he produced it not from the mind as it was busy foraging in the external world, but from the mind as it sat at home drawing on its stores. Working with pen in hand he produced his poetry as Milton produced his, and what differed between them was not so much the act of composition, as the whole process of preliminary experience. Perhaps Shakespeare, darting out into life, experienced it with only a latent thought of using it in writing, experienced it first of all for its own sake. Perhaps Milton's way was to experience for the sake of Milton, for the sake of one who was consciously a poet and consciously a great poet; perhaps Milton's way was to experience for the sake of writing. Shakespeare, therefore, is 'the chameleon Poet', Milton a poet exhibiting the 'egotistical sublime'.[2] If, as Longinus said, great literature is the echo of a great soul,[3] it is more than that for poets like Milton who, as it were, set

---

[1] *Biographia Literaria*, ii. 20.

[2] Keats's *Letters*, ed. M. B. Forman, ed. 1935, pp. 227 f. Keats was remembering the passage I have quoted from the *Biographia Literaria*, which had appeared a year earlier.

[3] *On the Sublime*, chap. ix.

more than their soul echoing. More, and therefore less—as egotism has a narrower resonance than selflessness.

As we should expect, Coleridge's distinction is one observable in the style, in so far as style—to stick to the more tangible items—is diction, arrangement of diction, phrasing, idiom, imagery, rhythm. Milton's style, we can say, is everywhere Miltonic; the dictum 'the style is the man' has more meaning when applied to the poetry of Milton than to that of Shakespeare, who, as Pope saw,[1] wrote as many different styles as his personages demanded.

Coleridge saw Shakespeare as 'standing alone, with no equal or second in his own class' and (with a change of image) as 'seated . . . on one of the two glory-smitten summits of the poetic mountain', the other summit being occupied by Milton, 'his compeer, not rival'.[2] He does not quite say that Shakespeare is the only poet who has the protean faculty; he says that no other poet can be called his 'second', no other having the faculty to a degree that is comparable, or exercising it over a comparable ground. If he had cared to look at the slopes below Shakespeare, he would have acknowledged the author of *The Seasons*; Thomson had no faculty for 'conceiving an Iago or an Imogen'[3] (for conceiving either, let alone the one as readily as the other); but if human nature was beyond him, nature external to the human was not. And higher up the same long slopes now, for us, stands Keats, who has a big share of the sort of Shakespearean powers that Thomson had, though he was to hope in vain for the sort that entered into Iagos and Imogens.[4] But if Shakespeare shares the slopes of his peak with certain other English poets, Milton shares his with all those many poets who, for good or ill and more or less, cannot get out of themselves. Among these poets are Donne, Shelley, and Wordsworth—as it happened it was Wordsworth, not Milton, who led Keats to invent the phrase 'egotistical sublime'. And among them, too, is Pope.

In the poems of these egotistical poets we can distinguish both indirect and direct expression of the self, both the egotistical sublime and sublime egotism. Look again at Milton.

---

[1] Preface to his ed. of Shakespeare, para. 4.   [2] *Biographia Literaria*, ii. 20.
[3] Keats's *Letters*, ed. cit., p. 228.   [4] Ibid.

Most of his poems are written in forms which admit the egotistical only indirectly and with reluctance: he writes mainly
epics and poetic plays. So far as that goes he is like Shakespeare, who also writes mainly in the impersonal kinds: plays
and narrative poems. Readers have sometimes thought they
have seen Shakespeare-the-man not only in the sonnets but
in the plays: notably in *The Tempest*, and in the characters of
Richard II, Hamlet, and Brutus. But the most positive of
them have been uncertain of the degree of visibility, partly
because as to Shakespeare-the-man external sources are so
empty of information. External sources are fuller as to Mil-
ton-the-man, and, besides, there are the ample autobiographical statements in the prose writings. The Milton,
therefore, who wrote *Samson Agonistes* in the impersonal kind
is seen to have been drawn to the theme because Samson and
himself occupied a common ground as persons. Even so, the
Miltonic in Milton does not depend on things so near to
direct statement of self as his Samson. Even if we did not
know that the Milton who wrote of Samson was himself
blind, aged, isolated, licking his wounds, we should still feel
Samson Agonistes to be very much Miltonic, just as we feel
Comus, written in an indirect kind uncharged with autobiography, to be so: and indeed 'L'Allegro' itself:

> And in his garland, as he stood,
> Ye might discern a cypress bud.[1]

Milton in the poems, as in the prose-works, gives echo and
voice together. Even in the midst of the egotistical-sublime
epic, of *Paradise Lost*, there is the sublime egotism of the
autobiographical introductions to four of its twelve books,
introductions which bulk as large as autobiographical passages in Chaucer, but which of course have none of his pre-
tended familiarity. If from the length and breadth of *Paradise
Lost* Milton's self 'rises like an exhalation', from these four
prologues it obtrudes like a head from draperies. And the
self expressed in those prologues covers, by the implication
of its spare details, pretty well the whole self—the self as it
looked up to the 'Heav'nly Muse',[2] and to 'Urania', a divine
power beside whom the muse, though heavenly, was merely

---

[1] Milton's 'Epitaph on the Marchioness of Winchester', ll. 21 f.
[2] *Paradise Lost*, i. 6; cf. ix. 21.

'an empty dreame';[1] and on a different plane, the poet as a
candidate for the highest honours of poetry and prophecy,
and also as engaged on peculiar technical problems; and, on
a different plane still, as he was the survivor, blind and solitary, of the Commonwealth.

Turning to Pope's poetry, we find likeness and difference.
The individual poetic mind of Pope is clearly discernible in
the style of all his poems, as Milton's in his, and I shall have
something to say later on the nature of that style.[2] And he is
also present, as Milton in the forms he mainly wrote in could
not be, when he writes moral and particularly satiric poetry.
His presence is as strongly felt in many of his poems as a
jailer's in his jail: a strong reason why he is never absent from
his *Dunciad* is because it is he who has put in all the other
living writers.

When we come to the sort of expression of Pope's self that
is direct expression, we find it covering as much of the self as
Milton's does, but covering it in far greater detail, and dis-
porting itself oftener and for longer a time: where Milton
indicates, Pope expatiates. And when it comes to the two
remaining matters, the direct expression of the authorial self
as engaged on problems of poetic technique, and as the presented self of an ordinary human being—the son, the friend
('virtuous men alone have friends'),[3] the lover, the social and
the solitary, the bringer-in and the layer-out of money, and
so on—the difference between Milton and Pope is immense.
If we were to judge by the mere quantity of this direct self-
expression, it is Pope not Milton who is the sublime egotist.
Pope gives us whole treatises about himself—*An Epistle from
Mr. Pope, to Dr. Arbuthnot*, several other Epistles, all the

---

[1] Op. cit. vii. 31 and 39.   [2] See below, pp. 164 ff.

[3] Voltaire, *Philosophical Dictionary*, ed. H. I. Woolf, ed. 1929, p. 150. For praise
of Pope as a friend, see De Quincey, *Collected Writings*, ed. Masson, 1890, iv. 276 f.
Two instances from the letters will suffice to show how Pope was valued as a friend:
Robert Digby, replying to a charming letter, begins 'I have read your letter over
and over with delight' (*Correspondence*, i. 473), and this from Swift (id. ii. 384):

'My Lord Peterborow spoiled every body's dinner, but especially mine, with
telling us that you were detained by sickness. Pray let me have three lines under any
hand or pothook that will give me a better account of your health; which concerns
me more than others, because I love and esteem you for reasons that most others
have little to do with, and would be the same although you had never touched a
pen, further than with writing to me.'

'Imitations of Horace'—several shorter poems, many parts of poems, and letters by the hundred.

Pope made some of his poetry out of his personal characteristics and affairs. I shall say something later of his moral character as it is shown in the poems,[1] here I am concerned with what we call his personality. The assemblage of his personal characteristics and affairs is more various, more splendid and civilized, more exquisitely collected and manipulated, more closely lived-with and thoroughly valued—and also more subject to vexations and contentions—than any drawn on by any other English poet: in a word an assemblage which delighted those connoisseurs of human goodness, Thackeray and Charles Lamb—Thackeray, who found in Pope's letters 'the finest company in the world', a 'Delightful and generous banquet!',[2] and Lamb whose cheek grew hectic over what, at first sight, seems a mere list of early friends,[3]

[1] See below, pp. 217 f.

[2] ' . . . the finest company in the world. A little stately, perhaps; a little *apprêté* and conscious that they are speaking to whole generations who are listening; but in the tone of their voices—pitched, as no doubt they are, beyond the mere conversation key—in the expression of their thoughts, their various views and natures, there is something generous, and cheering, and ennobling. You are in the society of men who have filled the greatest parts in the world's story—you are with St. John the statesman; Peterborough the conqueror; Swift, the greatest wit of all times; Gay, the kindliest laugher—it is a privilege to sit in that company. Delightful and generous banquet! . . . He who reads these noble records of a past age, salutes and reverences the great spirits who adorn it' (*The English Humourists of the Eighteenth Century*, 1853, pp. 185 ff.).

[3] Hazlitt records how in a conversation with Ayrton, Lamb (who could read Pope 'over and over for ever') spoke particularly of Pope's compliments. His examples concluded with 'his list of early friends' from the *Epistle to Arbuthnot*. Lamb recited 'with a slight hectic on his cheek and his eye glistening':

> But why then publish? *Granville* the polite,
> And knowing *Walsh*, would tell me I could write;
> Well-natur'd *Garth* inflam'd with early praise;
> And *Congreve* lov'd, and *Swift* endur'd my lays;
> The courtly *Talbot, Somers, Sheffield* read;
> Ev'n mitred *Rochester* would nod the head,
> And *St. John*'s self (great *Dryden*'s friends before)
> With open arms receiv'd one Poet more.
> Happy my Studies, when by these approv'd!
> Happier their Author, when by these belov'd!
> From these the world will judge of Men and Books,
> Not from the *Burnets, Oldmixons,* and *Cooks.*
>   [text of Twickenham ed., ll. 135 ff.]

'Here his voice totally failed him, and throwing down the book, he said "Do you think I would not wish to have been friends with such a man as this?"' ('Of Persons one would wish to have seen', *Works*, xvii. 127 f.).

discerning its devotion, its golden possessiveness and yet its beautiful manners, the smiles and shrewdness of its Homeric epithets.

If, therefore, we were to lose all external materials for a biography of Pope, materials that exist in prose, whether in Pope's letters or elsewhere, we should still be well informed simply by drawing on his verse. Sometimes we should be well mis-informed! or we should be at a loss as to which meaning among several possible ones was that which best represented the complicated fact. In most autobiographies an inevitable lack of impartiality matters less because the material concerned is not presented, so to speak, in a court of law; but some of Pope's is: it is part, as I shall show,[1] of a course of personal attack and defence. But even allowing— as in our knowledge of his biography we are able to allow— for the misleading, the dubious, and the ambiguous, we should still be able to construct a brief biography from among the couplets: from couplets like

> Bred up at home, full early I begun
> To read in Greek, the Wrath of Peleus' Son;[2]
>
> But (thanks to *Homer*) since I live and thrive,
> Indebted to no Prince or Peer alive;[3]
>
> Weak tho' I am of limb, and short of sight,
> Far from a Lynx, and not a Giant quite;[4]
>
> Hopes after Hopes of pious Papists fail'd,
> While mighty WILLIAM's thundring Arm prevail'd;[5]
>
> Me, let the tender Office long engage
> To rock the Cradle of reposing Age;[6]
>
> I am not now, alas! the man
> As in the gentle Reign of My Queen *Anne*;[7]
>
> Hibernian Politicks, O Swift, thy doom,
> And Pope's translating three whole years with Broome;[8]
>
> Hibernian Politics, O Swift! thy fate;
> And Pope's, ten years to comment and translate.[9]

---

[1] See below, pp. 215 ff.   [2] *Imitations of Horace*, Ep. II. ii. 52 f.
[3] Id., 68 f.   [4] Id., Ep. I. i. 49 f.   [5] Id., Ep. II. ii. 62 f.
[6] *Epistle to Dr. Arbuthnot*, ll. 408 f.
[7] 'The First Ode of the Fourth Book of Horace: To Venus', ll. 3 f.
[8] *Dunciad* (1728), iii. 327 f.   [9] *Dunciad*, final version, iii. 331 f.

Other couplets hold equally good evidence,of the history and
uses of Pope's mind:

> I lisp'd in Numbers, for the Numbers came;[1]

> Then teach me, Heaven! to scorn the guilty Bays;
> Drive from my Breast that wretched Lust of Praise;[2]

> I love to pour out all myself, as plain
> As downright *Shippen*, or as old *Montagne*;[3]

> As drives the storm, at any door I knock,
> And house with Montagne now, or now with Lock;[4]

> Thoughts, which at Hyde-Park-Corner I forgot,
> Meet and rejoin me, in the pensive Grott.
> There all alone, and Compliments apart,
> I ask these sober questions of my Heart.[5]

And, to speak of bigger things than couplets, the *Imitations
of Horace* exist to demonstrate Pope's subscription to the
philosophy of Horace, to 'the Horatian standard of Temper-
ance, of Contentment with a modest Competence'.[6] And
there are all the other epistles addressed to friends, and those
of the epitaphs that express a near sorrow. Moreover, if the
couplets are of use to the biographer of Pope, so they are to his
critic: four long poems discuss the ethics of his participation
in satire,[7] and scores of poems and passages deal with the art
of writing verse, and say what are the marks of the true poet.

Here and there, we still find people prefixing the 'Mr.' to
Pope's name. This may imply merely the wish to seem
familiar with the great dead, as when people speak of 'Will'
Shakespeare, 'Kit' Marlowe, 'Kit' Smart, and so on. There
is, however, another reason for the persistence of 'Mr.' Pope,
a reason as disinterested as that behind the persistence of
'Dr.' Johnson. To say 'Mr. Pope' when you mean the author
of the poems is to recall that the author exists as a person in
his poems. To put it another way: Shelley and Keats, as
Keats was quick to see, were very different persons, and so

---

[1] *Epistle to Dr. Arbuthnot*, l. 128.   [2] *Temple of Fame*, ll. 521 f.
[3] *Imitations of Horace*, Sat. II. i. 51 f.   [4] Id., Ep. I. i. 25 f.
[5] Id., Ep. II. ii. 208 ff.
[6] From 'The Life of Pope' by John Butt, *The Rape of the Lock*, ed. Geoffrey
Tillotson, 1941, p. 95.
[7] i.e. *Imitations of Horace*, Sat. II. i, *Epistle to Dr. Arbuthnot*, the two dialogues
known as the 'Epilogue to the Satires'. I shall be concerned with them below,
pp. 219 ff.

the poetry of the one greatly differs from the poetry of the other. But if, for the sake of argument, we can suppose that the 'Ode to the West Wind' was written by Keats, and the 'Ode to a Nightingale' by Shelley, the supposition would greatly affect our criticism of them as poets, and also our view of them as 'personalities', but it would affect nothing else. If, however, we can suppose that either of them had written *An Epistle to Dr. Arbuthnot*, we should have to crown our adjustments by rewriting their biographies. Since we have all heard the nightingale and all felt the west wind, we could all have written odes to celebrate them 'if', as Lamb would say, 'we had the mind to'. But no one else in the history of the world has 'been in a position' to write the *Epistle to Dr. Arbuthnot*. And the same is true of many other poems of his.

Pope's poetry, then, contains much that is the concern of his biographer and critic. Such material does not promise well for poetry, being more like the material drawn on in a court of law than like that drawn on by Wordsworth for his *Prelude*. Yet we have nothing to fear on this account for Pope's poetry, because in expressing it he used his mind with no diminishing of its intensity: it was the reading of a passage of autobiography, we remember, that made Lamb's cheek hectic. His best biographer speaks of his 'glow [of] mind',[1] and the glow was habitual whatever the mind was turned to. And so we see a mind that glowed as warmly as Keats's often engaged on an unusual work, that of presenting a personality. Indeed it is possible that when so employed its mental glow was at its warmest. In the twentieth century we are not likely to underestimate the part played by his abnormal body in sharpening the psychological conditions that made a personal victory very much desired. Anyone who has a short, slight, crooked body, and means to hold his own, may need to contrive a good share of the egotistical sublime. For a cripple, holding his own was harder in Pope's day than it is in ours. We can scarcely hope to imagine the insults he suffered in an age when men had not yet come to question their right to pelt physical malformation with laughter. Even Pope's friends could not help looking on him as a toy, and referring, however affectionately, to his 'little, tender, and crazy car-

[1] Sherburn, *The Early Career of Alexander Pope*, 1934, p. 43.

case'.[1] If his friends could not help condescending a little, his
enemies of course made a pleasure out of it. A fair instance of
their manner is Dennis's *Remarks on Mr. Pope's Rape of the
Lock* (1728), which deliberately sets out to be temperate in
abuse. Throughout this pamphlet Pope is referred to by
phrases such as 'the Folly, the Pride, and the Petulancy of
that little Gentleman *A.P-E*', 'the little facetious Gentleman', 'the only foul-mouthed Fellow in *England*', 'a little
conceited incorrigible Creature, that like the Frog in the
Fable, swells and is angry because he is not allow'd to be as
great as the Ox', 'this little Creature who is as diminutive an
Author as he is an Animal', 'a little Monster'. Pope therefore
needed all the encouragements and compensations he could
contrive. And the best of all came from being a great poet,
and from being seen to be one actually in the poems. If we
cannot hope to imagine the tortures he suffered, we cannot
hope to imagine the satisfaction he enjoyed—the satisfaction,
say, of being able to write such lines as these, and to know
they would be read universally:

> *Fr[iend]* You're strangely proud.
>   *P[ope]* So proud, I am no Slave:
> So impudent, I own myself no Knave:
> So odd, my Country's Ruin makes me grave.
> Yes, I am proud; I must be proud to see
> Men not afraid of God, afraid of me.[2]

Egotism has never touched a higher sublimity, and it is possible that the jibes of Dennis and the rest aided the ascent.

Pope's physique helped his fame, which in turn helped his
poetry. It happened that, just as he began to publish, people
were beginning to formulate their interest in the self of
authors. In 1709, the year of Pope's first publication, or at
least, of his first signed one, Rowe affixed a biography of
Shakespeare to his edition of the plays. It is a sad instance of
interest springing up hopelessly too late, since Rowe craves
a Shakespeare 'in his habit as he lived':

It seems to be a kind of respect due to the memory of excellent men,
especially of those whom their wit and learning have made famous, to

---

[1] Id., p. 44. Cf. *Correspondence*, iii. 296.
[2] 'Epilogue to the Satires', dial. ii. 205 ff.

deliver some account of themselves, as well as their works, to Posterity
. . . even their shape, make, and features have been the subject of
critical enquiries. How trifling soever this Curiosity may seem to be, it
is certainly very Natural; and we are hardly satisfy'd with an account
of any remarkable person, 'till we have heard him describ'd even to the
very cloaths he wears.[1]

Addison remembered this paragraph when launching *The
Spectator* a year or so later:

I have observed, that a Reader seldom peruses a Book with Pleasure,
'till he knows whether the Writer of it be a black or a fair Man, of a
mild or cholerick Disposition, Married or a Bachelor, with other Particulars of the like nature, that conduce very much to the right understanding of an Author.

The growth of this interest in the persons of poets was partly
due to the new status of the writer, who became more noticeable as the patron dwindled. This Natural interest came
too late to benefit the fame even of Pope's immediate predecessor: about Dryden as a person we know little more than
that he had cherry-coloured cheeks. Pope himself was mainly
responsible for the revolution. And, by a coincidence, the
curiosity about poets as persons grew warm at a time when
the object of the interest was peculiarly interesting. What
were the poet's 'shape, make, and features'? was he 'Married
or a Bachelor'? 'of a mild or cholerick Disposition'? The
answers were more interesting than could have been expected; and further questions discovered that Pope was a
Papist, had great men (and remarkable women) for friends,
and smaller men for enemies, had built a garden which he
ended by decorating with a grotto; and so on through the
hundred details all furnished by the poems themselves.

3

Late in his forties Pope arranged that this sort of fame
received a powerful impetus from self-expression in prose.
He arranged for the publication of his letters. These letters
were of two sorts, formal and informal; and the formal sort
was itself subdivisible—into the letter that was an essay addressed, as it were accidentally, to a friend, and into the letter
that was merely the pen-and-ink aspect of the extreme civi-

[1] *Eighteenth Century Essays on Shakespeare*, ed. D. Nichol Smith, 1903, p. 1.

lization of the time, as pleasant but as impersonal as a bow on a social occasion. All the letters together were found delightful, the 'essays' and letters of formal greetings being among the best of their kind, and the informal showing the same hand warmer and without its glove. Altogether Pope could rightly claim that they showed 'a history of myself'.[1] Passages of that prose history had already appeared, for when the big collection of letters was published in 1735 it was not the bolt from the blue it has sometimes been thought. Certain letters of his had been printed by Curll in 1726, apparently without Pope's knowledge[2]—he had published the pretty batch that Pope as a youth had sent to Henry Cromwell, describing them accurately as 'On Wit and Humour, Love and Gallantry, Poetry and Criticism'. What was remarkable about the 1735 Letters was the many grounds on which they were remarkable: their large number, their literary worth, the degree of Pope's mastery of the civilities, the social splendour of their first recipients, and the amiable light they flooded on their writer (that was why Pope so badly needed to publish them just then: his war with the dunces had left him sorer and shabbier than was comfortable). Before they were printed he subjected them to severe revision and rearrangement, treating them as the works of literature which from the start he had laboured to make them.[3] With whatever mixed feeling the public received these letters, it received them on the grand scale. Edition piled on edition and, as has been suggested,[4] they are partly responsible for the emergence of the great letter-writers of the latter half of the century, and of the epistolary novelists.

Pope's letters solidly seconded the poems in improving the public grasp of his identity.

4

The spectacle of the man Pope, whenever he uses 'I' in his poems, is so much before us that, as I have said, Nature itself

---

[1] *Correspondence*, iii. 38.   [2] Griffith, I. ii. 267.

[3] Since Pope published them for the sake of his good name, some of them were offered as something more than literature; i.e. as historical documents. Their value as such, however, is sometimes that of showing what Pope's scissors and paste did in the 1730's rather than what he originally posted as letters. On their essential truthfulness, however, see *On the Poetry of Pope*, p. 6 n.   [4] Griffith, I. ii, p. xl.

shrinks in importance. Where indeed is the 'I' absent? Only
from those poems which are either too brief or forbidding to
admit it—like the single couplet designed for the collar of
Prince Frederick's dog,[1] or the epitaphs, or certain translations, or the poems designed for anonymous publication.
From the first poem (the 'Ode on Solitude' with its personal
last stanza) to the last (the four-book *Dunciad* of 1743), the
poet keeps up a written account of himself. No wonder, then,
if this persistence makes for variety and range. The reader
will have discovered this variety and range for himself, but I
may recall it by a few examples in roughly chronological order.
Some of them show Pope supplementing his account of the
poet as a skilled writer. In *An Essay on Criticism* we see the
poet as a young writer, not scrupling to bring up the rear of
the age-long procession of great poets, fearful as he looks
before him, but prouder as he looks to right and left at his
contemporaries:

> Still green with bays each ancient Altar stands,
> Above the reach of sacrilegious hands;
> Secure from Flames, from Envy's fiercer rage,
> Destructive War, and all-involving Age.
> See, from each clime the learn'd their incense bring!
> Hear, in all tongues consenting Pæans ring!
> In praise so just let ev'ry voice be join'd,
> And fill the gen'ral chorus of mankind.
> Hail, Bards triumphant! born in happier days;
> Immortal heirs of universal praise!
> Whose honours with increase of ages grow,
> As streams roll down, enlarging as they flow;
> Nations unborn your mighty names shall sound,
> And worlds applaud that must not yet be found!
> Oh may some spark of your celestial fire,
> The last, the meanest of your sons inspire,
> (That on weak wings, from far, pursues your flights;
> Glows while he reads, but trembles as he writes)
> To teach vain Wits a science little known,
> T' admire superior sense, and doubt their own![2]

Or the conclusion of the *Temple of Fame*, for which there is
little beyond a cue in the original Chaucer:

---

[1] See above, p. 39.   [2] *Essay on Criticism*, ll. 181 ff.

While thus I stood, intent to see and hear,
One came, methought, and whisper'd in my Ear;
What cou'd thus high thy rash Ambition raise?
Art thou, fond Youth, a Candidate for Praise?
'Tis true, said I, not void of Hopes I came,
For who so fond as youthful Bards of Fame?
But few, alas! the casual Blessing boast,
So hard to gain, so easy to be lost:
How vain that second Life in others' Breath,
Th' Estate which Wits inherit after Death!
Ease, Health, and Life, for this they must resign,
(Unsure the Tenure, but how vast the Fine!)
The Great Man's Curse without the Gains endure,
Be envy'd, wretched, and be flatter'd, poor;
All luckless Wits their Enemies profest,
And all successful, jealous Friends at best.
Nor Fame I slight, nor for her Favours call;
She comes unlook'd for, if she comes at all:
But if the Purchase costs so dear a Price,
As soothing Folly, or exalting Vice:
Oh! if the Muse must flatter lawless Sway,
And follow still where Fortune leads the way;
Or if no Basis bear my rising Name,
But the fall'n Ruins of Another's Fame:
Then teach me, Heaven! to scorn the guilty Bays;
Drive from my Breast that wretched Lust of Praise;
Unblemish'd let me live, or die unknown,
Oh grant an honest Fame, or grant me none![1]

Or the instances of his courage: 'My brother', marvelled Mrs. Rackett, 'does not seem to know what fear is.'[2] He had the courage that attacked those in power, addressing George II with the epistle 'To Augustus', and the disgraced Oxford with the epistle that ends:

Thro' Fortune's Cloud One truly Great can see,
Nor fears to tell, that MORTIMER is He.

—an epistle that Grattan was to commend for its courage;[3] he attacked the court as often as he attacked Grub Street. This courage was not lost on Byron, but it has been lost on

---

[1] ll. 497 ff.   [2] Sherburn, *Early Career*, p. 43.
[3] *Recollections of the Table-Talk of Samuel Rogers*, 1859, p. 94: '[Grattan] Repeated Pope's lines to Lord Oxford with great enthusiasm. They required courage in Pope.'

those who, instead of seeing Pope as a man, see him as Lytton
Strachey saw him, as a monkey that dropped spoonfuls of
boiling lead from the safe station of an upper window. If boiling lead did hit his victims, it was usually discharged man
to man. Many virtues he claimed for himself, but admitted
to faults, however grand the company they kept:

> But touch me, and no Minister so sore.[1]

And to end, as befits the general picture, with the last paragraph of *An Epistle to Dr. Arbuthnot*:

> O Friend! may each Domestick Bliss be thine!
> Be no unpleasing Melancholy mine:
> Me, let the tender Office long engage
> To rock the Cradle of reposing Age,
> With lenient Arts extend a Mother's breath,
> Make Languor smile, and smooth the Bed of Death,
> Explore the Thought, explain the asking Eye,
> And keep a while one Parent from the Sky!
> On Cares like these if Length of days attend,
> May Heav'n, to bless those days, preserve my Friend,
> Preserve him social, chearful, and serene,
> And just as rich as when he serv'd a QUEEN!
> Whether that Blessing be deny'd, or giv'n,
> Thus far was right, the rest belongs to Heav'n.

It was in the confident knowledge of the august stature of
this complete literary personality that Pope assumed a grand
public voice. We have just heard it sounding forth from the
Satires. The extraordinary thing is that he could command
it even when, in years, he was scarcely more than a boy, and
duly sustain it. It is the voice of certain paragraphs in *An
Essay on Criticism*:

> But if in noble minds some dregs remain
> Not yet purg'd off, of spleen and sour disdain;
> Discharge that rage on more provoking crimes,
> Nor fear a dearth in these flagitious times.
> No pardon vile Obscenity should find,
> Tho' wit and art conspire to move your mind;
> But Dulness with Obscenity must prove
> As shameful sure as Impotence in love.

[1] *Imitations of Horace,* Sat. II. i. 76.

In the fat age of pleasure wealth and ease,
Sprung the rank weed, and thriv'd with large increase:
When love was all an easy Monarch's care;
Seldom at council, never in a war:
Jilts rul'd the state, and statesmen farces writ;
Nay wits had pensions, and young Lords had wit:
The Fair sate panting at a Courtier's play,
And not a Mask went unimprov'd away:
The modest fan was lifted up no more,
And Virgins smil'd at what they blush'd before.
And following licence of a Foreign reign
Did all the dregs of bold Socinus drain;
Then unbelieving priests reform'd the nation,
And taught more pleasant methods of salvation;
Where Heav'n's free subjects might their rights dispute,
Lest God himself should seem too absolute:
Pulpits their sacred satire learn'd to spare,
And Vice admir'd to find a flatt'rer there!
Encourag'd thus, Wit's Titans brav'd the skies,
And the press groan'd with licens'd blasphemies.
These monsters, Critics! with your darts engage,
Here point your thunder, and exhaust your rage!
Yet shun their fault, who, scandalously nice,
Will needs mistake an author into vice;
All seems infected that th' infected spy,
As all looks yellow to the jaundic'd eye.[1]

The voice sounds in 'The Messiah', and in *Windsor Forest*:

Thy trees, fair Windsor! now shall leave their woods,
And half thy forests rush into thy floods,
Bear Britain's thunder, and her Cross display,
To the bright regions of the rising day;
Tempt icy seas, where scarce the waters roll,
Where clearer flames glow round the frozen Pole:
Or under southern skies exalt their sails,
Led by new stars, and borne by spicy gales!
For me[2] the balm shall bleed, and amber flow,
The coral redden, and the ruby glow,

---

[1] ll. 526 ff. Pope was to improve on the quality of technique used in this passage. In some couplets there is too much unrewarding disturbance of the prose order, with uncertainty of rhythm as a consequence: the rimes have too much control. Nor would the maturer Pope have allowed the 'Did' in l. 545.
[2] 'Old Father Thames' is speaking.

The pearly shell its lucid globe infold,
And Phœbus warm the ripening ore to gold.
The time shall come, when, free as seas or wind,
Unbounded Thames shall flow for all mankind,
Whole nations enter with each swelling tide,
And seas but join the regions they divide;
Earth's distant ends our glory shall behold,
And the new world launch forth to seek the old.
Then ships of uncouth form shall stem the tide,
And feather'd people crowd my wealthy side,
And naked youths and painted chiefs admire
Our speech, our colour, and our strange attire!
O stretch thy reign, fair Peace! from shore to shore,
Till Conquest cease, and Slav'ry be no more;
Till the freed Indians in their native groves
Reap their own fruits, and woo their sable loves,
Peru once more a race of kings behold,
And other Mexico's be roof'd with gold.
Exil'd by thee from earth to deepest hell,
In brazen bonds shall barbarous Discord dwell;
Gigantic Pride, pale Terror, gloomy Care,
And mad Ambition, shall attend her there:
There purple Vengeance bath'd in gore retires,
Her weapons blunted, and extinct her fires:
There hateful Envy her own snakes shall feel,
And Persecution mourn her broken wheel:
There Faction roar, Rebellion bite her chain,
And gasping Furies thirst for blood in vain.[1]

This is the voice of the poet who rose to writing *An Essay on Man* and the last page of the *Dunciad*. To characterize it we can appeal to Milton, if we see that to Milton's grandeur Pope adds a coruscation of detail, and that whereas Milton thunders things unattempted yet in prose or rime, Pope's loud uplifted trumpets speak of men and himself as they find themselves.

Hobbes had said that the epic poem gives us 'a familiar and easie view of our selves'.[2] In Pope's day a view of ourselves that was more familiar and easy was beginning to be afforded by the novel, which was then coming into prominence, and also by biography, then coming into greater prominence. Pope's elaborate picture of himself in his poems quali-

---

[1] ll. 385 ff.   [2] See above, p. 20.

fies for some of the praise Johnson accorded to works in this
latter category:

> I have often thought that there has rarely passed a life of which a
> judicious and faithful narrative would not be useful. For, not only every
> man has, in the mighty mass of the world, great numbers in the same
> condition with himself, to whom his mistakes and miscarriages, escapes
> and expedients, would be of immediate and apparent use; but there is
> such an uniformity in the state of man, considered apart from adventi-
> tious and separable decorations and disguises, that there is scarce any
> possibility of good or ill, but is common to human kind. A great part of
> the time of those who are placed at the greatest distance by fortune, or
> by temper, must unavoidably pass in the same manner; and though
> when the claims of nature are satisfied, caprice, and vanity, and ac-
> cident, begin to produce discriminations and peculiarities, yet the eye
> is not very heedful or quick, which cannot discover the same causes still
> terminating their influence in the same effects, though sometimes ac-
> celerated, sometimes retarded, or perplexed by multiplied combinations.
> We are all prompted by the same motives, all deceived by the same
> fallacies, all animated by hope, obstructed by danger, entangled by
> desire, and seduced by pleasure.[1]

This being so, Pope's account of himself is partly an account
of ourselves, and so not wholly apart from Nature.

[1] *The Rambler*, No. 60.

X

MAN, POETRY, AND POPE'S POETRY

NATURE, then, was seen as the best material for poetry, and was in the possession of men. By the act of writing poetry, however, Pope had passed beyond the limits of the ordinary man. By virtue of what powerful difference was he enabled to do so? The question is the less difficult to answer because from Pope's time onwards people came to pay more attention to such differences. 'Metaphysicians', said John Stuart Mill—and the remark had a wider application—'have busied themselves for two thousand years, more or less, about the few *universal* laws of human nature [and] have strangely neglected the analysis of its *diversities*.'[1] And to cap this came William James with 'There is very little difference between one man and another, but what little there is, *is very important*'.[2] Obviously the little difference between one man and another is vividly noticeable when one of them is a poet.

An answer to the question was proposed by Wordsworth in the Preface to the *Lyrical Ballads* in their 1802 form. 'What is meant by the word Poet?' he asked. His answer does men splendid honour because, to begin with, it claims little for the poet beyond his precious possessions as a man.

What is a Poet? To whom does he address himself? And what language is to be expected from him? He is a man speaking to men. . . .

Loath to forgo the enormous advantages of being a man, Wordsworth begins by suggesting that the poet is to be singled out no more specially than one might single out a marble from a pocketful. And if he has to follow this up by admitting something special in the human specimen he admits it grudgingly:

[1] *Early Essays*, ed. J. W. M. Gibbs, 1897, p. 224.
[2] *The James Family*, ed. F. O. Matthiessen, New York, 1947, p. 673.

He is a man speaking to men: a man, it is true, endued with more lively sensibility, more enthusiasm and tenderness, who has a greater knowledge of human nature, and a more comprehensive soul, than are supposed to be common among mankind; a man pleased with his own passions [i.e. feelings] and volitions, and who rejoices more than other men in the spirit of life that is in him. . . .

The undeniable difference is represented as one rather of degree than kind, and of quantity than quality—the poet increases his amount of experience by taking pleasure in a deliberate and wide use of his memory, and speaking of the result:

To these qualities [the poet] has added a disposition to be affected more than other men by absent things as if they were present; an ability of conjuring up in himself passions, which are indeed far from being the same as those produced by real events, yet (especially in those parts of the general sympathy which are pleasing and delightful) do more nearly resemble the passions produced by real events, than any thing which, from the motions of their own minds merely, other men are accustomed to feel in themselves; whence, and from practice, he has acquired a greater readiness and power in expressing what he thinks and feels, and especially those thoughts and feelings which, by his own choice, or from the structure of his own mind, arise in him without immediate external excitement.

The man and the poet have essentially the same material before them. The man deals with it as it comes up and moves on to more. The poet keeps his experience fresh and adds to it by going on living his own life, and also by keeping his eyes open to as much as possible of the experience of others. He gives an account of his comprehensive store of experience in language. But here he is seen to be at a disadvantage, so thoroughly is Wordsworth in love with those actual things— a man undergoing his own lot of experience:

But, whatever portion of this faculty we may suppose even the greatest Poet to possess, there cannot be a doubt but that the language which it will suggest to him, must, in liveliness and truth, fall far short of that which is uttered by men in real life, under the actual pressure of those passions, certain shadows of which the Poet thus produces, or feels to be produced, in himself. However exalted a notion we would wish to cherish of the character of a Poet, it is obvious, that, while he describes and imitates passions, his situation is altogether slavish and mechanical, compared with the freedom and power of real and substantial action and suffering. So that it will be the wish of the Poet to bring his feelings near to those of the persons whose feelings he describes, nay, for short spaces of time perhaps, to let himself slip into an entire delusion, and even confound and identify his own feelings with theirs; modifying only the language which is thus suggested to him, by a consideration that he describes for a particular purpose, that of giving pleasure. Here, then, he will apply the principle, on which I have so much insisted, namely, that of selection; on this he will depend for removing what would otherwise be painful or disgusting [i.e. distasteful] in the passion; he will feel that there is no necessity to trick out or to elevate nature: and, the more industriously he applies this principle, the deeper will be his faith that no words, which his fancy or imagination can suggest, will be to be compared with those which are the emanations of reality and truth.

Surely this is outrageous. Man is superior to the poet, and the poet as a man is superior to the poet as a poet, because the emotion prompted by actual experience issues in a more lively and true language than any the poet can come by as a person imagining experience. Such is Wordsworth's reverence for truth, for fact, that he endows the man experiencing it, whoever the man may be, with a 'power' of expressing it which is 'free' to be original and exact. That is his claim: otherwise we might suppose that the men in whom the emotions are aroused would react with such unoriginal and inexact means of expressing emotion as empty vocalic exclamations of delight or, alternatively, cursing and swearing. Wordsworth ignores the vast bulk of the evidence that men are not endowed with great utterance, even when greatly moved, except as they are poets already—for, as Coleridge was to point out, 'the property of passion [i.e. emotion] is not to *create*; but to set in increased activity'.[1] Wordsworth did not see how much of special qualification lay in the verb of his famous phrase 'a man speaking to men'. The poet has speech. If men do not lack powers adequate for expressing their emotions it is because they have several means besides speech. Their expression is lively, original, exact, free, and powerful only because it draws on so many means—words, tones of voice, looks, bodily gestures and actions. The poet has words and words alone. This limitation, however, is severe only if he cannot use a golden opportunity, an oppor-

---

[1] *Biographia Literaria*, ii. 42.

tunity to use his single means to make something that exists
on a different plane, that is capable of widely surviving the
occasion as a thing published.

The poet, I conclude, is superior to men because he is finer
as a human being when language (rather than deeds with or
without some scraps of language) is called for, and because
of the durability and universality of his language when written down, printed, and published.

What has been so far said of the poet applies equally to the
writer of prose. Wordsworth's Preface is again to the point.
Having given out that the subject of his ballads is Nature, he
asks 'why have I written in verse?' when

what confessedly constitutes the most valuable object of all writing
whether in prose or verse, the great and universal passions of men, the
most general and interesting of their occupations . . . may be as vividly
described in prose.

As before, however, the answer is not entirely satisfactory, in
that at bottom metre is represented as something 'superadded' to prose language. This explanation would account
for those notorious lines of Wordsworth's in which super-
addition is the process only too obviously resorted to, for at
his poetical (though not necessary philosophical) worst, he
wrote prose which, because its words are pushed around to
fit a metre, is prose that is the worse for its regular pulsations.
On the other hand, the obvious way of showing up the fallacy
of his account is to exhibit those thousands of superb lines of
his in which the metre is part and parcel of the language.

The prose of speech is one of the media of expression open
to man, and it does not matter that it is usually mishandled
because man has access, as I have said, to many extra-verbal
means for the completion of his expression. The man who
goes farther, and gives his prose a written form, must, if he is
competent, satisfy our demand for expression that is complete in a single medium, and is also accurate, elegant, and
ordered, unless there are special reasons why not—prose of
a kind and quality Clough had in mind when he discussed
eighteenth-century prose:

finding our ordinary everyday speech rounded into grace and smoothed
into polish, chastened to simplicity and brevity without losing its

expressiveness, and raised into dignity and force without ceasing to be familiar; saying once for all what we in our rambling talk try over and over in vain to say; and saying it simply and fully, exactly and perfectly.[1]

But the man who goes beyond this writing of prose and starts, as it were, to sing his meaning, takes a step that places him across the frontier. When it is not a fool's step in the dark, he takes it because his meaning calls for rhythm as dances have rhythm, a rhythm which being regular is like the beating of the heart that men are conscious of when they are excited. The metre of the poet's words must seem no more a thing superadded to them than the heart-beat is superadded to the physical body. I say 'must *seem*'. For it is in accordance with the effect felt by the reader, and that alone, that the thing is to be judged. So long as the metre seems at one with the words, we need not inquire whether the poet achieved it by way of art or 'luck' or both. Often, it will be by means of art, if lucky art. For art is 'second nature' to the poet, as of effective makers in general.

It would be unwise to be particular on this score and to demand more of poets than this power to make metrical language, to try to specify sorts of metre and of language, for the sorts vary from age to age. At some times the fashion is for strictness, at others for freedom, and those fashions affect both language and metre, and usually both together. It is enough to require the poet to possess the sort of meaning which, being restricted to expression in words, cannot be expressed without rhythm—without rhythm, which, compared to the rhythm of speech, or of prose, is regular.

2

From an inquiry on these lines, the author of the many passages I have quoted in the foregoing chapters has nothing to fear. And first as to his language.

Like that of every poet, every writer, his language shows some of the effects of fashion. In the department of language that is diction, he followed fashion to the extent of making a certain use of what became known as 'poetic diction'. I have

---

[1] 'On the Formation of Classical English', in *Poems and Prose Remains*, 1869, i. 330 f.

already written on this matter,[1] and need only say here that in Pope's day different forms of poetry—the epic, the epistle heroic or familiar, the pastoral, the 'elegy', the satire—were felt to require different 'colours' of diction, i.e. different selections from the English vocabulary. Some of these sorts of diction became known as 'poetic' diction, and as fashions changed—partly no doubt because the view of the world as a stable finished thing gave way to the view of it as a developing thing—came to be objected to as literary in the bad sense: they had outstayed their long welcome and been used mechanically by out-of-date poets.[2] In their long day they were expected and called for, and, especially when used by good poets, were found to be as pleasurable as the newer diction was found in the nineteenth century. We can still recognize the presence of this poetic diction in the poems of the crowded years that stretch from Spenser to Wordsworth, and even in Tennyson, who seems to have returned to items of it because on second thoughts, as it were, they still seemed items of exact diction—'feathered prey', 'curling' or 'rolling' waters, 'vocal grove', and the applications of the periphrastic formula that is still in use today—e.g. 'iron squadrons' (cavalry), 'yellow dirt' (gold). The other sorts of diction are today not so easily recognized. Few of us can appreciate the practical bearing of the principle that Pope enunciated in conversation with Spence:

> After writing a poem, one should correct it all over, with one single view at a time. Thus for language; if an elegy; 'these lines are very good, but are not they of too heroical a strain?' and so *vice versa*. It appears very plainly, from comparing parallel passages touched both in the Iliad and Odyssey, that Homer did this; and it is yet plainer that Virgil did so, from the distinct styles he uses in his three sorts of poems. It always answers in him; and so constant an effect could not be the effect of chance;[3]

—an observation that is modified later:

---

[1] *Essays in Criticism and Research*, Cambridge, 1942, pp. 53 ff.
[2] How long has been well demonstrated by John Arthos in his *Language of Natural Description in Eighteenth-Century Poetry*, Ann Arbor, 1949, which shows the eighteenth-century diction as applied to physical matter to be common from the Greek authors downwards, often in translated form, sometimes in directly borrowed form.   [3] Spence, pp. 23 f.

Though Virgil, in his pastorals, has sometimes six or eight lines together that are epic: I have been so scrupulous as scarce ever to admit
above two together, even in the Messiah.[1]

Most of us only go the length of distinguishing the 'poetic'
diction from the rest of Pope's diction. But the diction of the
Horatian satires would be worth distinguishing from, say,
that of the *Dunciad*, and we may be sure Pope's competent
first readers appreciated that and other distinctions.

To investigate one instance. The diction of *An Essay on
Man* is *sui generis*, being designed to suit its cosmic and
Natural matter and its expository manner (which is tight to
the point of ellipsis). Its diction is of two sorts, and with distinctions of diction go distinctions of syntax. One style is
marked by the use of weighty words derived from the Latin
after the later manner of Milton—homage to Milton was
especially fitting in the cosmic portion of the Essay. There is
'yonder argent fields above',[2] and the line, quoted from
Paradise Lost and significantly altered:

> But vindicate the ways of God to man;[3]

there are also:

> And pours it all upon the peccant part;[4]
> 'Annual for me, the grape, the rose renew
> 'The juice nectareous, and the balmy dew . . .'[5]
> Or in the natal, or the mortal hour;[6]

and so on. Another Miltonic device is noticeable—the placing
near together of two similar-sounding words of contrasted
import:

> As full, as perfect, in a hair as heart;[7]
> Reason is here no guide, but still a guard;[8]

and, with less well-marked echo,

> His knowledge measur'd to his state and place;[9]

or the natal/mortal line I have just quoted for its latinate and
Miltonic weight. In the last Epistle, where Pope comes

---

[1] Spence, p. 312.   [2] i. 41.
[3] i. 16. Milton had the less militant 'justify'.   [4] ii. 144.
[5] i. 135 f.   [6] i. 288.   [7] i. 276.   [8] ii. 162.   [9] i. 71.

nearer to the affairs of ordinary life, his style is different
again. Its quality may best be described as Johnsonian: it is
still a style of Pope's, but has something of the golden-fisted
bluntness we associate with the *Vanity of Human Wishes*:

> Or Public Spirit its great cure, a Crown;[1]
> The rest is all but leather or prunella;[2]
> One self-approving hour whole years out-weighs
> Of stupid starers, and of loud huzzas;[3]
> What greater bliss attends their close of life?
> Some greedy minion, or imperious wife,
> The trophy'd arches, story'd halls invade,
> And haunt their slumbers in the pompous shade.[4]

These two sorts of words are not much used by Pope outside
An Essay on Man, and the above are instances only, not a
complete list.

We are apt to miss distinctions like this, but we cannot
miss the category that includes all Pope's diction apart from
the 'poetic' diction I have distinguished—the category of the
diction of modern English when modern English is written.
For almost all Pope's diction has remained standard. To
glance at the entries in Abbott's *Concordance* is to appreciate
how it has helped to form the core of the standard English
diction, whether of prose or poetry. Apart from inevitable
differences due to differences of subject-matter and the ex-
pansion of vocabulary to cope with the expression of new
matter, it is modern diction. When later writers like Carlyle
or Morris seek to substitute other sorts of diction, they are
merely transitory disturbers (whatever their success on their
own behalf or their influence) of what had become stable and
was to remain so. One of the virtues of Pope's diction, with
the exception I have named, is that it cannot be parodied: it
is diction without trace of mannerism. The diction he used
for his expression of Nature has continued to serve that end
ever since.

Pope, then, was a national benefactor in that his selection
from existing diction helped to establish a permanent standard for Englishmen. That achievement is his greatest in the
department of language, and it was the sort of achievement

[1] iv. 172.   [2] iv. 204.   [3] iv. 255 f.   [4] iv. 301 ff.

he set most store by. A few words he revived, or promoted
out of the obscurity of learned writing, for instance:

> Fire in each eye, and Papers in each hand,
> They rave, recite, and *madden* round the land;[1]

there was also 'casuistry' in the *Rape of the Lock*, 'obstetric',
beautifully placed in the *Dunciad*,[2] and 'anticlimax'—but this
last as it happens was for the purposes of prose. Pope, however, was more ambitious to make common words combine
as never before:

> There Affectation with a sickly Mien
> Shows in her Cheek the Roses of Eighteen,
> Practis'd to Lisp, and hang the Head aside,
> *Faints into* Airs, and languishes with Pride;[3]
> Some rising Genius *sins up to* my Song;[4]
> On *once a* flock-bed, but repair'd with straw,
> With *tape-ty'd* curtains, never meant to draw;[5]

and

> So watchful Bruin forms, with plastic care,
> Each growing lump, and *brings it to* a bear.[6]

Keats took over 'faints into', but that and the rest of these
expressions are essentially 'nonce' expressions. They are not
characteristic of his diction, for he wished to keep as near to
man as possible. Man does not create diction: he selects from
what he finds in use. The difference is that Pope's selection
has more authority.

Pope's power over diction is perhaps most evident in his
endowing of common words with a power to surprise us,
prompting us to pierce through the dimmer sense they have
acquired in common usage and to see them as if we had invented them ourselves, rediscovering the literal sense which
has been partly overlaid:

---

[1] *Epistle to Dr. Arbuthnot*, ll. 5 f.
[2] 'And Douglas lend his soft, obstetric hand' (iv. 394).
[3] *Rape of the Lock*, iv. 31 f. The original italicizes 'Affectation'.
[4] *Imitations of Horace*, 'Epilogue to the Satires', dial. ii. 9.
[5] *Moral Essays*, iii ('Of the Use of Riches', To Bathurst), 301 f.
[6] *Dunciad*, i. 101 f.

Explore the Thought, *explain* the *asking* Eye;[1]

The gayest Valetudinaire,
    Most thinking Rake *alive*;[2]

Die of a rose in aromatic pain?[3]

From the dry rock who bade the waters flow?
Not to the skies in useless columns tost,
Or in proud falls magnificently *lost*,
But clear and *artless* . . . . [4]

In these last lines the word 'lost' has another sort of power. We are not accustomed to think of water as something that can be lost, as a key or a shilling can, and we look at the abstracted sense of the word so as to see how it can apply to water. It would be well if the critics who have blamed Pope for using the 'poetic' diction demanded by some of his subject-matter could have credited him with this vital power over the kind of words that are most recalcitrant to innovation —those which, as it were, inhabit our everyday tongue. Here are more instances:

The Gods, to curse Pamela with her Pray'rs,
Gave the gilt Coach and dappled Flanders Mares;[5]

Try'd all hors-d'œuvres, all liqueurs *defin'd*;[6]

Stretch'd on the *rack* of a *too easy chair*;[7]

Fond to *spread* Friendships, but to *cover* Heats,
To help who want, to *forward* who excel;
This, all who know me, know; who love me, *tell*;[8]

---

[1] *Epistle to Dr. Arbuthnot*, l. 412. How deliberate is Pope's use of this complex sort of diction, and how difficult it is to attain to use it, may be appreciated by comparing an earlier form of the line:
       Explore my *Thought*, and watch my asking *Eye*.
                        (*Correspondence*, iii. 226.)

[2] 'A Farewell to London. In the Year 1715', ll. 39 f.

[3] *Essay on Man*, i. 200. See above, p. 25.

[4] *Moral Essays*, iii ('Of the Use of Riches', To Bathurst), 254 ff.

[5] 'Epistle to Miss Blount, with the Works of Voiture', ll. 49 f. The original text italicizes the two proper nouns.

[6] *Dunciad*, iv. 317. The original text italicizes the two French words.

[7] Id. iv. 342. The term 'easy chair', which Pope uses again at *Dunciad*, i. 22, was of recent invention—the earliest mention in the *O.E.D.* is 1707.

[8] *Imitations of Horace*, Sat. II. i. 136 ff.

> As Helluo, late Dictator of the Feast,
> The *Nose* of Hautgout, and the *Tip* of Taste;[1]
> The *Mob of Gentlemen* . . .[2]

—or almost any line from the 'character' of Atticus. But instances are frequent. As far as diction goes, Pope is a supreme master, selecting, promoting, preserving, pointing, and bestowing authority. Nothing, of course, is farther from the power of the common man, but it is in accordance with what he himself attempts in his own fumbling way.

When we leave diction as such and see it in its place in syntax we find that Pope gives us language, the result of this combination, in two kinds. First, pure English, by which I mean a form that most Englishmen recognize as happy and pleasantly handy for use, whether in speech, written prose, or verse. He improved the general confidence as to what is standard English sentence-structure:

> With nothing but a Solo in his head;[3]
> And she who scorns a Man, must die a Maid;[4]
> It may be reason, but it is not man;[5]
> He stuck to Poverty with Peace of Mind.[6]

In longer passages there is an inevitable intrusion of the sort of English that is only in place in metre, but even so a surprising amount of standard sentence-structure persists:

> I learn to smooth and harmonize my Mind,
> Teach ev'ry Thought within its bounds to roll,
> And keep the equal Measure of the Soul.
>   Soon as I enter at my Country door,
> My Mind resumes the thread it dropt before;
> Thoughts, which at Hyde-Park-Corner I forgot,
> Meet and rejoin me, in the pensive Grott.
> There all alone, and Compliments apart,
> I ask these sober questions of my Heart.[7]

---

[1] *Moral Essays*, ii ('Of the Characters of Women'), 79 f.

[2] *Imitations of Horace*, Ep. II. i ('To Augustus'), 108. *Mob*, being a new slang abbreviation of *mobile vulgus*, was unexpected in collocation with 'gentlemen'.

[3] *Dunciad*, iv. 324.   [4] *Rape of the Lock*, v. 28.

[5] *Moral Essays*, i ('Of the Knowledge and Characters of Men'), 36.

[6] *Imitations of Horace*, Ep. II. ii. 65. Pope is here probably using a recognized expression of the time, which has remained permanent: cf. Burnet's *Sermon preached at the Funeral of* [Archbishop Tillotson], 1694, p. 11: 'He still stuck to the stricture of life in which he was bred.'   [7] Id., Ep. II. ii. 203 ff.

Pretty! in Amber to observe the forms
Of hairs, or straws, or dirt, or grubs, or worms;
The things, we know, are neither rich nor rare,
But wonder how the Devil they got there?[1]
'Has she no Faults then (Envy says) Sir?'
    Yes she has one, I must aver:
When all the World conspires to praise her,
    The Woman's deaf, and does not hear.[2]

The order of the words in these pieces is mainly the order of
words in prose. It was Coleridge who noted in Pope's original
(i.e. not translated) poems, and especially in his later ones, an
'almost faultless position [as well as] choice of words'.[3] Coleridge's standard for word-order in verse is by and large that
for word-order in prose. According to that standard, his word
'almost' must stay. There are times when the needs of riming
led Pope to abandon the prose word-order though nothing
was gained thereby except rime, which therefore stands to
taunt his lack of contrivance.[4] The worst example was pointed
out by Rogers:

> In Pope's noble lines *To the Earl of Oxford* . . . there is an impro-
> priety which was forced upon the poet by the rhyme;
>> 'The Muse attends thee to the silent shade . . .
>> She waits, *or to the scaffold or the cell,*
>> When the last lingering friend has bid farewell.'
> It should be, of course, 'or to the cell or the scaffold'.[5]

But it is clear that Pope's use of this sort of language—his
choice of words and his placing of them, though in metre—
has had its effect on English as English has been written and
spoken by everybody during the last two centuries. When
Pope and Bolingbroke were shaking their heads over the un-
certainties of the vernacular, Bolingbroke urged Pope to
'continue to Write' and so 'contribute to fix it'.[6] Here we
touch again on Nature, for trying to speak of men, Pope

---

[1] *Epistle to Dr. Arbuthnot*, ll. 169 ff.
[2] 'On a Certain Lady at Court', ll. 9 ff.   [3] *Biographia Literaria*, i. 26 n.
[4] See above, p. 157, n. 1. See also my 'Manner of Proceeding in Certain Eighteenth-
and Early Nineteenth-century Poems' (Warton Lecture of the British Academy,
1948).
[5] *Recollections of the Table Talk of Samuel Rogers*, ed. 1856, p. 27. See, however,
addendum, p. 212 below.   [6] *Correspondence*, ii. 219.

sometimes made his speech the sort of speech that man himself would not have felt embarrassed to create if he had had
the wit, and did in fact use when created. For, as he knew,
men do not overlook words that help them to speak as they
would like to: they are much beholden to good writers, who
being 'their own strict Judges' do not spare to erase any word

> That wants or Force, or Light, or Weight, or Care,
> Howe'er unwillingly it quits its place,
> Nay tho' at Court (perhaps) it may find grace:
> Such they'll degrade; and sometimes, in its stead,
> In downright Charity revive the dead;
> Mark where a bold expressive Phrase appears,
> Bright thro' the rubbish of some hundred years;
> Command old words that long have slept, to wake,
> Words, that wise *Bacon*, or brave *Raleigh* spake;[1]
> Or bid the new be *English*, Ages hence,
> (For Use will father what's begot by Sense).[2]

It goes without saying that no writer can have a big effect on
something so national as language, but in so far as any effect
is possible for any one writer Pope has had as big an effect as
any. On this score he is in the same class as Shakespeare, the
composers of the Collects, and the translators of the Bible. If
the common reader were to read Pope aloud to friends he
would not feel unduly self-conscious, even though metre co-
incided with standard speech.

I have used the term 'nonce' expressions of some of Pope's
diction, and I have said that Pope's English is often standard.
We must not give too much emphasis to what is standard in
it. Often it is standard accidentally, as it were—it has rather
made a standard than conformed to one. All writers are concerned to express their meaning accurately and completely,
but writers of verse differ from writers of prose in that they
have more resources at command. They have the resources
of metre and of varieties of word-order improper to prose. I
have shown that occasionally Pope finds in metre an obstacle
to perfect expression: he departs from the prose order of
words without gain and therefore with loss. But usually his

---

[1] Cf. *Correspondence*, iv. 208: ' . . . a Hankering (tis a good expressive English word).'
[2] *Imitations of Horace*, Ep. II. ii. 160 ff.

expression is perfect, and therefore essentially nonce expression. If we look at his couplets we usually find that each one is unique in all respects. Write them out as prose, pretend that they have no metre in them, gabble them off, and the result is gaucherie and pidgin-English:[1] leave them as they stand, and take in their words as they come—words with all their peculiarities of sound, degree of emphasis, position, sense, associations—and they have the self-explanatory individuality of a man with his own physical and mental features. Because this nonce result seems in accordance with the genius of the language the common man takes it in, in all its strangeness, as if the words had fallen from his mother's lips. He often has the impression that he is reading standard English because he is reading perfectly expressed meaning.

One of the great services that Pope rendered to English lay in his cult of conciseness. 'I hate *words*', he said, 'without matter.'[2] A firm rule of his was to

> . . . show no mercy to an empty line.[3]

It is partly because of the concise force of his own lines that the opening couplet of the *Vanity of Human Wishes* has been so often pilloried. Conciseness, as Hobbes had remarked, is particularly appropriate to language in its written form:

> words that pass away (as in public orations they must) without pause, ought to be understood with ease, and are lost else: though words that remain in writing for the reader to meditate on, ought rather to be pithy and full.[4]

When the young Pope was engaged on revising Wycherley's poems, the process was partly one of inducing conciseness:

> Some [verses] I have contracted, as we do Sun-beams, to improve their Energy & Force; some I have taken quite away, as we take Branches from a Tree to add to the Fruit. . . .[5]

---

[1] In charging Pope's syntax with being 'faulty' De Quincey must have failed to allow it to create its own soundness by being read carefully (see *Works*, xi. 63). For an instance of Pope's using syntax to help express his meaning, see that of the 'Character' of Atticus where the syntax allows the sense to edge forward, as if a snake were jerking up to within striking distance.

[2] *Correspondence*, iii. 302.   [3] *Imitations of Horace*, Ep. II. ii. 175.
[4] *English Works*, VIII. xxxi.   [5] *Correspondence*, i. 16.

This ideal of conciseness has, I think, a relation to Nature: surely men prefer the laconic to the windy, believing with Pope that

> Words are like leaves; and where they most abound,
> Much fruit of sense beneath is seldom found.[1]

Conciseness, being found pleasurable by the reader, makes its contribution to the poetry. In reading poetry, we give words our conscious attention—'the words', as Coleridge saw, 'ought to attract our notice'[2]—and the pleasures that come of our being pleasurably conscious that they are composed of sounds, even of letters,[3] and that they fall or leap into place, contribute to that composite mental and sensuous pleasure readers of poetry are seeking. When writing is terse, we notice the hard work being done by a few syllables, are conscious that it exists apart from the matter receiving the terse expression, and, if other scores are satisfied, find the terseness pleasurable.

It was in the cause of conciseness that Pope complicated his expression. This complication varied between what may be called the knotted and the fused. His lines are sometimes full as a closed fan or tweezer-case is full. We pause and open them, confident that their contents are bright and clear. The process is like that of undoing a knot, when we know we can manage it. These lines may be said to contain the sort of meaning that Crabbe, say, could have expressed quite completely, given two or three times the number of Pope's words. Examples of this sort of complication are numerous, and would include much that showed Pope's verbal wit. Dryden had considered two sorts of wit—the wit that was dependent on words and the wit that was not. He had preferred the latter, which, concerned as he often was with translation, he called 'wit in all languages'.[4] There are triumphs of this sort of wit in Dryden's writings, and in Swift's, and particularly in their prose: as when Dryden exemplifies the effectiveness of fine raillery, in preference to butcherly satire, by speaking of the rapier's severance of head from trunk while leaving it

---

[1] *Essay on Criticism*, ll. 309 f.
[2] *Table Talk and Omniana*, Oxford, 1917, p. 256.
[3] Our response to 'Kubla Khan' would be different if its proper nouns were spelt *Coobler Can, Sannerdoo, Alf.*   [4] *Essays*, i. 53.

in place:[1] that would lose nothing essential in translation into another language, as it has lost nothing essential in my transmitting it without exact quotation. Pope's wit in prose—say in *Peri Bathous*—is of this kind. But in verse it is often otherwise. There he claimed the right of the poet to draw from words everything they can yield. In his theory he decried some part at least of this practice. In the *Peri Bathous*, for instance, he pilloried the poet who makes 'a Word, like the tongue of a jackdaw, speak .... twice as much by being split',[2] i.e. who produces puns. And yet his own puns are a recognizable part of the elaboration of the expression when he is not writing with that engraved and enforced plainness I have been speaking of. The multiplication of the sense of single words is sometimes a mark of Pope's sophistication as an artist; and on no other score do we find him departing so far from the ideal of literary use which we may ascribe to the Natural man.

Then there is his use of the antithesis. Again, he despised antitheses in theory, at least when much used. Lord Hervey's 'wit' was

> . . . all see-saw between *that* and *this*,
> Now high, now low, now Master up, now Miss,
> And he himself one vile Antithesis.[3]

But the laugh rebounds on himself, since he used the antithesis often, though without confining his wit, as he alleges against Hervey, to that sole means of expression—and then bounds away, because his antitheses are delightful. Instances will occur to every reader. That they are famous is a proof of their acceptability to the common reader.

There is a particular recipe for conciseness which deserves a moment's attention—that by which we are given enunciation and illustration in one. Pope did not invent this method, but he used it with uncommon skill: examples are the monosyllabic warning against the over-use of monosyllables:

> And ten low words oft creep in one dull line;[4]

and the last line of the simile that represents learning as like climbing mountains:

[1] Id., ii. 93.   [2] Chap. x.
[3] *Epistle to Dr. Arbuthnot*, ll. 323 ff.   [4] *Essay on Criticism*, l. 347.

Hills peep o'er hills, and Alps on Alps arise![1]

where one verb is, as it were, humped, and the other per-
pendicular. Here Pope's power is the power to see what exists
in the language ready-made: that once seen, use follows
without further effort.

Then there is the other sort of concise complexity, the
sort not so easily analysed, and which could not be entrusted
to Crabbe's means of expression. We pause and open couplets with this sort of complexity, as we do the other sort, but
the process is happily defeated by the way the contents spread
indeterminately through the mind. Their effect is of a richness which we feel to draw on our most intimate reserves of
mind, and to test the quality of our own way of experiencing
the external world. I shall have something to say later of some
of Pope's complex imagery; here I am speaking of meaning
that is subtle in feeling and intellectual content. There is, for
instance, the couplet for the dog-collar,[2] or this inscription
for a monument:

> This *SHEFFIELD* rais'd. The sacred Dust below
> Was *DRYDEN* once: The rest who does not know?[3]

Or these couplets, virtually the epitome of a whole chapter in
a biography:

> Offend her, and she knows not to forgive;
> Oblige her, and she'll hate you while you live:
> But die, and she'll adore you—Then the Bust
> And Temple rise—then fall again to dust.[4]

Or the couplet that concludes the account of the Lord
Mayor's show in the *Dunciad*:

> Now Night descending, the proud scene was o'er,
> But liv'd, in Settle's numbers, one day more.[5]

The first line of this last couplet has the *lacrimae rèrum* in it
as well as the sort of sensuous suggestion that lines of Milton
and Keats have. The second was the illustration Tennyson
chose for his remark that Pope's 'lancet touches are very

---

[1] Id., l. 232.   [2] See above, p. 39.
[3] For the evolution of this couplet from Atterbury's draft see *Correspondence*, ii. 55.
[4] *Moral Essays*, ii ('Of the Characters of Women'), 137 ff.   [5] i. 89 f.

fine';[1] on another occasion he reverted to the couplet as a whole:

It is dreadful to think how satire will endure. The perfection of that couplet brings tears to one's eyes, and it pillories Settle for ever.[2]

The lancet wound is obvious to everybody. But the wit reserves its completest laugh for those who see that 'numbers' is not merely a technical term that could as easily be 'verses': Pope takes advantage of a metrical term 'numbers' that can exist only in the plural, and follows it by an arithmetical term which, existing in the singular, expresses the unaccumulating mite of poor Settle, the official City Poet. As a whole the couplet is a fair instance of the couplets that are designed to be complex.

In our own age there is no risk that this kind of writing will lack appreciation: we are much given to trying to analyse complexity. When he so wished, Pope was a complex poet, and he was gifted with the power to make complexity of both the organic and the mechanical kinds. Taking a particular pleasure in his complexities, we must not fail to credit him with a power he also loved to exercise, the power to write lines that are simple. These simple lines have their own sort of aesthetic effect: they are simple not because they are casual, but because they are contrived, as a window of clear panes is contrived in a church built by Wren.

There are other pleasurable qualities in Pope's words. Musicalness sings out when needed: either for Keatsian purposes, as in the lines on Maeotis, which most pleased his ear,[3] or, for all those local reasons calling for glorious or dignified sound:

> Oh spring to light, auspicious Babe, be born![4]

or

> Nor fears to tell, that MORTIMER is He.[5]

or, for purposes of comic mimicry:

[1] *Alfred Lord Tennyson, A Memoir by his Son*, 1897, ii. 286.
[2] William Allingham, quoted in Johnson's *Lives of the Poets*, i. 376 n.
[3] Johnson, *Lives of the Poets*, iii. 250.
[4] 'The Messiah', l. 22.
[5] 'Epistle to Robert Earl of Oxford, and Earl Mortimer', l. 40.

Or if you needs must write, write Cæsar's Praise:
You'll gain at least a *Knighthood*, or the *Bays*.
    P[*ope*]. What? like Sir *Richard*, rumbling, rough and fierce,
With Arms, and George, and Brunswick crowd the Verse?
Rend with tremendous Sound your ears asunder,
With Gun, Drum, Trumpet, Blunderbuss & Thunder?
Or nobly wild, with *Budgell*'s Fire and Force,
Paint Angels trembling round his *falling Horse*?
    F[*riend*]. Then all your Muse's softer Art display,
Let *Carolina* smooth the tuneful Lay,
Lull with *Amelia*'s liquid Name the Nine,
And sweetly flow through all the Royal Line.[1]

Or this:

Now thousand tongues are heard in one loud din:
The Monkey-mimics rush discordant in;
'Twas chatt'ring, grinning, mouthing, jabb'ring all,
And Noise and Norton, Brangling and Breval,
Dennis and Dissonance, and captious Art,
And Snip-snap short, and Interruption smart,
And Demonstration thin, and Theses thick,
And Major, Minor, and Conclusion quick;[2]

or for a different purpose, comic and gently aesthetic com-
bined, when the close of the second Book of *The Dunciad*
uses onomatopoeia on an uniquely grand scale (for even
Spenser or Tennyson does not keep it up for so long):

Three College Sophs, and three pert Templars came,
The same their talents, and their tastes the same;
Each prompt to query, answer, and debate,
And smit with love of Poesy and Prate.
The pond'rous books two gentle readers bring;
The heroes sit, the vulgar form a ring.
The clam'rous crowd is hush'd with mugs of Mum,
'Till all tun'd equal, send a gen'ral hum.
Then mount the Clerks, and in one lazy tone
Thro' the long, heavy, painful page drawl on;
Soft creeping, words on words, the sense compose,
At ev'ry line they stretch, they yawn, they doze.
As to soft gales top-heavy pines bow low
Their heads, and lift them as they cease to blow:

---

[1] *Imitations of Horace*, Sat. II. i. 21 ff.   [2] *Dunciad*, ii. 235 ff.

Thus oft they rear, and oft the head decline,
As breathe, or pause, by fits, the airs divine.
And now to this side, now to that they nod,
As verse, or prose, infuse the drowzy God.
Thrice Budgel aim'd to speak, but thrice supprest
By potent Arthur, knock'd his chin and breast.
Toland and Tindal, prompt at priests to jeer,
Yet silent bow'd to Christ's No kingdom here.
Who sate the nearest, by the words o'ercome,
Slept first; the distant nodded to the hum.
Then down are roll'd the books; stretch'd o'er 'em lies
Each gentle clerk, and mutt'ring seals his eyes.
As what a Dutchman plumps into the lakes,
One circle first, and then a second makes;
What Dulness dropt among her sons imprest
Like motion from one circle to the rest;
So from the mid-most the nutation spreads
Round and more round, o'er all the sea of heads.
At last Centlivre felt her voice to fail,
Motteux himself unfinish'd left his tale,
Boyer the State, and Law the Stage gave o'er,
Morgan and Mandevil could prate no more;
Norton, from Daniel and Ostrœa sprung,
Bless'd with his father's front, and mother's tongue,
Hung silent down his never-blushing head;
And all was hush'd, as Folly's self lay dead.[1]

3

The result of all these values in the words is the more thrilling because the words, as it were, happen to be in metre. I have shown that Pope often represents the office of poet as that of a skilled worker.[2] He hoped that readers would not be put off by his metre, would not feel it to be hieratic and mysterious. The heroic couplet, to which he almost entirely restricted himself, was, and is, a reassuring metre, readily cognizable, open to inspection, and manageable without tax-·ing the lungs. On the basis of its frank merits Pope leads his readers a dance. The versions of his single metre are too numerous for convenient classification. I do not need to add much to what I said in my former book. There I used the baffled words 'as if magically' to characterize the way Pope

---

[1] *Dunciad,* ii. 380 ff.   [2] See above, pp. 136 ff.

handled the circumscribed modulations of his metre, especially in the later poems. If the analytical critic were to do proper justice to his designing of couplets in themselves, and to his placing of the designed couplets in the paragraphs they contribute to build, he would have to face the examination of everything Pope wrote, and at the end of a short while would see that in Pope's hands the heroic couplet becomes at once the subtlest and most various instrument used in English poetry—with the exception of the free verse (which is sometimes rimed) of Mr. Eliot's *Waste Land*: Pope's couplets are as subtle as Milton's blank verse and have the advantages of rime. For rime is indeed an advantage when used according to that exquisite science understood by Pope. The rimes of his couplets are not all equally prominent. They clang like bells, or they come near effacing themselves, according to local demands or to his general liking for variety. Pope liked rimes for their own sake, for the aesthetic effect of sound and echo: but he saw to it that the sounds and the echoes varied in strength and not always pair by pair: a weak sound may be followed by a strong echo. For he conceived rime as a medium of sense, as a means contributing to express the varying strength of the meaning. The prominence accorded the rimes in his couplets depends on how the sense expressed in them is shaded. A couplet of Pope's is like a range of hills with rises and falls, with sometimes a plateau in prominence, sometimes a peak. If the peak comes at the rime, then the rime is prominent, but not otherwise. This is verifiable on any page. In the following random instances I have italicized the most prominent item(s):

> Bred up at home, full early I begun
> To read *in Greek*, the Wrath of Peleus' Son;[1]

> Who loves a Lye, lame slander helps about,
> Who writes a Libel, *or who copies out*:[2]

> That harmless Mother thought *no Wife a Whore,*—
> *Hear this!* and spare his Family, *James More!*[3]

In these couplets the emphatic item or items are very em-

---

[1] *Imitations of Horace*, Ep. II. ii. 52 f.
[2] *Epistle to Dr. Arbuthnot*, ll. 289 f.   [3] Id., ll. 384.

phatic. Where items receive a weaker emphasis, or where
there are several of them receiving such emphasis—as in

> Thy shady empire shall retain no trace
> Of war or blood, but in the sylvan chase;[1]

or

> Ah hopeless, lasting flames! like those that burn
> To light the dead, and warm th' unfruitful urn;[2]

—in couplets such as these rime cannot be said to protrude.
In all the couplets instanced it retires into the background,
or stands out in company with other words. In either sort it
is not so prominent as in lines where the rime falls on the
peak of sense:

> Down, down they larum, with impetuous whirl,
> The Pindars, and the Miltons of a *Curl[l]*;[3]

or

> To help who want, to forward who excel;
> This, all who know me, know; who love me, *tell*.[4]

This means that, as Pope used them, rimes have some of the
flexibility they have in the freer heroic couplet of Marlowe
and Keats—a flexibility of sound but not often of time: Pope's
syntax usually needs a pause at the end of a couplet, if not
always at the half-way point. And the rimes sometimes have
a casual look by being imperfect. Among those appendages to
the *Concordance* where E. A. Abbott classified some of Pope's
metrical characteristics is one that lists his imperfect rimes.
Many of these rimes were 'true' rimes in his own day, as we
know from H. C. Wyld's valuable little book,[5] but even in
the early eighteenth century *appear'd* cannot have rimed with
reward nor *fool* with all of the following: *cowl, dull, ridicule,*
and *skull*. 'I am angry', wrote Swift,

at some bad Rhymes [in the first volume of the *Homer*], and pray in
your next do not let me have so many unjustifiable Rhymes to *war* and
gods.[6]

---

[1] *Windsor Forest*, ll. 371 f.   [2] *Eloisa to Abelard*, ll. 261 f.
[3] *Dunciad*, iii. 163 f.   [4] *Imitations of Horace*, Sat. ii. i. 137 f.
[5] *Studies in English Rhymes*, 1923. Wyld does not draw on the evidence of the
riming dictionaries, for which see A. Dwight Culler, 'Edward Bysshe and the
Poet's Handbook', *Publications of the Modern Language Association of America*,
lxiii (1948), 865 ff.   [6] [Pope's] *Correspondence*, i. 301.

I am not sure how Pope saw these imperfect rimes. But if they were deliberately made so—and we have a duty to infer deliberation of a poet so conscious of his purposes and effects —there is one principle by which they can be explained. That principle is as much a social as an aesthetic one. The formal manners of Pope's time alternated with a calculated informality. To take some instances. The grand rows of houses built in Bath by the elder Wood had it said of them (the reign was stretched for the sake of a joke) that they were Queen Anne in front, and Mary Ann behind. In the garden planning of the time, there is the studied negligence of builded ruins and follies. In music the harpsichordist was required to improvise long creaky arpeggios while the strings sustained the chord that marked the transition from one movement to another. In the field of textual scholarship Pope cared little for what he saw as a merely mechanical accuracy:

> Comma's and points they set exactly right,
> And 'twere a sin to rob them of their Mite.[1]

Or there is the use, on solemn occasions as well as light, of 'em as an alternative for *them*. All things considered, it is possible that Pope planned his rimes to vary between false and true, so that he should not appear too vulgarly exact.

I have said that for Pope there was a 'science' of rime: he saw rimes as requiring to be monosyllabic, with a long vowel (which he often made an [ei] as in *state*, or an [ai] as in *light*), to fall on a verb, and, very occasionally and for particular effects, to be disyllabic. Much can be said of his rimes, and much of it has already been well said.[2] It is to Abbott's credit that he noted the frequent use in the *Dunciad* of curt short-vowelled rimes like 'mud', 'mum', 'bug', 'sink', 'in', 'bog', which are introduced to express disgust.[3]

The danger for the couplet, a short endlessly recurrent metre, is an effect of sameishness. The charge against Pope on this head was vigorously made by Leigh Hunt. In his magazine *The Reflector* of 1812 appeared his 'Feast of the Poets', which contained the couplet:

---

[1] *Epistle to Dr. Arbuthnot*, ll. 161 f.
[2] See especially W. K. Wimsatt, *The Verbal Icon*, Kentucky, 1954, pp. 157 ff.
[3] *Concordance*, p. xiii.

> . . . Pope spoil'd the ears of the town,
> With his cuckoo-song verses, one up and one down;[1]

and when, two years later, he reprinted the poem in book
form he substantiated its criticisms by means of notes. That
on Pope, a brilliant essay occupying twelve octavo pages, is
a discussion of metre: it urges poets 'to bring back the real
harmonies of the English heroic [i.e. the five-beat line], and
to restore to it half the true principle of its music,—variety'.
Hunt does not like the heroic couplet of the eighteenth
century, and in any event thinks Pope 'no master' of it, being

a very indifferent practiser, and one whose reputation will grow less
and less, in proportion as the lovers of poetry become intimate with his
great predecessors, and with the principles of musical beauty in general.

And so to his proof:

Let the reader take any dozen or twenty lines from Pope at a
hazard, or if he pleases, from his best and most elaborate passages, and
he will find that they have scarcely any other pauses than at the fourth
or fifth syllable, and both with little variation of accent. Upon these the
poet is eternally dropping his voice, line after line, sometimes upon
only one of them for eight or ten lines together. . . . See, for instance,
the first twenty lines of Windsor Forest, the two first paragraphs of
Eloisa to Abelard, and that gorgeous misrepresentation of the exquisite
moonlight picture in Homer. The last may well be quoted:—

> As when the moon—refulgent lamp of night,
> O'er Heav'ns clear azure—spreads her sacred light,
> When not a breath—disturbs the deep serene,
> And not a cloud—o'ercasts the solemn scene;
> Around her throne—the vivid planets roll,
> And stars unnumber'd—gild the glowing pole,
> O'er the dark trees—a yellower verdure shed,
> And tip with silver—ev'ry mountain's head;—
> Then shine the vales—the rocks in prospect rise,
> A flood of glory—bursts from all the skies:
> The conscious swains—rejoicing in the sight,
> Eye the blue vault—and bless the useful light.

Yet this is variety to the celebrated picture of Belinda in the Rape
of the Lock:—

---

[1] *The Reflector*, ii (1812), 314. It is ironical that Hunt's criticism of Pope's metre
is indebted to an instance of Pope's manner of expression: 'one up and one down'
recalls Pope's line on the wit of Lord Hervey (see above, p. 175).

> Not with more glories—in th' ethereal plain
> The sun first rises—o'er the purpled main,
> Than issuing forth—the rival of his beams,
> Launch'd on the bosom—of the silver Thames.
> Fair nymphs and well-dress'd youths—around her shone,
> But ev'ry eye—was fix'd on her alone.
> On her white breast—a sparkling cross she wore
> Which Jews might kiss—and infidels adore.

[and so on for ten lines more]. This is a very brilliant description of a drawing-room heroine; but what are the merits of it's versification, which are not possessed by even Sternhold and Hopkins [doggerel versifiers of the Psalms]? Out of eighteen lines, we have no less than *thirteen* in *succession* which pause at the fourth syllable,—to say nothing of the four *ies* and the six *os* which fall together in the rhymes; and the accent is all so unskilfully managed, or rather so evidently and totally forgotten, that the ear has an additional monotony humming about it,—

> Quìck as her eyes,
> Fàvours to none,
> 'Oft she rejects,
> Brìght as the sun.

It does not follow that the critic who objects to this kind of sing-song, should be an advocate for other extremes. . . . Let the varieties, like all the other beauties of a poet, be perfectly unaffected: but passion and fancy Naturally speak a various language; it is monotony and uniformity alone that are out of Nature. When Pope, in one of his happy couplets, ridiculed. the old fashion of gardening, he forgot that on principles common to all the arts, he was passing a satire on himself and his versification; for who can deny, that in the walks of his Muse

> Grove nods at grove—each alley has it's brother,
> And half the platform—just reflects the other?

[And so to a renewed plea for] that proper mixture of sweetness and strength,—of modern finish and ancient variety,—from which Pope and his rhyming facilities have so long withheld us.[1]

Hunt's role is that of a crusader, hacking at an infidel. He does not like Popean couplets, and we can do no more than leave him to his preference for stanzas and blank verse. Modern readers, after all the intervening stanzas and blank verse, and also free verse, are ready to readmit the couplets of Pope. Again there is no more to be said: fashion imposes its

---

[1] *The Feast of the Poets, with notes . . . 1814*, pp. 28 ff. Hunt makes several verbal errors in his transcriptions.

demands on us. But whether liking or disliking, critics must
try to see things as they are. In the first place, seeing Hunt as
he was, we allow his need to encourage in himself and his
contemporaries a liking for the couplets he was soon to try to
write in the *Story of Rimini*—to try, for he cannot quite escape
the older measure. But in turn, seeing Pope as he was, we see
that Hunt did not deal fairly by him. I grant that it is impossible to read those couplets of Pope in the form Hunt
printed them without a nauseating sense of sing-song. But if
we remove the cruel dashes, some of the lines are found to be
without a pause, others to have a faint one, and only a few to
have the clear pause represented by a comma. Because of his
dashes Hunt is himself pinioned by a remark of Johnson's,
which he quoted to dissent from, and which I omitted from
my transcript—Johnson had defended Pope against those
who judged of his versification 'by principles rather than
perception'.[1] Hunt himself is one of these offenders. His
criticism sprang, I grant, from a dislike of the couplet which
in the historical circumstances was reasonable, but he un-
reasonably proceeded to misrepresent Pope's couplets in
accordance with the *a priori* principle that couplets are sing-
song. Of course, if you want metre to be 'perfectly unaffected'
you will not go to couplets to find that effect—though in the
couplets of Pope that are meant to look like conversation you
come near to thinking that you get it. But the desire for the
'perfectly unaffected' is surely illegitimate, and the trouble
with much nineteenth-century versification is precisely that
it is not affected enough, not being enough a thing of art,
achieving, where it needs to, a look of the 'perfectly unaffected', but, more often, needing to achieve an effect of art.
Of course Pope's couplets cannot do everything: they cannot,
of necessity, give the impression of being loose. The loose has
its charms. Pope could not afford to allow them, because they
existed in his time in a debased form: they had succumbed to
the danger which not many loose metrists escape, that of being
loose and uncontrolled. Before Pope began to write, Atterbury, who was to become his friend, had written that discerning 'Preface to the Second Part of Mr. Waller's Poems,
Printed in the Year 1690', which contained these remarks:

---

[1] *Lives of the Poets*, iii. 248.

[The verses of the poets before Waller] ran all into one another, and hung together, throughout a whole copy, like the hooked atoms that compose a body in Des Cartes. There was no distinction of parts, no regular stops, nothing for the ear to rest upon; but as soon as the copy began, down it went like a larum, incessantly; and the reader was sure to be out of breath before he got to the end of it: so that really verse, in those days, was but downright prose tagged with rhymes.[1]

—a passage Pope recalled in his lines on the bogus Pindars and Miltons of the day,[2] and which prompted the laugh at the 'slip-shod Sibyl' (slip-shod because her *feet* were uncontrolled).[3] When controlled, looseness has obvious merits—as in *Paradise Lost*. Even looseness, however, tends to repeat its effects. One of these is the closing of the sense in mid-line and with an unaccented syllable, an effect associated with the later plays of Shakespeare and the seventeenth-century dramatists:

> The barge she sat in, like a burnish'd throne,
> Burn'd on the water.[4]

With this device went that other which added a weak syllable at the end of most lines, and so formed the metre which, right down to the nineteenth century, remained the metre of poetic drama. These devices are repeated *ad nauseam* even by the good poets, and they come to irritate a lover of the loose versification.

What is needed, by both tight and loose metres, is the effect of variety. Looseness does not guarantee this effect, and the surprising thing about Pope's closed, or mainly closed, couplets is that they frequently achieve it: sometimes with jubilant obviousness, as towards the end of 'The Messiah':

> No more the rising Sun shall gild the morn,
> Nor ev'ning Cynthia fill her silver horn;
> But lost, dissolv'd in thy superior rays,
> One tide of glory, one unclouded blaze
> O'erflow thy courts: the light himself shall shine
> Reveal'd, and God's eternal day be thine!

but more often with 'niceties' of a quieter sort.

---

[1] *The Poems of Edmund Waller*, ed. G. Thorn-Drury, 1901, I. xxi.
[2] See above, p. 181.
[3] *Dunciad*, iii. 15.
[4] *Antony and Cleopatra*, II. ii. 195 f.

In conclusion I agree there is monotony in the lines Hunt quotes from the *Iliad*, even when read without their dashes (a monotony that may be traceable in the last analysis rather to the poverty of the sense than to the metre), but not in those from the *Rape of the Lock*; and *a fortiori* not in the lines of Pope's 'most elaborate passages', which Hunt invites us to bring into the argument, and of which I have given many examples in the course of my book.

Two observations with which to close this section of my argument. First, Hunt's method of cutting each line in two has the authority of the youthful Pope. In a letter to Walsh of 22 October 1706[1] his observations on metre start on the assumption that every line in English verse falls into two parts.[2] To confine ourselves to the instances chosen in this letter, we should agree that the following line pauses a little in the middle:

> Homage to thee, and peace to all she brings;

though we should prefer to say that it pauses twice. We should not agree, however, that there is a pause in the line:

> Where'er thy navy spreads her canvas wings.[3]

Pope spoke in that letter of 'certain Niceties',[4] of which his remarks on versification are instances. I think he deceived himself on some points, and was a victim of the 'cant' Johnson referred to—the judging by principle rather than perception. The judgement in question, however, is that of Pope the theorist, and perhaps mainly the youthful theorist, rather than the practitioner. In remarks to Spence he showed where his real criterion lay, and had lain, I think, from the start:

one must tune each line over in one's head, to try whether they go right or not.[5]

---

[1] *Correspondence*, i. 22 ff.

[2] He seems to have drawn on the 'rules for making English verse' in Bysshe's *Art of English Poetry* (1702, &c.). For a description and discussion of Bysshe's handbook see A. Dwight Culler, *Publications of the Modern Language Association of America*, lxiii, 1948, 858 ff.

[3] It is interesting to find Pope drawing his instances from Waller, not Dryden: these two lines form the opening couplet of 'To the King, on his Navy'. As a 'child', Pope 'was a great admirer of Waller' (*Correspondence*, i. 97).

[4] Cf. 'little niceties', *Correspondence*, i. 106.   [5] Spence, p. 312.

It was because of the rarity of this sort of head that Hunt was
not alone in his strictures. Cowper had declared that Pope

> Made poetry a mere mechanic art;
> And ev'ry warbler has his tune by heart,

though 'mere mechanic' was rather hard on the poet whom
the same poem allowed to have great 'musical finesse', a very
'nice . . . ear', a very 'delicate . . . touch'.[1] Evidently, as I have
said, Pope had overdone his account of himself as a skilled
worker. The belief that his couplets were produced mechanically merely shows that 'every warbler' of crude versions of
his sort of couplet had contributed to dulling the ear of
readers, who during the latter half of his century came to
want a change at whatever cost. Not all readers and not all
poets: even the lines that dub his couplets merely mechanic
are lines written in the same measure: and no verses have
been loved more than those of the *Deserted Village*, both at
the time and later, and few liked more heartily than Crabbe's.
Nearer our own day there is Mr. Eliot, who tells us that he
destroyed a set of satiric couplets when Mr. Pound objected
that Pope had done satiric couplets once for all.[2] Even if Mr.
Eliot had aimed at a strict imitation, I suspect that the result,
like those achieved by other poets, was by any fine scale independent of Pope. If we want to shock ourselves into seeing
Pope's couplets for what they are, we may study the recalcitrant originality of couplets purporting to imitate them in
the literary competitions of our weekly periodicals.

Pope turned his lines with the result that, in general, the
rules dissolved away, except where he wished to flourish
them, as here:

> Happy my Studies, when by these approv'd!
> Happier their Author, when by these belov'd![3]

—or to ignore them equally with a flourish, as, for instance,
in the swift line with three stresses:

[1] Cowper, *Table Talk*, 1781, ll. 654 f.
[2] Ezra Pound, *Selected Poems*, 1928, p. xxi: 'incidentally, I remember that Pound
once induced me to destroy what I thought an excellent set of couplets; for, said he,
"Pope has done this so well that you cannot do it better; and if you mean this as a
burlesque, you had better suppress it, for you cannot parody Pope unless you can
write verse better than Pope—and you can't".'
[3] *Epistle to Dr. Arbuthnot*, ll. 143 f.

Unfinish'd things, one knows not what to call,
Their generation's so equivocal;[1]
Down, down they larum, with impetuous whirl,
The Pindars, and the Miltons of a *Curl*[*l*];[2]

or the subtly irregular line

And the pale Ghosts start at the Flash of Day![3]
Light quirks of Musick, broken[4] and uneven,
Make the soul dance upon a Jig to Heaven;[5]
Steer'd the same course to the same quiet shore,[6]
In quiet flow from Lucrece to Lucrece.[7]

The test of the vitality of Pope's versification is, as John-son saw, the test of perception, or the test of reading, and preferably of reading aloud. Coleridge erred badly, for once, when he compared Pope on this head with seventeenth-century poets:

In Massinger, as in all our poets before Dryden, in order to make harmonious verse in the reading, it is absolutely necessary that the meaning should be understood;—when the meaning is once seen, then the harmony is perfect. Whereas in Pope and in most of the writers who followed in his school, it is the mechanical metre which deter-mines the sense.[8]

Against this I recall an occasion when the late Sir Henry Ainley, then advanced in years, recited some Pope without mastering his meaning in advance. It was as if he agreed with Coleridge: his sing-song sense of the metre dictated the em-phasis, with the result that the metre was insulted and the meaning made nonsense. There is the record of Hannah

---

[1] *Essay on Criticism*, ll. 42 f.   [2] *Dunciad*, iii. 163 f.

[3] *Rape of the Lock*, v. 52.

[4] Pope uses 'broken' in the sense of irregular, jerky, and also in the sense of music on stringed instruments.

[5] *Moral Essays*, iv ('Of the Use of Riches', To Burlington), 143 f.

[6] 'Epitaph on the Monument of the Hon(ora)ble Robert Digby, and of his sister Mary', l. 13.

[7] *Essay on Man*, iv. 208. The stress given to 'Lucrece' on each of its appearances in this line is an indication of the subtlety of Pope's system of stress in his mature work. If we forced the line into regularity, the first 'Lucrece' would be stressed as a strong-weak, the second as a weak-strong. Read properly, the line has an appropriately quiet flow in which strong accents are reduced in strength: we linger on the two 'Lucreces' and give them two half-strength accents apiece.

[8] *Miscellaneous Criticism*, ed. T. M. Raysor, 1936, p. 94.

More that another actor wisely took the opportunity to school himself:

> Yesterday Mr. Garrick called upon us; a volume of Pope lay upon the table; we asked him to read, and he went through the latter part of the 'Essay on Man'. . . . He read several lines we had been disputing about with regard to emphasis, in many different ways, before he decided which was right.[1]

An Essay on Man is especially planned to be a crowdedly emphatic poem, but Garrick would have found a similar difficulty in most of Pope's poems. The power so to 'tune' the lines is a faculty proper to the poet, and though by the same rule improper to the man, the common reader knows well enough when it is done to good effect. Of course the reader will have to work in the attempt to complete his understanding of what he is reading. Pope desiderated repeated readings of his poems:

> [The *Dunciad*] will bear a second reading, or (to express myself more justly and modestly) will be better borne at the second than first reading. . . .[2]

and

> I want to know your opinion of [*An Essay on Man*] after twice or thrice reading.[3]

Those remarks are both from letters to Caryll, who was not the most intelligent of Pope's friends. But the intelligent Garrick also recognized the need of re-reading. And if contemporaries did, then all the more ourselves, who are distant from Pope's English by two hundred years.[4] We happen to know how Pope himself practised the art of reading, and had practised it from a boy:

> Mr. Pope thought himself the better, in some respects, for not having had a regular education.—He, (as he observed in particular), read originally for the sense; whereas we are taught, for so many years, to read only for words.[5]

---

[1] William Roberts, *Memoirs of the Life of Mrs. Hannah More*, ed. 1839 (abridged), p. 24.   [2] *Correspondence*, iii. 36.
[3] Id., iii. 354.
[4] Some of the difficulties in the way of present-day readers of Pope's poetry are the subject of Appendix 2, pp. 252 ff. below.
[5] Spence, pp. 279 f.

Attending first, or, as it were, in the middle of the mind, to the sense of his poems, the reader usually finds the expression fitting each line like the finger of a glove. Taking the couplets all together, one might describe them as oratorical and yet often conversational, intricate and yet forceful, constructed and yet alive. Except rarely, they are not instances of metre 'superadded' to meaning.

4

In speaking of both language and versification I have sometimes had to leave the common reader, who must take what he can, being the 'test' of Pope's art only in so far as he can give it a general approval. Molière had reasons for trying out on his cook those plays that he did not design for the court,[1] reasons that may not have been binding or appropriate for a writer who designed his poems not only to be read by all but to be read in private—clearly the act of reading in private allows a closer attention to the niceties of language than the act of hearing in a theatre. Some passages Pope might well have tried out on his. cook, with the object of altering what was found not immediately or sufficiently comprehensible. We might imagine the experiment as suitable in particular for *Eloisa to Abelard*, *An Essay on Man*, the *Moral Essays*, and the *Imitations of Horace*, but if passages in other poems that use words elaborately had undergone the experiment, they might well have survived it because, as in Shakespeare, they have enough of firm obvious sense, when read well, for the cook, though in addition they have niceties beyond the cook's powers. Or rather beyond the cook's conscious powers—the common reader is aware that niceties exist even when he cannot lay hold on them: they contribute to the pleasantness of the firm sense he is consciously taking in.

This general approval from the common reader Pope very

---

[1] Cf. the practice of Lucius Cary, Lord Falkland (1610?–43), as reported in Swift's *Letter to a Young Gentleman, Lately entered into Holy Orders*, para. 5: 'he used to consult one of his Lady's Chambermaids, (not the Waiting-woman, because it was possible she might be conversant in Romances,) and by her Judgment was guided, whether to receive [a word] or reject it'; and of Swift himself, who tested the intelligibility of his writings by having them read to his serving-men (see Colin J. Horne, *Swift on his Age*, 1953, p. 258).

much sought, but he made his effects also for the *un*common reader. He wrote for poets and critics as well as for the man in the street.

Because his matter was of the business-and-bosom kind he saw the need to make it come home to all his readers as a new thing—cleansing the stuffed bosom by presenting the old, tried sense under new colours, or by taking the old and tried and presenting new aspects of it. It is to Johnson that we owe the useful term 'mere Nature'. The thing it denoted in literature he always greatly disliked. He found it at its worst in the mimic 'Ballad of Hardyknute', written by Lady Wardlow, who had died in 1721. Bishop Percy, who, unlike Johnson, admired balladry, called this piece a 'fine morsel of heroic poetry [which] hath generally past for ancient',[1] but Johnson, before it was certainly known to be mimic, allowed it

no great merit, if it be really ancient. People talk of Nature. But mere obvious Nature may be exhibited with very little power of mind.[2]

In actual life Nature can never be 'mere', simply because each instance falls on our living selves. But in literature there is no such infallible vividness. While drawing its best material from Nature, literature must avoid at all costs the stale and flat and therefore unprofitable, and it does so by giving Natural sense a newness like that which Nature cannot but have for us in actual life. Being only too ready for the touch of Nature, we resent being touched by it rawly at the hands of weak or lazy writers: we are so exposed that we wish to be respected. Instead of insipidly repeating what we have heard before, the writer must

. . . mark that point where sense [i.e. Nature] and dulness meet,[3]

mark it and avoid it. In avoiding mere repetition a storyteller has a task not very difficult. He can touch us with the Nature of an incident, which simply because it is a new incident wins our response sufficiently. Pope did not often avail himself of narrative: he suspected it as flowing from a writer too easily. Unlike the narrator, he usually preferred to see Nature already generalized into a comment, or as part of an argument, or as record of actual experience. 'I will tell . . .

---

[1] Boswell's *Life of Johnson*, ii. 91 n.   [2] Ibid.   [3] *Essay on Criticism* l. 51.

the story as shortly as I can', he promises in one of his letters;[1] and when he gives us narratives in the poems they are either as brief as he could make them (being illustrative fable), or, if longer, weighty with reflection and sophistication. Even when he was committed to long narrative in translating Homer, he subjected Homer's Nature to an intellectualiza- tion, a process that Johnson justified on the grounds of this very principle of avoiding what by that date had become mere Nature.

Pope's standards of the new are high. Though he called in the poor Indian because his 'simple Nature' was what was needed as an illustration, he worked up the description into a fine paragraph.[2] Usually his method was to provide Nature with a sensuous surface. And one of the attractions of satire for him was that it satisfied the joint demands of newness and Nature by the angle at which Nature was approached. Pope also justified his use of Nature by 'dressing' what might otherwise be mere Nature 'to advantage' in an expression 'ne'er so well'.

And so I return to remark on the extraordinary complexity of Pope's expression, line by line, its density and intensity. Some of this complexity I sought to explore in my former book, and Professor Maynard Mack has since produced his splendid analytical essay, 'Wit and Poetry and Pope'.[3] Nice- ties of expression exist by the thousand in his poems. Twen- tieth-century readers have come to delight in noting them.

5

In the earlier chapters I discussed the sense Pope attached to certain terms that related closely to Nature. The content he found in *truth* and *sense* has usually prompted the sort of thought that goes most fittingly into prose. Another term of his was *beauty*, and the content of that might seem to offer more obvious hope for a poet; but he related it to those other terms so that it came to mean a fittingness in the appurtances of the things approved as Natural. Another term *man* is

---

[1] *Correspondence*, ii. 308.   [2] See below, p. 256.

[3] Included in *Pope and His Contemporaries. Essays presented to George Sherburn*, ed. J. L. Clifford and L. A. Landa, 1949. On the danger of reading into Pope's poems a complexity that does not exist, see Appendix 2, pp. 252 ff. below.

obvious ground for both the poet and prose writer: we can all remember scores of great passages of poetry and prose— prose with the sort of matter Hume or John Stuart Mill gave it—which speak of man. Pope's usual subject-matter, however, was a of sort that might be thought incorrigibly prosaic, and yet he made poetry out of it.

To claim the product as poetry requires no boldness when one lives in an age in which Pope's metrical writings are widely agreed to be that subtle quantity. If, however, the claim had been made at any time from his own to ours, it would not have lacked warm supporters. In every age Pope has had many readers who never supposed him not a poet, and no age has lacked assenting voices among 'the few who know' to give a fine authority to the claim. Pope, as I have said, played down the poet in him. But if in a Horatian imitation, on which he collaborated with Swift, he prays that he should be found to have written

> Something in Verse as true as Prose,[1]

that was rather because he revered prose than that he placed it above poetry: poetry for him was, as it were, prose with poetry fused into it. If he described himself as a mechanic, he enjoined, as Keats might have done, that a poet must forget father and mother and cleave to poetry alone,[2] and his brief account of becoming a poet describes an initiation that reads as authentically as any:

> . . . the kind Muses met me as I stray'd
> And gently pressd my hand, and said, Be Ours![3]

His claim to be a great poet lies in what he has to say, and also in what is implied in the fine phrase about himself as a poet in the ending of a letter to Burlington:

I am, in the sincerity of a Philosopher, & with the Flame and Warmth of a Poet, My Lord, your most faithfull, obedient humble servant, A. Pope.[4]

How, then, did he make his partly recalcitrant matter into poetry? What faculties of mind determined that his considerations of Nature should issue as poetry?

---

[1] *Imitations of Horace*, Sat. II. vi. 26.   [2] See below, pp. 231 f.
[3] Twickenham ed., vi. 194.   [4] *Correspondence*, iii. 342.

He used the usual terms when discussing his 'making'. In the note on the rock of ice he invoked *fancy*,[1] on other occasions the terms *invention* and *imagination*.

To start with *invention*. Johnson defined it as the power 'by which new trains of events are formed and new scenes of imagery displayed'.[2] 'Trains' denotes sequence in narrative, 'scenes' description. Johnson's instance—his definition comes in his Life of Pope—is the *Rape of the Lock*. For that poem Pope drew his materials from events and scenes actual and imaginary. Both sorts existed, as it were ready-made, before his poem came to use them. His friend Caryll, charging him to heal the quarrel between the Petres and the Fermors, told him how the quarrel arose; the sylphs and gnomes, though imaginary, existed in de Villars' *Le Comte de Gabalis*. There was little to choose, therefore, between the two sorts of material in regard to the work Pope had to do on them in the first place, if I may represent a complex process as if chronological—the making of the materials into something which his mind could gaze at as if on an actual moving scene encountered, say, as he walked along the Strand. The power to see in that way is, we may suppose, the power to describe. Where Caryll's material was concerned there was need, in addition, to understand minds in order to understand the actions they prompted, actions that were in this instance given. This different power we might call the power of psychology. The actions were given, but they were not given as the poem presents them, for it makes them take the form of an imitation in little of the action of an epic poem. Some other power, then, was necessary by which Pope discerned the rudiments of a possible epic action in the gossipy history furnished by Caryll. Perhaps we could call this the power of partly finding and of partly making literary jokes. Once Pope had imposed on himself the requirement to imitate the epic, he had to work on his given material, to adjust and to add. Performing this part of his work entitled him to invention as Johnson defined it: he was making of a given train of events a train of events that was partly new. It was the same sort of power, I think, which enabled him to see that the poem required sylphs and gnomes. In its first version he had provided

---

[1] See above, p. 61.   [2] *Lives of the Poets*, iii. 247.

machinery of the most august kind—the gods, Fate—but
that was machinery appropriate to epic rather than to mock-
epic. It was only later that he saw how to complete the
mockery by adding the sylphs and gnomes, creatures that
were to the epic gods what his human actors were to the
human actors of the epic. He took the opportunity to choose
the sylphs because of his power of discerning all the problems
inherent in a projected poem, and because of his 'divine discontent' with anything less than the best solution of them.
For Pope the problems were the more difficult in that he
could not invent his solution by creating it as if by the wave
of a wand; it was felt as a condition of the problem that his
need must be met by something already made by someone
else. Coming to see the need for mimic machinery, he did
not invent a new race of fairies. He would have felt that
solution to show

a weakness . . . since the serious epic took its machinery from established mythology, and since 'Truth, or at least . . . that which passes
for such', is best parodied by something else in the same . . . category.[1]

To read the essay from which these words are taken is to see
Pope collecting from the inventions of others. The principle
is important, and I shall have more to say of it later on. It
accounts for the presence in the poem of the game of ombre:
Pope went to the length of working out a course of play,
according to the rules, which fitted his psychological and
narrative purposes, and which also furthered his purposes of
epic mimicry.

A further point of the same sort. His laugh at epic is
sometimes the sharp-pointed laugh of parody—he contrived
the introduction of speeches which, while they would appear
to the unlearned to be happily invented for the occasion,
closely follow speeches in actual epics.

I have said that Pope preferred not to write narrative, not
to make 'new trains of events'. But the very conditions of
writing made him rely on something that often comes near to
being narrative, particularly when he is describing a crowd
of figures, each engaged on showing his nature by appearance

---

[1] Twickenham ed., ii. 357. The quotation within the quotaton comes from *The
Spectator*, No. 523. Cf. Hobbes, p. 205 below.

and action. His great scenes are among the finest things he
did. We think of them as more warmly sensuous, more
variously coloured counterparts of the crowded paintings and
engravings of Hogarth—of Gin Lane or the Strolling
Players. He might have preferred to present them as Hogarth did his, but words cannot escape the law that they must
form themselves into a sequence, into a 'new train'. The result, however, is so animated that the effect is of narrative
rather than of description: the scenes fall under Johnson's
category of 'new trains of events' rather than of 'new scenes
of imagery'. His poems contain a score or so of these great
living scenes, and I have already cited and quoted some of
them. A number of them do have a thread of narrative in
them—the account of the coming on of sleep at the close of
the second Book of the *Dunciad*, or the account of the grand
tour in the fourth—but we are more conscious of what the
thread is supporting, of the weight of picture and sense (of
sense primary and secondary, for the scenes are allegorical).
One of the finest instances has no narrative thread: I quote
the whole paragraph to show the way the scene emerges from
the argument:

> Let modest *Foster*, if he will, excell
> Ten Metropolitans in preaching well;
> A simple Quaker, or a Quaker's Wife,
> Out-do *Landaffe*, in Doctrine—yea, in Life;
> Let humble ALLEN, with an aukward Shame,
> Do good by stealth, and blush to find it Fame.
> *Virtue* may chuse the high or low Degree,
> 'Tis just alike to Virtue, and to me;
> Dwell in a Monk, or light upon a King,
> She's still the same, belov'd, contented thing.
> *Vice* is undone, if she forgets her Birth,
> And stoops from Angels to the Dregs of Earth:
> But 'tis the *Fall* degrades her to a Whore;
> Let *Greatness* own her, and she's mean no more:
> Her Birth, her Beauty, Crowds and Courts confess,
> Chaste Matrons praise her, and grave Bishops bless.
> In golden Chains the willing World she draws,
> And hers the Gospel is, and hers the Laws:
> Mounts the Tribunal, lifts her scarlet head,
> And sees pale Virtue carted in her stead!

Lo! at the Wheels of her Triumphal Car,
Old *England*'s Genius, rough with many a Scar,
Dragg'd in the Dust! his Arms hang idly round,
His Flag inverted trails along the ground!
Our Youth, all liv'ry'd o'er with foreign Gold,
Before her dance; behind her crawl the Old!
See thronging Millions to the Pagod run,
And offer Country, Parent, Wife, or Son!
Hear her black Trumpet thro' the Land proclaim,
That 'Not to be corrupted is the Shame.'
In Soldier, Churchman, Patriot, Man in Pow'r,
'Tis Av'rice all, Ambition is no more!
See, all our Nobles begging to be Slaves!
See, all our Fools aspiring to be Knaves!
The Wit of Cheats, the Courage of a Whore,
Are what ten thousand envy and adore.
All, all look up, with reverential Awe,
On Crimes that scape, or triumph o'er the Law:
While Truth, Worth, Wisdom, daily they decry—
'Nothing is Sacred now but Villany'.[1]

Other poems of Pope drew on some or all of the powers I
have noted. In the *Dunciad* he chose from existing literary
and social materials and arranged his choice in accordance
with the demands of epic mimicry. For the *Imitations of
Horace* the process was different, though within limits: Pope
was given the course of his argument, not in vague outline by
Caryll, but, for the most part, inch by inch by Horace. His
contribution was that of imagining Horace writing his poem
in English in Hanoverian England, saying the same sort of
thing but making it vivid to readers of Pope's day. In *Eloisa
to Abelard* he chose existing materials—a contemporary version of the correspondence of the medieval lovers[2]—and by
selection, addition, and arrangement gave them the sort of
shape Ovid had given his *Heroides*. As in the *Rape of the Lock*
he had to use the power of psychology, and he used it
gloriously.

Some of his poems, however, show him engaged on a
different sort of work from any I have yet noted, the poems
that are essays (on criticism, man, the characters of men and

---

[1] 'Epilogue to the Satires', dial. i. 131 ff.
[2] See Twickenham ed., ii. 277 ff.

women, the use of riches) and the poems that are familiar
epistles (to Dr. Arbuthnot or Martha Blount). Here he had
the freedom to construct an argument for himself. He constructed each one carefully, sometimes starting by drawing
up a plan in prose. The kind to which most of the long poems
that are not 'imitations' belong forbade any plan other than
the plan of an essay, which is satisfied, and indeed happy,
if it gracefully gathers certain related matters into a sort of
sequence; it does not need to achieve an unbroken argument.[1]
In these longer poems, no doubt, some of the paragraphs
might be transposed without undue disturbance, unless of
course they begin with a transition that pins them in one place
rather than another.

In these poems, and indeed in Pope's poems of all kinds,
there is often a remarkable organization that fuses together
—the word is not too strong— the paragraph-sections of the
matter in ways other than the strictly logical or narrative.
When it was assumed that the heroic couplet could achieve
nothing more complex than separate epigrams, even Pope's
power of constructing a paragraph was not credited to him.
That his paragraphs are designed as wholes may be demonstrated by trying to remove a couplet without loss to quality
(the aesthetic shapeliness and substance) as well as to quantity (amount of sense and mere size). But he also provided
'niceties' of interrelation between paragraph and paragraph.
He gave them, to begin with, as firm a link as possible at the
point of contact. Some of his skill in the making of transitions
I noted in my former book.[2] How much meaning can lie in
the link may be seen from the 'Epistle to Miss Blount, on her
leaving the Town, after the Coronation':

> As some fond virgin, whom her mother's care
> Drags from the town to wholsom country air,
> Just when she learns to roll a melting eye,
> And hear a spark, yet think no danger nigh;

---

[1] Elder Olsen, 'Rhetoric and the Appreciation of Pope' (*Modern Philology*, xxxvii,
No. 1, 1939), has demonstrated the happy blocking out of the material in *An
Epistle to Dr. Arbuthnot*. He thinks that Pope bore in mind the orations of Greece
and Rome when planning it. If this is so, the arrangement came later in the day
than he allows—the poem of 1734 was largely made up from fragments written
much earlier.

[2] *On the Poetry of Pope*, pp. 49 ff.

From the dear man unwilling she must sever,
Yet takes one kiss before she parts for ever:
Thus from the world fair *Zephalinda* flew,
Saw others happy, and with sighs withdrew;
Not that their pleasures caus'd her discontent,
She sigh'd not that They stay'd, but that She went.

    She went, to plain-work, and to purling brooks,
Old-fashion'd halls, dull aunts, and croaking rooks,
She went from Op'ra, park, assembly, play,
To morning walks, and pray'rs three hours a day;
To pass her time 'twixt reading and Bohea,
To muse, and spill her solitary Tea,
Or o'er cold coffee trifle with the spoon,
Count the slow clock, and dine exact at noon;
Divert her eyes with pictures in the fire,
Hum half a tune, tell stories to the squire;
Up to her godly garret after sev'n,
There starve and pray, for that's the way to heav'n.[1]

Here the second 'She went', which is made more emphatic
by being followed by a comma, is a repetition of words but
not of tone, or pace; it is weighty and slow because the first
removes the girl *from* the town that she loves and the second
removes her *to* the country that she detests. And the same
poem contains an instance of planning on a larger scale, an
instance of how a whole paragraph may owe its fullest, or
detailed, meaning entirely to what it is related to. The last
two paragraphs of this short poem are as follows:

In some fair evening, on your elbow laid,
You dream of triumphs in the rural shade;
In pensive thought recall the fancy'd scene,
See Coronations rise on ev'ry green;
Before you pass th' imaginary sights
Of Lords, and Earls, and Dukes, and garter'd Knights;
While the spread Fan o'ershades your closing eyes;
Then give one flirt, and all the vision flies.
Thus vanish sceptres, coronets, and balls,
And leave you in lone woods, or empty walls.

    So when your slave, at some dear, idle time,
(Not plagu'd with headachs, or the want of rhime)
Stands in the streets, abstracted from the crew,
And while he seems to study, thinks of you:

---

[1] ll. 1 ff. For the aunts and rooks cf. Harriet at the close of Etherege's *Man of Mode.*

Just when his fancy points your sprightly eyes,
Or sees the blush of soft *Parthenia* rise,
Gay pats my shoulder, and you vanish quite;
Streets, chairs, and coxcombs rush upon my sight;
Vext to be still in town, I knit my brow,
Look sow'r, and hum a tune—as you may now.[1]

Some part of the meaning of the last paragraph is reserved,
and only to be brought into the light by investigation—by
investigating how it is related to the meaning of the paragraph that precedes it. That fuller sense is seen to exist even
on a first reading, but just how clearly defined it is only becomes apparent on investigation. It goes without saying that
investigation is not a necessity: any one reading and re-
reading these paragraphs is beautifully aware of complexity,
and this awareness is the effect Pope aimed at. It is surely
open to us, however, to look closely at complexity, if only because it invites attention by making itself felt as firm, as the
result of 'art not chance'.[2] The effect of richness of meaning
is the result of something so conscious as to be constructed.
The penultimate paragraph shows Miss Blount to be idle,
but the 'idle time' of her experience is vexed with envy and
worldly ambition. The idle time of the author, however, is
'dear' as well as idle because filled with imagining her.
Moreover, it is implied that she is self-deceived. Her vision
is romantic in the sense of being wilfully rosy and incomplete. Pope's reference to his headaches and poetic frustra-
tions over rime, all the more so for being references to things
absent, show him as a real complete person; and, after all, it
is a real complete person a girl marries, not a Duke glorified
at a coronation; he is thinking of a fully known person, herself, while she, on her part, is thinking of strangers at their
most unreal. He is standing in the streets, where she wishes
she stood, but is abstracted from the 'crew'—the 'low' word
reiterates that he detests the town as she the country—
whereas she has been engrossed in them and would be again.
Wakened from his 'study', he is vexed to be still in the town
she is envious of, and even Gay is no compensation for his
lack of her. Both he and she relieve their frustration by humming a tune or a part of one: both, that is, have their frail

[1] ll. 31 ff.   [2] *Essay on Criticism*, l. 362.

resources against frustration. But for him it is a lover's frustration. His poem, then, is all the more a love poem because a sad one—his love is for someone whose imagination is haunted by the wrong things. The full sense of this last paragraph only becomes complete when it relates itself to that of its predecessor. It exists in neither but, as it were, on a series of bridges connecting the two.

The same poem contains a good example of Pope's application of the principle of contrast. That principle owed at least its name to the painters, from whom Pope borrowed it consciously: he used it when explaining to Tonson why, not being able to show him a whole poem, he was unwilling to show him a piece of one, the 'character' of the Man of Ross:

> To send you any of the particular verses will be much to the prejudice of the whole [poem]; which if it has any beauty, derives it from the manner in which it [i.e. the 'character'] is *placed*, and the *contrast* (as the painters call it) in which it stands, with the pompous figures of famous, or rich, or high-born men.[1]

In the third paragraph of the poem—the first showed Miss Blount leaving town and the second her dull life out of it—there comes this amplification of a country item, already mentioned:

> Some Squire, perhaps, you take delight to rack;
> Whose game is Whisk, whose treat a toast in sack,
> Who visits with a gun, presents you birds,
> Then gives a smacking buss, and cries—No words!
> Or with his hound comes hollowing from the stable,
> Makes love with nods, and knees beneath a table;
> Whose laughs are hearty, tho' his jests are coarse,
> And loves you best of all things—but his horse.[2]

The squire is in contrast to the 'dull aunts' and 'croaking rooks' of the paragraph that precedes, and to the passive character of the squire who has already been mentioned (unless the squires are meant to be the same person); he is also in contrast to the visionary lords and gartered knights who occupy the paragraph that follows. Pope makes much use of this principle of arrangement. It has even been called his 'usual method', and compared to that of a suite of Purcell or Handel

---

[1] *Correspondence,* iii. 290.   [2] Op. cit., ll. 23 ff.

in which 'an allegro is followed by an andante or a courante by a rigadoon'.[1] The principle of contrast is itself a principle of cohesion: to contrast is to relate.

And to revert to the question of Pope's architecture within the paragraph, there is a remarkable instance of it in the last paragraph of this same poem, where the third person in the first two couplets suddenly becomes first person in the third couplet—'your slave . . . *my* shoulder'. Here are couplets which only reveal their brilliant sense as they are taken as a unit. It is only as third person becomes first that we appreciate the reality of the little scene—what was an abstraction and 'study', so detached as to be third person, breaks off on the sudden tap of the shoulder, and brings Pope back to himself.

Another instance, from 'An Elegy on the Death of an Unfortunate Lady'. 'From these', that is, from the generality of mankind, whose 'souls . . . but peep out once an age',

> From these perhaps (ere nature bade her die)
> Fate snatch'd her early to the pitying sky.
> As into air the purer spirits flow,
> And sep'rate from their kindred dregs below;
> So flew the soul to its congenial place,
> Nor left one virtue to redeem her Race.
>   But thou, false guardian of a charge too good,
> Thou, mean deserter of thy brother's blood!
> See on these ruby lips the trembling breath,
> These cheeks, now fading at the blast of death:
> Cold is that breast which warm'd the world before,
> And those love-darting eyes must roll no more.
> Thus, if eternal justice rules the ball,
> Thus shall your wives, and thus your children fall:
> On all the line a sudden vengeance waits,
> And frequent herses shall besiege your gates.[2]

At first we take 'kindred dregs' as a chemical term—when certain substances are heated some of their constituents evaporate and become 'spirits', which are 'purer' than the 'dregs' left behind, which, having been a part of their former self, may be said to be 'kindred'. We take 'kindred', that is,

[1] G. Sherburn, '*The Dunciad*, Book IV', *Studies in English, 1944*, Austin, Texas, pp. 175, 184.   [2] ll. 23 ff.

as metaphorical. But it prepares us for the appearance of 'kindred' in its non-metaphorical sense, first in the vague 'Race' (i.e. family), then in the particular uncle:

> But thou, false guardian of a charge too good,
> Thou, mean deserter of thy brother's blood! . . .

We see, therefore, how seriously Pope believed that

Most little poems should be written by a plan: this method is evident in Tibullus, and Ovid's Elegies, and almost all the pieces of the ancients.[1]

If little poems, then longer ones, equally or more so.

6

In general, the long story of Pope's creativeness is a story of limitation of one sort and another. Pope either chose limitation as a positive advantage or forwent the chance to make the most of freedom when it was allowable. We do not expect him to have achieved freedom of thought, where it was possible, in the essay and original epistles, because he was a poet of Nature, and for such a poet freedom was suspect as likely to be merely freedom to be wrong, or cheap, or callow, or silly. The poet of Nature can be sure that he is talking sound sense only if he talks 'what oft was thought'. He thinks of readers as seeking to tread the old familiar highway, with eyes refreshed. In the other poems the choice to take existing forms and to fill them with existing materials was a choice as deliberate. Pope believed that readers seek the aesthetic pleasure of seeing difficulties overcome, and he made the problems he had to solve as difficult as he could by pledging himself not to invent when he could find. Men he saw as creatures 'Naturally . . . desirous of Truth',[2] and if Truth was not available at first hand, he resorted to someone else's report of it—to something which simply by existing already was guaranteed as of interest to men. It is almost as if he were trying to meet the objection of Plato by showing that poetry need not be lies, if only because the poet can point to an existing authority. He belonged to the school that was suspicious of invention. Hobbes had made the wild sort of invention look foolish in a modern epic poem:

[1] Spence's *Anecdotes*, p. 1.   [2] See above, p. 61.

There are some that are not pleased with fiction, unless it be bold, not onely to exceed the *work*, but also the *possibility* of nature [i.e. the external world]: they would have impenetrable Armors, Inchanted Castles, invulnerable bodies, Iron Men, flying Horses, and a thousand other such things, which are easily feigned by them that dare. [Let us not think that] the Beauty of a Poem consisteth in the exorbitancy of the fiction. For as truth is the bound of Historical, so the Resemblance of truth is the utmost limit of Poeticall Liberty. . . . Beyond the actual works of nature a Poet may now go; but beyond the conceived possibility of nature, never. I can allow a Geographer to make in the Sea a Fish or a Ship which by the scale of his Mapp would be two or three hundred mile long, and think it done for ornament, because it is done without the precincts of his undertaking; but when he paints an *Elephant* so, I presently apprehend it as ignorance, and a plain confession of *Terra incognita*.[1]

The transgression of probability that Hobbes deprecated was the sort that Horace had ridiculed in the first words of the *Ars Poetica*:

> Should some ill Painter in a wild design
> To a Mans Head an Horses Shoulders joyn,
> Or Fishes Tail to a fair Womans Waste,
> Or draw the Limbs of many a different Beast,
> Ill match'd, and with as motly Feathers drest;
> If you by chance were to pass by his Shop;
> Could you forbear from laughing at the Fop,
> And not believe him whimsical, or mad?[2]

Obviously this laugh was raised only against a painter who madly thought that in joining incompatibles he was painting probabilities—if it had been his object to paint a centaur or a mermaid, there would have been no madness and so no laugh. And yet for Horace and Hobbes, and for Pope too, the matter could not have been allowed to rest on that basis, on that appeal to fancy, even to fancy racial and Natural. They would have felt called on to improve the painter's conception of his office, appealing to him to approach nearer to

---

[1] Hobbes, 'Answer . . . to . . . D'Avenant's *Preface* before *Gondibert*', Spingarn, ii. 61 f.

[2] John Oldham, 'Horace His Art of Poetry, Imitated in English', ll. 1 ff. (*Poems and Translations*, 1684, p. 1). In the first line we note the reappearance of Hobbes's 'wild': see above, p. 61, n. 3.

Natural man, taking for his object either mankind itself or
what interested mankind more immediately and completely
than centaurs and mermaids ever could. There was one occasion when Pope released this very laugh of Horace:

> . . . Amphitrite sails thro' myrtle bow'rs;
> There Gladiators fight, or die, in flow'rs;
> Un-water'd see the drooping sea-horse mourn,
> And swallows roost in Nilus' dusty Urn.[1]

He laughed, as Horace did, where there was a flouting of
everyday sense. Here was invention employed by gardeners
to achieve nonsense just as it was employed by the supremely
vicious beyond any degree of it Pope felt like claiming for
himself:

> Vice with such Giant-strides comes on amain,
> Invention strives to be before in vain;
> Feign what I will, and paint it e'er so strong,
> Some rising Genius sins up to my Song.[2]

For Pope the invention had no more freedom than it enjoys
as a novelist uses it, the freedom that Hazlitt summed up
when he spoke of 'feigning according to Nature'.[3] The
novelist—Fielding, Jane Austen, George Eliot, and so on—
makes up his story, but he draws, as all writers must, on his
memory, though with no intent to disorganize what he finds
there and to recombine the dismembered fragments into a
Mustardseed, an Ariel, a Caliban, a Jabberwock, or into
such magical adventures as Ariosto delighted to fancy. He
respects the contents of his imagination as they stand. He
assumes that mankind gets most satisfaction from literature
when it reassembles everyday images in a probable action.
He agrees, therefore, with Hobbes. And with Wordsworth,
who when he came to publish *Peter Bell* used it partly as a protest against the magic-powered action of poems of Southey;
his prologue shows him rejecting improbabilities; he will not
continue to use the magic shallop that is touring in among
the heavenly bodies:

---

[1] See above, p. 101.
[2] *Imitations of Horace*, 'Epilogue to the Satires', dial. ii. 6 ff.
[3] *Works*, ed. P. P. Howe, 1930–4, xx. 390.

There was a time when all mankind
Did listen with a faith sincere
To tuneful tongues in mystery versed;
Then Poets fearlessly ·rehearsed
The wonders of a wild career.

Go—(but the world's a sleepy world,
And 'tis, I fear, an age too late)
Take with you some ambitious Youth!
For, restless Wanderer! I, in truth,
Am all unfit to be your mate.

Long have I loved what I behold,
The night that calms, the day that cheers;
The common growth of mother-earth
Suffices me—her tears, her mirth,
Her humblest mirth and tears.

The dragon's wing, the magic ring,
I shall not covet for my dower,
If I along that lowly way
With sympathetic heart may stray,
And with a soul of power.

These given, what more need I desire
To stir, to soothe, or elevate?
What nobler marvels than the mind
May in life's daily prospect find,
May find or there create?

Wordsworth begins this passage by noting an historical change; there had been a time when man liked stories of marvels. But he thinks that man has come to prefer his fiction to be invented 'according to Nature'. If the interest shown today in detective fiction and space-travel fiction is felt to suggest that man is slipping back into a liking for marvels, we may remember that these kinds of fiction claim to be probable down to the last finger-print and space-helmet. One of the reasons for the dislike, in Pope's time, of invented improbabilities was that they were felt to be too easy to concoct. In *A Tale of a Tub* one of the recurrent charges against the Moderns is that they prefer inventing to the harder duty of remembering: "tis manifest', Swift noted ironically,

what mighty Advantages Fiction has over Truth; and the Reason is just at our Elbow; because Imagination can build nobler Scenes, and produce more wonderful Revolutions than Fortune or Nature [human and external] will be at the Expence to furnish.[1]

In *Gulliver's Travels* Swift only invented when he could not draw on history. In the land of Brobdingnag Gulliver has a travelling-box made for him, and most readers have assumed it to be an invention of Swift's. But he was doing something more clever: he was borrowing the travelling-box that some-one else had been at pains to invent, in this instance so prominent a person as Archbishop Cranmer, whose wife, when the celibacy of clergy was being enforced, had to be carried about secretly.[2]

The invention in the *Rape of the Lock* or the *Dunciad* did not function with more freedom than Pope found necessary. He followed precedent wherever possible.

There were times when he hankered after other principles, for a holiday from the hard work he insisted on doing when making poems. In the 1730's he told Spence that he had once intended to write

a Persian fable; in which I should have given a full loose to description and imagination. It would have been a very wild thing if I had executed it; but might not have been unentertaining.[3]

But when he spoke earlier of the same, or a similar, project he postulated clearness of moral meaning, even though the enthusiasm for 'wildness' was even stronger:

I have long had an inclination to tell a Fairy tale; the more wild & exotic the better, therefore a *Vision*, which is confined to no rules of probability, will take in all the Variety & luxuriancy of Description you will. Provided there be an apparent moral to it. I think, one or 2 of the Persian Tales would give one Hints for such an Invention. . . .[4]

This confession shows Pope in a pleasant light—it is always pleasant to see principles come near to breaking down! But, in the first place, he did not write his exotic fiction; and, in the second, had he done so, he would not have found his in-

<hr/>

[1] Op. cit., ed. A. C. Guthkelch and D. Nichol Smith, 1920, p. 172.
[2] See *D.N.B.*, s.v. Cranmer, v. 23*a*. One recalls Thackeray's account of Mme la Duchesse d'Ivry, the ridiculous authoress of *Les Cris de l'Ame*, who 'hesitates at nothing, like other poets of her nation; not profoundly learned, she invents where she has not acquired' (*The Newcomes*, chap. xxxi).
[3] Spence, p. 140.　　　　　[4] *Correspondence*, ii. 202.

vention free. It was not free to roam among the improbabilities when he wrote his dream-poem, the *Temple of Fame*. The
note on Zembla, from which I have already quoted, assumed
that the conditions of such a poem made that freedom available. The matter is of less importance for Pope because he
has not full authority when his poem is 'imitated' from a
poem already in existence, Chaucer's *Hous of Fame*. But an
imitation allowed of additions, and Pope took advantage of
this, though not in the direction of freedom. For invention
is tied with unusual strictness in a dream-poem. In his
note Pope spoke of invention as he was to speak on a later
occasion of the same faculty under another name, *imagination*. Writing to Swift in 1734, he announced that he was
nearing the end of his work on *An Essay on Man*, and continued: 'My system is a short one, and my circle narrow.'
This prompted a general observation ('you', 'one', and 'we'
are careless 'incorrect' variations, I think, for a single meaning, that of 'poets'):

> Imagination has no limits, and that is a sphere in which you may
> move on to eternity; but where one is confined to Truth (or to speak
> more like a human creature, to the appearances of Truth)[1] we soon
> find the shortness of our Tether.[2]

The tether was even shorter in a dream-poem. Pope did not
see this. His note speaks of its admitting 'every wild Object
that Fancy may present'. In the twentieth century we well
know that dreams are not so wildly unconnected with 'sense'
as Pope seems to have supposed—on this occasion, though
not on all: elsewhere he speaks of:

> . . . the last image of that troubled heap,
> When Sense subsides, and Fancy sports in sleep,
> (Tho' past the recollection of the thought)
> Becomes the stuff of which our dream is wrought.[3]

A dream-poem, if written by one of ourselves, could not but
be allegorical: it would be taken as carrying a 'prose' statement about the affairs or psychological state of its author: if

[1] Pope is recalling Hobbes: see above, p. 205.
[2] *Correspondence*, iii. 445.
[3] *Moral Essays*, i ('Of the Knowledge and Characters of Men'), 45 ff. By 'sense'
Pope of course means the five physical senses.

in that poem elephants were represented as walking the water our prose conclusion would be drawn only too plainly. But for Pope, as for any medieval dream-poet, the prose statement had to be something very precise indeed. It had to be a moral statement. And the making of so precisely sensed a statement imposed hard conditions on the invention. The product of the invention might be 'wild' or tame: whether one or the other was irrelevant beside its need to further the moral statement. Pope's wish for wildness, however, did not go unfulfilled. He found it, as Emily Brontë did, in the wildness of Nature—in the extremes of human passion in Eloisa and Atossa, in the human freaks of Flavia and Villiers, in the 'Madness, Pride, Impiety'[1] of men. And he also drew wildly on Nature external to man when he came to make his imagery, and so displayed the sort of creative power to which Coleridge could alone allow the name *imagination*.

It goes without saying that nothing in Pope's poetry is the exact copy of an object existing for him in the external world, but a copy modified as his poetic needs directed. Sometimes greatly modified. To take an instance, the insects to which in a late poem Pope compared courtiers:

> Ye tinsel Insects! whom a Court maintains,
> That counts your Beauties only by your Stains,
> Spin all your Cobwebs o'er the Eye of Day!
> The Muse's wing shall brush you all away.[2]

Courtiers are dubbed insects, but not by any exact analogy with a single sort of actual insect—the insect they resemble is both butterfly (or moth) and spider, having both beauties and cobwebs. They are further removed from actual insects by being made by art: they are tinsel insects. Further, what is natural beauty on the wings of a butterfly is sophisticated beauty in courtiers: what are beautiful dyes and stains on the butterfly's wings[3] are moral stains on courtiers, stains which they are encouraged to flaunt as proudly as if the stains were beautiful colours, shutting out the true standard of conduct, as cobwebs do the watching eye of heaven. This passage is

[1] *Essay on Man*, i. 258.
[2] *Imitations of Horace*, 'Epilogue to the Satires', dial. ii. 220 ff.
[3] 'stains': Cf. *Imitations of Horace*, Ep. ii. i ('To Augustus'), 215. Keats may have recalled Pope's line in his lines on the stained window in 'The Eve of St. Agnes'.

one of those in Pope which could have illustrated Coleridge's sense of the imagination as an esemplastic power as properly as the passages he chose from Shakespeare and Wordsworth. We are in a different world when we read Addison's bid for this sort of effect. In his *Letter from Italy*, comes

> I bridle in my struggling Muse with pain,
> That longs to launch into a bolder strain,

of which Johnson remarked, in the manner of Pope's *Peri Bathous*:

> To *bridle* a *goddess* is no very delicate idea; but why must she be *bridled*? because she *longs to launch*; an act which was never hindered by a *bridle*: and whither will she *launch*? into a [*bolder*] *strain*. She is in the first line a *horse*, in the second a *boat*; and the care of the poet is to keep his *horse* or his *boat* from *singing*.[1]

The imagery of Addison's lines deserves Johnson's pillorying of its parts, because they remain parts. They are stuck together in the fancy, and lack the effects of the fusing power Coleridge demanded before he allowed fancy the name of imagination. Pope's imagery, where it consists of more than a single image, is always cohesive. If it has parts, they fuse as they join what we have already taken into our minds.

One prominent instance may seem an exception to this, the imagery of

> Estates have wings, and hang in Fortune's pow'r
> Loose on the point of ev'ry wav'ring Hour.[2]

In this particular instance, however, we may make a division between the first image and the rest. The first three words echo Proverbs xxiii. 5 (I quote the Authorized Version; the Douai does not vary from it significantly):

> Wilt thou set thine eyes upon that which is not? for riches certainly make themselves wings: they fly away as an eagle toward heaven.

It is as if Pope's couplet began with 'Riches, as Solomon said, grow wings, and so do estates; to which I add my own image, namely that they hang . . .'. When the reader has finished with the eagle and its wings, he is asked to start again and

---

[1] *Lives of the Poets*, ii. 128.   [2] *Imitations of Horace*, Ep. ii. ii. 248 f.

picture a something, an x standing for estates, insecurely
placed on the tip of one of the hands of a clock—the hands
of a clock are made of light thin metal, they increase the in-
security of anything laid on them, let alone anything heavy,
by moving through a circle that will dislodge them simply by
the law of gravity. There are reasons, then, for the disparate-
ness of the images of this couplet.

Usually Pope's complicated clusters of images do not ask
to be worked out in complete visualization as we work out,
say, the picture in a limerick of Edward Lear. We take them
as we take Shakespeare's—or, if the analogy be allowed,
the various flavours in a Christmas cake. For all its contrivance, its sharp wit, its hard brain-work, Pope's poetry,
like that of Shakespeare's poet and of Shakespeare himself,
'is a gum, which oozes'.[1] Being often so complex, it must
partly mystify the common reader, whom Pope wished to
reach and has reached. But, as I have said, the common
reader does not mind mystification if it is not the result of in-
competence, and if it promises a sufficient clarity as the
reward for looking into it.

[1] *Timon of Athens*, I. i. 21.

Addendum to p. 171 above, note 5

My friend, Dr. Harold Brooks, has defended the order of the words: 'Is Pope not
thinking of what Oxford may be *sentenced* to (so that no question arises of the
scaffold's coming *after* the cell in time). He may not be counting Oxford's incarceration before sentence; his order of thought may be: the Muse attends you whether
you are sentenced to present execution, or to life-long, or at any rate a long, term of
imprisonment.' I admit that from 'prison' to 'death' seems the natural crescendo—
and the opposite may seem an anticlimax: yet as the incarceration would stretch on
into the future, I'm not sure that to pass from imminent execution to long imprisonment is not a natural order of ideas. Milton has something like it, on the fates of
divinely elected leaders, in *Samson* (693 ff.):

<blockquote>
their carcases
To dogs and fowls a prey, or else captiv'd . . .
</blockquote>

XI

MAN AND POPE'S SATIRIC POETRY

I

IN the passages quoted above[1] as illustrations of Pope's
concern with morality there were illustrations also of his
concern with rebuke. In the third of them, and even in the
second, appeared an ingredient that he seldom wished or
managed to keep out of his poetry, any more than Dryden
did, the ingredient of satire. He could not contemplate the
good without rounding on its 'strong Antipathy', the bad.[2]
When quoting his lovely lines on 'Virtue's prize',[3] I detached
them from what followed in completion of them:

> What nothing earthly gives, or can destroy,
> The soul's calm sun-shine, and the heart-felt joy,
> Is Virtue's prize: A better would you fix?
> Then give Humility a coach and six,
> Justice a Conq'ror's sword, or Truth a gown,
> Or Public Spirit its great cure, a Crown.[4]

Humility, the good, would have gone bad, Pope is saying, if
it were found possessing the furniture of the proud. But he
did not stop at good and bad as general qualities. He seldom
saw the good without seeing good men, or the bad without
seeing bad men; and he sometimes went on to name particular persons. In the passages quoted on p. 37 above, you
not only get the comprehensive jibe at 'graver mortals', but
in the words 'our Gen'rals' come closer to individuals (closer
because the number of retired generals at any one time is a
small number), and finally touch the skin of a particular person in the word 'Cibber', and not only touch but pierce, because a man who is known to be self-assertive is awarded the
inappropriate epithet 'modest'.

Here are some further instances, illustrating degrees of

---

[1] pp. 36 f.   [2] 'Epilogue to the Satires', dial. ii. 198.
[3] See above, p. 42.   [4] *Essay on Man*, iv. 167 ff.

particular satire. The first is about three insipid pastoralists, and reading it is like being made to eat more than we want of a semolina pudding, till Pope dashes the dish down on the floor:

> Of *gentle Philips* will I ever sing,
> With *gentle Philips* shall the Vallies ring.
> My Numbers too for ever will I vary,
> With *gentle Budgell*, and with *gentle Carey*.
> Or if in ranging of the Names I judge ill,
> With *gentle Carey* and with *gentle Budgell*:
> Oh! may all *gentle* Bards together place ye,
> Men of good Hearts, and Men of Delicacy.
> May *Satire* ne'er befool ye, or beknave ye,
> And from all Wits that have a Knack[1] Gad save ye.[2]

Or this about a pompous patron of the arts:

> Proud, as *Apollo* on his forked hill,
> Sate full-blown *Bufo*, puff'd by ev'ry quill;
> Fed with soft Dedication all day long,
> *Horace* and he went hand in hand in song.
> His Library, (where Busts of Poets dead
> And a true *Pindar* stood without a head)
> Receiv'd of Wits an undistinguish'd race,
> Who first his Judgment ask'd, and then a Place:
> Much they extoll'd his Pictures, much his Seat,
> And flatter'd ev'ry day, and some days eat:
> Till grown more frugal in his riper days,
> He pay'd some Bards with Port, and some with Praise,
> To some a dry Rehearsal was assign'd,
> And others (harder still) he pay'd in kind.
> *Dryden* alone (what wonder?) came not nigh,
> *Dryden* alone escap'd this judging eye:
> But still the Great have kindness in reserve,
> He help'd to bury whom he help'd to starve.[3]

Or this from one of his two essays on the use of riches, as fierce a passage as he ever wrote:

---

[1] A reference may be intended to the gift which even Dennis allowed Pope ('a notable knack of Rhimeing and Writing smooth Verse': *Critical Works*, ed. E. N. Hooker, ii (1943), 108) and also Curll (see Bowles's note, *The Works of Alexander Pope*, 1806, ii. 394). In anonymous prose, Pope had claimed the knack for himself, see *Guardian*, 40 (*Prose Works*, ed. N. Ault, 1936, i. 101).
[2] 'The Three *gentle* Shepherds.'   [3] *Epistle to Dr. Arbuthnot*, ll. 231 ff.

What Riches give us let us then enquire,
Meat, Fire and Cloaths. What more? Meat, Cloaths, and Fire.
Is this too little? would you more than live?
Alas! 'tis more than Turner finds they give.
Alas! 'tis more than (all his Visions past)
Unhappy Wharton, waking, found at last!
What can they give? to dying Hopkins Heirs;
To Chartres, Vigour; Japhet, Nose and Ears?
Can they, in gems bid pallid Hippia glow,
In Fulvia's buckle ease the throbs below,
Or heal, old Narses, thy obscener ail,
With all th' embroid'ry plaister'd at thy tail?
They might (were Harpax not too wise to spend)
Give Harpax self the blessing of a Friend;
Or find some Doctor that would save the life
Of wretched Shylock, spite of Shylock's Wife:
But thousands die, without or this or that,
Die, and endow a College, or a Cat:
To some, indeed, Heav'n grants the happier fate,
T'enrich a Bastard, or a Son they hate.[1]

2

When a man shows himself to be a poet he cuts himself off, as I have shown, from his fellows, though the gap will be bridged if he wins respect or honour from his readers—if in short he achieves readers numerous enough. When the poetry written is satiric, the relation is more complicated.

In attempting an analysis I begin with 'general' satire. Whether general or particular, satire would seem to be poetry trying to be more than poetry. It is sometimes charged against poetry that it is 'only' poetry. There is sometimes a feeling—in the nineteenth century, for instance—that it is not in earnest. Satire claims to have the merit of earnestness. The satiric poet sets himself up as judge as if in a public court, dealing with the morals and actions of his fellow men. He seems to be trying to annihilate the psychical distance between the page and its readers, and to 'mean business'. We must not exaggerate, however, the degree of his personal animus, or misconceive the kind of his poem, especially when it is a general satire. Usually, I suggest, the earnest-

[1] *Moral Essays*, iii (Of the Use of Riches, To Bathurst), 81 ff.

ness of the poet and his satire exists rather in the claim to

ness of the poet and his satire exists rather in the claim to earnestness than in the actuality. No doubt the deepest reason why a poet writes general satire is a literary and psychological, not a moral and intellectual, reason. He may write it—and we infer this from his choosing to write in a form so public and obtrusive—because he wants to increase the number of his readers and to engage them intensely. The darkest dread of a poet is that the reader will idly 'twirl over' his pages—as Swift said of the reader of the fulsome prefaces and dedications in most of the books of his time.[1] We have already seen Pope himself reading certain pastorals in that contemptuous sort of way. Electing to write general satire, the poet at bottom may be electing to write what he knows in advance—I am assuming that he has the power to write it well—will be read with eagerness and relish. Even a poem so lacking in pugnacity as *An Essay on Man* was seen as all the better for having a dash or two of general satire, the sort of ingredient Pope added to the lines about the soul's calm sunshine, which I began by quoting:

> the seasoning of satire renders it more palatable to the generality.[2]

This remark, I think, hits the nail on the head. At bottom the satirist is a poet hungry for readers. His deepest motive is literary. As for the reader, he is wholly free to accept the satire as literature and nothing more, because, as Swift noted, no one applies general satire to himself:

> . . . Satyr being levelled at all, is never resented as an offence by any, since every individual Person makes bold to understand it of others, and very wisely removes his particular Part of the Burthen upon the shoulders of the World, which are broad enough, and able to bear it. [General satire] is but a *Ball* bandied to and fro, and every Man carries a *Racket* about Him to strike it from himself among the rest of the Company.[3]

What sort of difference does it make when the satire ceases to be general and becomes particular? When this happens we have to distinguish the named victims from the readers who are not named. For the named victims satire is hardly literature in the first place—I shall show later that it may be

---

[1] *A Tale of a Tub*, p. 131.   [2] *Correspondence*, iii. 354.
[3] *A Tale of a Tub*, pp. 51 f.

literature in the second. They have no option but to respond
as persons. For the rest of its readers the experience of reading
is first of all literary, but with an increasing sense that more
than literature is concerned. Along with the pure impersonal
pleasure in the poetry exists a concern with the personal, not
for themselves, but for both the victim and the satirist. While
the victim bleeds and decides what to do about it, the general
reader comes to take a sort of sporting interest in how things
will go. Punishment presupposes rules and rules a lawgiver,
and both the victim and the general reader, though at different temperatures, inquire as to the credentials, the moral
character, of the self-appointed executive of the law. As he
put in the names of his victims, the satirist could not but
know that these inquiries would arise, and his act presupposes a decision to bear the brunt in the interests of his fame,
even though he may not feel quite sure that his credentials
will be found to pass muster. The question will arise, lazily
or more in earnest, What sort of man was Pope?

3

I have used the past tense 'was'. For there is a distinction
between how the question appeared to Pope's contemporaries and to later readers. Any personal rebuke that satire
may make is one thing when the person rebuked is alive, and
another when both he and the rebuker are dead. In the first
place, then, what sort of man did Pope seem to his contemporaries?
Few of them would have any first-hand knowledge of him,
and the image they formed was no doubt formed mainly
from the poems. Here the following of Nature stood Pope in
good stead. He seemed to his first readers more like one of
themselves than some later poets have seemed to theirs. He
felt as they felt, though at greater depth; he subscribed,
though more vividly, to their moral system, code of manners,
and way of life. On the whole he behaved beautifully in the
poems, charming the women, often in the slightly risqué way
that was still fashionable, and speaking grandly on occasion
for the men. The few things that readers may not have cared
for—say, the cruelty that was apparent even if only on such
occasions as anybody would admit to be provoking—those

few unpleasantnesses were surely swallowed up for Pope's
first readers in their gratitude for the general pleasures the
poetry afforded them. For the common reader respects the
poets he reads, sees them as heroes and geniuses. All told,
the common reader probably took the satire calmly and sided
with Pope. When the 'character' of Atticus was beginning to
trickle out among friends, this is how Atterbury, a bishop,
wrote to Pope:

> Permit me, Dear Sir, to break into your retirement and to desire
> of you a Compleat copy of those Verses on Mr. Addison,[1] which you
> wrote down in an imperfect manner for me. When you send it, send
> me also your last Resolution, which shall punctually be observ'd, in
> relation to my giving out any Copy of it: for I am again Sollicited by
> another Lord; to whom I have given the same Answer, as formerly.
> No small piece of your writing has been ever sought after so much;
> it has pleas'd every man without Exception, to whom it has been read.
> Since you now therefore know, where your real Strength lyes, I hope,
> you will not suffer that Talent to ly unemploy'd. For my part, I should
> be glad to see you finish something of that kind, that I could be con-
> tent to be a little sneer'd at in a Line, or so, for the sake of the pleasure
> I should have in reading the rest. I have talk'd my Sense of this matter
> to you, once, or twice, and now I put it under my hand, that you may
> see it is my deliberate Opinion. What weight that may have with you,
> I cannot say: but it pleases me to have an Opportunity of shewing you,
> how well I wish you, and how true a friend I am to your Fame.[2]

In view of this degree of literary admixture and complication it seems beside the point for anyone to take up the
view that the writing of satire, even when particular satire,
is reprehensible absolutely. The Reverend William Lisle
Bowles took this view—though we have just seen that a
bishop did not—and it can cite the highest morality in its
favour. Few men can live up to that New Testament morality,
and the satirist writes for men either as they have failed or
never tried to. He writes for them as they are Natural, and,
alas, it seems that the Nature in men prefers to see pain dealt
out rather than rosy garlands. There is more truth in La
Rochefoucauld's view of man than all men like to admit, and
it was Charles Reade—to quote as high an authority in these

---

[1] For the early version of the 'character' of Atticus, see Twickenham ed., vi.
142 ff.   [2] *Correspondence*, ii. 104 f.

matters as exists in English—who noted that 'People find no pleasure in proving an accused person innocent; the charm is, to detect guilt'.[1] Men prefer particular satire to satire in its less wounding general form. As we have seen, no small piece of Pope's had been so much sought after as the 'character' of Atticus. And to take an instance from the following century, we find Thackeray remarking that when Disraeli published his *romans à clef* readers were little interested in the matters the author had most at heart—things like his 'discovery of the Venetian origin of the English constitution'— but in 'those amusing bitter sketches of Tadpole, Rigby, Monmouth, and the rest, of which the likeness proved irresistible, and the malice tickled everybody':

What were those keys to 'Coningsby' with which certain publishers undertook to furnish simple people in the country, at the rate of 'a shilling including the postage stamp'? They were not, we take it, keys to the... Caucasian or Venetian theories, or to the Young England mystery (which, Heaven knows, wants a key as much as any problem hitherto unexplained in this world); but such a key as you buy at Epsom of the running horses, with the names, weights, and colours of the riders.[2]

Pope discussed similar matters further in the 'Epilogue to the Satires'. His friend is represented as expostulating with him to this effect:

F[riend]. Yet none but you by Name the Guilty lash;
Ev'n *Guthry* saves half *Newgate* by a Dash.
Spare then the Person, and expose the Vice.
    P[ope]. How Sir! not damn the Sharper, but the Dice?
Come on then Satire! gen'ral, unconfin'd,
Spread thy broad wing, and sowze on all the Kind.
Ye Statesmen, Priests, of one Religion all!
Ye Tradesmen vile, in Army, Court, or Hall!
Ye Rev'rend Atheists!—*F*. Scandal! name them, Who?
    P. Why that's the thing you bid me not to do.
Who starv'd a Sister, who forswore a Debt,
I never nam'd—the Town's enquiring yet.
The pois'ning Dame—*Fr.* You mean—*P.* I don't—*Fr.* You do.
    P. See! now I keep the Secret, and not you.[3]

---

[1] *Foul Play*, chap. lx. Cf. the evidence of Samuel Rogers, p. 142 above.
[2] *Contributions to the Morning Chronicle*, ed. Gordon N. Ray, Urbana, 1955, pp. 78 f.   [3] 'Epilogue to the Satires', dial. ii, 10 ff.

When Pope published his last *Moral Essay* he met a storm of criticism on the ground that what he had left veiled, and therefore general, was in reality particular, that 'Timon' was Brydges, Duke of Chandos. The charge, as Professor Sherburn has shown,[1] was ill founded, and imputed to Pope ineptitude and worse—Chandos was a close friend of many of Pope's close friends, including Burlington himself, to whom the essay was addressed. The outcry was another example of the Natural wish to find a victim where none in particular was intended. And, indeed, a recurring item of Popiana is the 'Key' to Mr. Pope's latest satire. Nor did this avid victimizing cease when Pope's contemporaries died off: it continued as an interest of scholars. We can see a counterpart of it active today in the general use made of Pope's expression. New victims for his satire are hauled forward from time to time. In the *Spectator* of 6 November 1920, for instance, a review of the autobiography of Margot Asquith quotes as epigraph the character of Calypso from Pope's second *Moral Essay*, 'Of the Characters of Women':

> 'Twas thus Calypso once each heart alarmed,
> Awed without sense, and without beauty charmed;[2]
> Her tongue bewitched as oddly as her eyes,
> Less wit than mimic, more a wit than wise;
> Strange graces still, and stranger flights she had,
> Was just not ugly, and was just not mad;
> Yet ne'er so sure our passion to create,
> As when she touched the brink of all we hate.

And not only do men still continue to apply Pope's charges to modern victims, they also re-apply his praise. But not so often. It remains true that where Pope has left a general portrait, men have often sought to pin it down to a particular person. Even so, their practical concern cannot usually have been more than tepid. Particular satire for the common reader is more highly spiced than general satire, but it does not leave the plane of 'pure' literature.

It was different for the victims. They were not free to like Pope's satiric poems—or not free in the first place, for I shall show later that this remark requires some modification. They

---

[1] *The Huntingdon Library Bulletin*, viii. 1935, pp. 131 ff.
[2] ll. 45 ff.; Pope wrote 'Aw'd without Virtue, without Beauty charm'd'

were free, of course, to reply or not. Some of them, despair-
ing of the pen, tried physical retort. Ambrose Philips is said
to have bought a rod, and have 'stuck [it] up at the Bar of
Button's Coffee-house' for the purposes of retaliation.[1] And
there was the story, which Professor Sherburn discredits,[2]
that a son of John Dennis, brandishing a drawn sword,
challenged Pope to leave the dinner table of Bathurst and
meet him in a nearby lane. Others, the bold ones, put their
faith in what Pope depressingly described as their 'gray
goose quill'.[3] Many were the charges brought up against him
in writing. To sift the truth in these angry charges is the task
for biographers, but from the start it was obvious that there
was more ground for charges against Pope than against, say,
Persius, whom Dryden had commended in these terms:

> The philosophy in which Persius was educated, and which he pro-
> fesses through his whole book [of satires], is the Stoic; the most noble,
> most generous, most beneficial to human kind, amongst all the sects,
> who have given us the rules of ethics, thereby to form a severe virtue
> in the soul; to raise in us an undaunted courage against the assaults of
> fortune. . . . And this [philosophy] he expressed, not only in all his
> satires, but in the manner of his life. . . . What he has learnt, he teaches
> vehemently; and what he teaches, that he practises himself. There is
> a spirit of sincerity in all he says; you may easily discern that he is in
> earnest, and is persuaded of that truth which he inculcates.[4]

Pope was no Persius. What sort of moral character did he
have?

The worst thing that can be brought up against him is his
double-dealing, and the amount of it. Early in his career his
friend Caryll, an older and much simpler man, had caught
him in what he rose to calling his 'popish tricks'.[5] Later these
tricks seem to have gone to all lengths, sometimes amounting
to treachery. Professor Sherburn, annotating the letters, cannot but remark that Pope's machinations for the publication
of the joint letters of Swift and himself 'are painful to record'.[6]
Pope expended much brilliant art on phrasing things so as to
convey the wrong meaning without actually being charge-
able with its conveyance.

---

[1] Sherburn, *Early Career*, p. 120.   [2] *Correspondence*, iv. 364 n.
[3] *Epistle to Dr. Arbuthnot*, l. 249; it was the term for a certain sort of pen.
[4] 'A Discourse concerning the Original and Progress of Satire' (*Essays*, ii.
75 ff.).   [5] See *Correspondence*, i. 165.   [6] Id., iv. 214.

The objects of his trickery were the satisfactions of success, financial and literary. There is ample evidence that he could be generous with money on occasion, but some of his financial gains were not quite on the square. But always there are extenuations we feel we have to make. The most weighty, of course, is that on the score of Pope's physique. Both he and his friends spoke of his 'crazy carcase', and it seems almost a miracle that—used as Pope used it, as gaily and even as recklessly as possible—it lasted for so long as fifty-six years. On top of this was his religion, a severe handicap which his literary genius was able to ignore, but which nevertheless did not smooth his social lot. Further, he was the son of a linen-draper on terms of pleasant intimacy with the aristocracy—pleasant, but expensive and not without anxieties. All these do something to take the edge off the heinousness of his trickery. And usually there was the excuse that his deceits were in the service of great literature. The end may never justify the means, but ends do vary, and the end for Pope was a splendid contribution to the general happiness of readers. If there lay trickery behind certain publications, at least they were of the order of the translated *Odyssey*, the *Dunciad*, and the Swift–Pope correspondence.

A further shortcoming was what Mark Pattison phrased as 'spreading his plumes and hinting at his own virtues'.[1] And it was often more than hinting. The claim to honesty sometimes followed without a break on prevarication. To take one instance. When his *Sober Advice from Horace* appeared, anonymously, he wrote to Caryll:

> Here is a piece of poetry from Horace come out, which I warn you not to take for mine, tho' some people are willing to fix it on me. In truth I should think it a very indecent Sermon, after the *Essay on Man*.[2]

To this Professor Sherburn appends the note:

> Pope uses his high skill in the art of genteel equivocation in this re-

---

[1] *Essays*, ed. H. Nettleship, 1889, ii. 384.

[2] *Correspondence*, iii. 447. When he actually is honest, we get such acceptable, such Natural, aphorisms as the following: 'Thus passes Day after Day, & we do with the Men we esteem, as we do with the Virtues we esteem, think we can reach them another Time, & So live & dye without the possession of them' (id., iii. 490).

mark: he does not flatly deny authorship of his *Sober Advice*, but only a very thin partition divides the warning from a lie.

Pope continued:

> But in a week or so, you'll have a thing, which is mine, and I hope not unworthy an honest man, in his own just vindication from slanders of all sorts, and slanderers of what rank or quality whatsoever.

It is a pity that he could not rest satisfied with successful trickery, covering it with what decency silence can afford. These quotations come from a private letter not published in his lifetime. In the letters that were so published self-imputed honesty is even found fortifying itself in lofty scorn for the dishonest:

> I wish I had nothing to trouble me more [than 'the railing papers about the *Odyssey*']: an honest mind is not in the power of any dishonest one. To break its peace, there must be some guilt or consciousness, which is inconsistent with its own principles. Not but malice and injustice have their day, like some poor part-lived vermin that die of shooting their own strings. Falsehood is folly (says Homer) and liars and calumniators at last hurt none but themselves, even in this world. In the next, 'tis charity to say, God have mercy on them! They were the devil's vicegerents upon earth, who is the father of lies, and I fear has a right to dispose of his children.[1]

The claim also recurs in the poems, which also presuppose honesty in the claim to other virtues. So frequently does the particular claim recur that we are tempted to impute to the word a special sense. Perhaps Pope meant it to bear the sense of *honnête*: in downright English 'honest' means the sort of virtue that belonged to Arthur Hugh Clough, or Anthony Trollope, or William Cobbett, or Thackeray, but *honnête* carries no such plain sense—it shades off into the graceful decency we expect of that indefinable creature the 'gentleman'. My own comment on Pope's complex moral character, in so far as it concerns his tricks, is one that he would not have cared to accept, and which in any event is an explanation scarcely to be hazarded of one so shrewd. I do not think he really understood himself, being, as I think, bemused by his own brilliance. At any rate there is a frequent

[1] Id. ii. 353.

relish in his letters for his versatility. The ground of its exercise varies. Here are some instances:

I have been lying in wait for my own imagination this week and
more, and watching what thoughts of mine came up in the whirl of
fancy that were worth communicating to you in a letter. But I am at
length convinced that my rambling head can produce nothing of that
sort; so I must e'en be contented with telling you the old story, that
I love you heartily. I have often found by experience that Nature and
truth, tho' never so low or vulgar, is yet pleasing when openly and
without artifice represented; insomuch that it would be diverting to
me to read the very letters of an infant, could it write its innocent in-
consistencies and tautologies, just as it thought 'em. . . .

You can't wonder my thoughts are scarce consistent, when I tell
you how they are distracted! Every hour of my life, my mind is
strangely divided. This minute, perhaps, I am above the stars, with a
thousand systems round about me, looking forward into the vast abyss of
eternity, and losing my whole comprehension in the boundless spaces
of the extended Creation, in dialogues with Whiston and the astrono-
mers; the next moment I am below all trifles, even grovelling with
Tidcombe in the very center of nonsense: now am I recreating my
mind with the brisk sallies and quick turns of wit, which Mr. Steele
in his liveliest and freest humours darts about him; and now levelling
my application to the insignificant observations and quirks of grammar
of Mr. Cromwell and Dennis.

Good God! what an Incongruous Animal is Man? how unsettled in
his best part, his soul; and how changing and variable in his frame of
body? The constancy of the one, shook by every notion, the temperament of the other, affected by every blast of wind. What an April
weather in the mind! In a word, what is Man altogether, but one
mighty inconsistency.[1]

That, no doubt, is too much a show-piece—inspired by
Montaigne, and Hamlet's description of man—for it to count
weightily as evidence here. That it embroiders a characteristic account of himself there are other passages to show,
passages that read more simply and so more sincerely. The
following, written in the previous year to the same corre-
spondent, has more simplicity, if not much more:

You see my letters are scribbled with all the carelessness and in-
attention imaginable: my style, like my soul, appears in its natural

---

[1] *Correspondence,* i. 185 f.

undress before my friend. 'Tis not here I regard the character of a wit.
Some people are wits all over, to that degree that they are fools all over.
They are wits in the church, wits in the street, wits at a funeral, nay
the unmannerly creatures are wits before women! There is nothing
more wrong than to appear always in the pontificalibus of one's pro-
fession, whatever it be. There's no dragging your dignity about with
you every where, as if an alderman should constantly wear his chain
in his shop. Mr. Roper, because he has the reputation of keeping the
best pack of fox hounds in England, will visit the ladies in a hunting
dress. And I have known an author, who for having once written a
tragedy has never been out of buskins, since he can no more suffer a
vulgar phrase in his own mouth than in a Roman's; and will be as much
out of countenance if he fail of the true accent in his conversation, as
an actor would, were he out upon the stage. For my part, there are
some things I would be thought besides a wit; as a Christian, a friend,
a frank companion, and a well natured fellow, and so forth.[1]

Here is part of a letter, a little later in date, to Martha
Blount:

I do suppose you will not show this Epistle out of Vanity, as I doubt
not your said Sister does all I writ to her. Indeed to correspond with
Mr. Pope may make any one proud who lives under a Dejection of
Heart in the Country. Every one values Mr. Pope, but every one for
a different reason. One for his firm adherence to the Catholic Faith,
another for his Neglect of Popish Superstition, one for his grave be-
havior, another for his Whymsicalness. Mr. Tydcomb for his pretty
Atheistical Jests, Mr. Caryl for his moral and christian Sentences,
Mrs. Teresa for his Reflections on Mrs. Patty, and Mrs. Patty for his
Reflections on Mrs. Teresa.[2]

This versatility, which he prided himself on, went deeper in
his nature than he knew. And at bottom it was a confusion,
which, I think, he enjoyed. He twice speaks of himself in his
letters as 'clouded' or 'cloudy', and it is worth while to look at
the context:

'The unwearied diligence', he says, which I observe at this season
in the country people about me affords one good lesson: that I ought
to make hay whilst the sun shines. No fair day in the fancy is to be
neglected, considering what a climate what a right English climate,
there is in my head, where few days pass without being clouded, or
feverish;[3]

[1] Id. i. 155 f.   [2] Id. i. 208 ¶.   [3] Id. i. 292.

and on the later occasion he speaks of 'such a whining, valetudinary, cloudy, journalier[1] Companion as my Self'.[2] He also speaks in the same terms in the poem quoted above.[3] And writing to Swift with longing to be with him we get:

> If I liv'd in Ireland, I fear the wet climate wou'd indanger more than my life, my humour, and health, I am so Atmospherical a creature—[4]

He was often, I believe, in the state of mind he described in a letter of 1715: 'a wild, distracted, amused, buried state, both of mind and body'.[5] No doubt it was a state of mind conducive to poetry, but not so conducive to honesty on the more practical plane. Encouraging atmosphericalness and versatility in himself, Pope may have shaken the centre of his character, failing to see where the aesthetic and purely intellectual ended and the moral began. His famous words 'Know, then, thyself . . .' may have been ready with a sharp practical sense for him, had he cared to attend to it.

At first sight there are certain things in Pope that seem the reverse of lacking in self-knowledge. For instance, the infamous remark in a private letter to Martha Blount. Pope had written an obscene version of Psalm 1 which had unfortunately got into print. It created enough stir to make him feel the need to disown it, which he did in the following terms:

> Whereas there have been publish'd in my Name, certain scandalous Libels, which I hope no Person of Candor[6] would have thought me capable of, I am sorry to find myself obliged to declare that no Genuine Pieces of mine have been printed by any but Mr. Tonson and Mr. Lintot. And in particular, as to that which is entituled, A Version of the first Psalm; I hereby promise a Reward of three Guineas to any one who shall discover the Person or Persons concerned in the Publication of the said Libel, of which I am wholly ignorant. A. Pope.[7]

And his comment on this in the letter to Martha Blount ran:

---

[1] 'daily', or 'humdrum'; a word recently imported from France, denoting 'day-labourer', 'journal published daily'.   [2] *Correspondence*, iii. 218.
[3] See above, p. 35.   [4] *Correspondence*, ii. 522.
[5] Id. i. 322.   [6] 'kindliness.'
[7] See *Correspondence*, i. 350 n.

If you have seen a late Advertisement, you will know that I have not told a lye (which we both abhominate) but equivocated pretty genteely.[1]

But far from instancing his self-knowledge was not this praise of his cleverness seriously damaging to the rest of himself? Is it a good thing for the interests of the whole man to claim that sort of brilliance? Can he have thought how the remark would look to Martha Blount and also, when his immediate pleasure had subsided, to himself? But, as so often, we cannot leave this instance without noting the extenuations. In a letter to Swift published in 1740 he made no claim to an unblemished authorial record:

> There is nothing of late which I think of more than mortality, and what you mention of collecting the best monuments we can of our friends, their own images in their writings: (for those are the best, when their minds are such as Mr. Gay's was, and as yours is.) I am preparing also for my own; and have nothing so much at heart, as to shew the silly world that men of Wit, or even Poets, may be the most moral of mankind. A few loose things sometimes fall from them, by which censorious fools judge as ill of them, as possibly they can, for their own comfort: and indeed, when such unguarded and trifling *Jeux d'Esprit* have once got abroad, all that prudence or repentance can do, since they cannot be deny'd, is to put 'em fairly upon that foot; and teach the publick (as we have done in the preface to the four volumes of miscellanies) to distinguish betwixt our studies and our idlenesses, our works and our weaknesses.[2]

That is most acceptable—and would that Pope had always been so sound and frank! The version of Psalm 1, parodied not from the text of the Authorized Version or the Douai version but, less reprehensibly, from the debased form given it by Sternhold and Hopkins,[3] comes under the category of 'loose things' and 'weaknesses'. And surely, for a thing of this kind, it makes a difference whether or not the poet was responsible for its publication. Pope did not publish this poem, and was therefore justified in repudiating it. Whether by direct lie or prevarication mattered little.[4] He chose prevarication, and did so, I think, because he enjoyed it, be-

---

[1] Id. i. 350.   [2] Id. iii. 347.

[3] See N. Ault, *New Light on Pope*, 1949, pp. 156 ff.

[4] See appendix 8 to Newman's *Apologia pro Vita Sua*, ed. W. Ward, 1931 ed., pp. 436 ff., for a discussion of these and other casuistic terms.

cause, as he said of himself, he liked to contrive 'deep Whim-
sies',[1] and because, as Johnson said of him, 'He hardly drank
tea without a stratagem'.[2] Indeed we sometimes feel that,
tiresome as his tricks were found at the time, they had at
bottom a childish delight in the exercise of what, after all,
was a gift for making misleading statements that had brilliance as well as having power to mislead.

    This, then, is what could have been charged against him
by his contemporary victims. And if they made charges at all,
of course they improved on them. Pope was thoroughly
blackened. This meant that his virtues were ignored, simply
as not in question. Those virtues are seen to be sound when
we are free to see them. It is harder to see them because his
faults are of the sort that throw a colour over everything else.
If you are once found constructing a clever trick, it is difficult ever to be allowed to be innocent again. To look at the
matter in another quarter and from the other end, much that
looks sinister may be read into the records of Wordsworth's
authorial biography if we start from the assumption that he
was dishonest. If we give Pope a fair hearing, his virtues are
as obvious as his shortcomings.

    I have already referred to his charms as a companion and
friend,[3] but there is one important matter, which I have reserved till now, his capacity for deep feeling of the amiable
sort, especially towards his mother and many friends. Here
are some instances:

Let me tell you I am the better acquainted with you [Swift] for a
long Absence, as men are with themselves for a long affliction;[4]

    The Loss of a Friend is the Loss of Life; after that is gone from us,
'tis all but a Gentler Decay, & wasting & lingring a little longer. I was
tother day forming a Wish for a Lady's happiness, upon her Birthday:
and thinking of the Greatest Climax of felicity I could raise, step by
step, to end in This—a Friend;[5]

    I find my other Tyes dropping from me; some worn off, some torn
off, others relaxing daily: My greatest, both by duty, gratitude, and
humanity, Time is shaking every moment, and it now hangs but by a
thread! I am many years the older, for living so much with one so old;

---

[1] 'A Farewell to London. In the Year 1715', l. 38.
[2] *Lives*, iii. 200: Johnson was adapting a line from one of Young's satires.
[3] See above, pp. 146 ff.   [4] *Correspondence*, ii. 349.   [5] Id., ii. 180.

much the more helpless, for having been so long help'd and tended by her; much the more considerate and tender, for a daily commerce with one who requir'd me justly to be both to her; and consequently the more melancholy and thoughtful; and the less fit for others, who want only in a companion or a friend, to be amused or entertained;[1]

And you [Gay], whose Absence is in a manner perpetual to me, ought rather to be remembered as a good man gone, than breathed after as one living.[2]

So will the death of my Mother be! which now I tremble at, now resign to, now bring close to me, now set farther off: Every day alters, turns me about, and confuses my whole frame of mind;[3]

It is indeed a Grief to mee which I cannot express, and which I should hate my own Heart if it did not feel, & yet wish no Friend I have ever should feel;[4]

and again, a few days later:

I found you [Caryll] too true a prophet; but God's will be done, Reason and religion both tell me it is best; but affection will not be on their side, and I'm really more troubled than I would own. The very habitude of so many years, if there were little affection would have this effect, for men are creatures more of habit than principle. But in a word not [to] seem a better man than I am, my attendance upon her living was not virtue, but only duty, and my Melancholy for her dead, is not virtue but weakness.[5]

Of course we can take the line that Pope's feelings were a literary fiction. Being a poet, he was less dependent than other men on direct experience: having gifts as a narrative poet, he could have imagined feelings such as he expresses, and expressed them with as convincing particulars. But even if this might possibly explain Pope's, there is also the external evidence of his friends, who thought the feelings genuine enough. Swift, Gay, Arbuthnot, Burlington, Edward Earl of Oxford, Martha Blount, and the rest did not think his feeling was a literary fiction: their letters give us clear evidence that they knew he meant the wonderful things he said.

My reading of Pope's moral character is a development of that of Johnson and of Leslie Stephen. Stephen wrote:

Pope, let us again admit, was a liar; but human nature (the remark is not strictly original) is often inconsistent; and, side by side with

---

[1] Id. ii. 480.   [2] Id. iii. 131.   [3] Id. iii. 336.
[4] Id. iii. 374.   [5] Id. iii. 375.

degrading tendencies, there sometimes lie not only keen powers of intellect, but a genuine love for goodness, benevolence, and even for honesty. Pope is one of those strangely mixed characters. . . .[1]

Modern researchers into Pope's biography are finding that his nineteenth-century critics saw him as worse than he was. But though, on balance, Pope was morally better than Stephen's biographical and historical knowledge allowed him to appreciate, Stephen does see that a 'genuine love' of various good things was at least possible for him. This being so, I do not see why he proceeds to say:

our pleasure in reading [Pope] is much counterbalanced by the suspicion that those pointed aphorisms which he turns out in so admirably polished a form may come only from the lips outwards.[2]

Stephen has found a truth and throws it away.

It is something the same with Johnson: he finds the truth but applies it only by half:

When Pope murmurs at the world, when he professes contempt of fame, when he speaks of riches and poverty, of success and disappointment, with negligent indifference, he certainly does not express his habitual and settled sentiments, but either wilfully disguises his own character, or, what is more likely, invests himself with temporary qualities, and sallies out in the colours of the present moment.[3]

Why that word 'invests'? Pope's 'contempt of fame' ('contempt' is a crude word, Pope's emotions being always of a complicated kind) is no more 'invested' than his love of it. He does not invest himself in emotions; instead, contempt and love and all the emotions graded between them gain predominance in turn. Pope stated his belief in the theory of 'the ruling passion', but because one passion ruled in moments that mattered most did not mean that its overborne competitors were not native, active, and strong.

The rest of Pope's virtues are those he possessed as an author. I have shown that he often represented the work of a poet as that of a skilled worker, but there is evidence, some of which I have also shown, of claims very different. Indeed no

---

[1] *Hours in a Library* [first series], 1874, pp. 129 f.: this passage does not occur in the first version of the essay, *The Cornhill Magazine*, xxviii, July–Dec. 1873.
[2] This passage, like the one just quoted, does not occur in the first version.
[3] *Lives of the Poets*, iii. 212.

poet has represented the calling of poet as more sacred and severe. When as a young man he wrote of Crashaw, it was in silent contrast with himself:

I take this Poet to have writ like a Gentleman, that is, at leisure hours, and more to keep out of idleness, than to establish a reputation: so that nothing regular or just can be expected from him. All that regards Design, Form, Fable, (which is the Soul of Poetry) all that concerns exactness, or consent of parts, (which is the Body) will probably be wanting; only pretty conceptions, fine metaphors, glitt'ring expressions, and something of a neat cast of Verse, (which are properly the dress, gems, or loose ornaments of Poetry) may be found in these verses. This is indeed the case of most other Poetical Writers of *Miscellanies*; nor can it well be otherwise, since no man can be a true Poet, who writes for diversion only. These Authors shou'd be consider'd as *Versifiers* and *witty Men*, rather than as *Poets*; and under this head will only fall the Thoughts, the Expression, and the Numbers. These are only the pleasing parts of Poetry, which may be judg'd of at a view, and comprehended all at once. And (to express my self like a Painter) their *Colouring* entertains the sight, but the *Lines* and *Life* of the Picture are not to be inspected too narrowly.[1]

Crashaw seemed at bottom one of

> . . . the Wits of either Charles's days,
> The Mob of Gentlemen who wrote with Ease;
> Sprat, Carew, Sedley, and a hundred more,
> (Like twinkling Stars the Miscellanies o'er).[2]

Four years later he wrote as Keats was to write:

I have the greatest proof in nature at present of the amusing [i.e. absorbing] power of Poetry, for it takes me up so intirely that I scarce see what passes under my nose, and hear nothing that is said about me. To follow Poetry as one ought, one must forget father and mother, and cleave to it alone.[3]

Ten years later still, this dedication is expressed still more strikingly, with the same echo from the Gospels:

To write well, lastingly well, Immortally well, must not one leave Father and Mother and cleave unto the Muse? Must not one be prepared to endure the reproaches of Men, want and much Fasting, nay Martyrdom in its Cause. 'Tis such a Task as scarce leaves a Man

[1] *Correspondence*, i. 109 f.
[2] *Imitations of Horace*, Ep. II. i. 107 ff.   [3] *Correspondence*, i. 243.

time to be a good Neighbour, an useful friend, nay to plant a Tree,
much less to save his Soul;[1]

which stands in contrast to the passage from the *Imitations
of Horace* I have already quoted.[2]

All told, Pope is the poet of the couplet:

> . . . how severely with themselves proceed
> The Men, who write such Verse as we can read![3]

He had the heavenly gift that makes a man a poet, but had
enough moral character not to presume on it. He worked
hard before he was satisfied, before he could earn the praise
of being 'the most *faultless* of Poets'. That praise was from
Byron,[4] who was not the last judge of the particular virtue.
Other poets have been as faultless as Pope, some even more
wholly so: but they are few; and in speaking of faultlessness
we must also speak of difficulties in the way of it. It is easier
to be faultless as Herrick is than as Milton is. Pope's poems
are the sort that are supremely difficult to write, because
complex, large, and concentrated and because part of their
material lies as it were casually and uninspiringly in newspapers. His near-faultlessness therefore is the index of application: it is not only inspired but laboured at, not only
given but earned.

Pope subscribed to the old belief[5] that to practise the art
of poetry severely was to have some claim to be a good man.
He took up this position in the Preface to his *Works* of 1717:

> If I have written well, let it be consider'd that 'tis what no man can
> do without good sense, a quality that not only renders one capable of
> being a good writer, but a good man. And if I have made any acquisi-
> tion in the opinion of any one under the notion of the former, let it be
> continued to me under no other title than that of the latter.[6]

And believing that goodness was exercised mainly in friendship, he asserted that

---

[1] *Correspondence*, ii. 227.   [2] Above, pp. 137 ff.
[3] *Imitations of Horace*, Ep. II. ii. 157 f.   [4] *Letters and Journals*, v. 109.
[5] For the history of this ethical claim on behalf of the poet see S. H. Butcher,
Aristotle's Theory of Poetry and Fine Art, ed. 1898, pp. 200–2, and J. E. Spingarn,
A History of Literary Criticism in the Renaissance, New York, ed. 1930, p. 53.
[6] Cf. *Correspondence*, iii. 340; and cf. him on Newton, id. ii. 459.

I have ever believd this as a sacred maxime, that the most Ingenious [endowed with genius] Natures were the most Sincere, & the most Knowing & Sensible Minds made the Best Friends;[1]

and conversely that bad writers made poor friends:

these Authors, whose incapacity is not greater than their insincerity, and of whom I have always found (if I may quote myself)

> That each bad *Author* is as bad a *Friend*.[2]

And when bad writers he had punished turned and sought his friendship, they were rewarded with the couplet:

> A Fool quite angry is quite innocent;
> Alas! 'tis ten times worse when they *repent*.[3]

If the writings and the man stand or fall together, the man Pope stands the firmer for the writings. And we can prove that Pope's integrity as a writer did help him to be a better man. Take, for instance, the matter of times and seasons ('hours, days, months, and years are the medium of the art of life').[4] Pope did not rush his attacks and defences into print, though, as he tells us, 'I don't very well bear Retardments'.[5] Instead he kept them by him till he was sure they were poems.[6] How many of those who have expressed detestation for the wasp of Twickenham see the personal context of the *Dunciad* for what it was? Professor Sherburn's account of it is not well enough known in England:

---

[1] *Correspondence*, ii. 138.

[2] Letter to Swift, 23 Mar. 1727–8 (*Correspondence*, ii. 481): Pope is quoting (with a difference) *An Essay on Criticism*, l. 519.

[3] *Epistle to Dr. Arbuthnot*, ll. 107 f. Twickenham ed., v. 445, suggests that the couplet had special reference to Aaron Hill; another possible candidate is Thomas Cooke (see *Correspondence*, ii. 509 f.).

[4] Lane Cooper, *Experiments in Education*, 1943, N.Y., p. 91.

[5] *Correspondence*, iv. 431.

[6] Cf. Johnson, *Rambler*, no. 169:

'There were in those days no weekly or diurnal writers; *multa dies, et multa litura*, much time, and many rasures, were considered as indispensable requisites; and that no other method of attaining lasting praise has been yet discovered, may be conjectured from the blotted manuscripts of Milton now remaining, and from the tardy emission of Pope's compositions, delayed more than once till the incidents to which they alluded were forgotten, till his enemies were secure from his satire, and, what to an honest mind must be more painful, his friends were deaf to his encomiums.'

Many people think of [Pope] as leaping to a reply when attacked; but the truth is that in most cases he paused before a retort. Theobald, for example, attacked Pope in 1726; two years later the *Dunciad* appeared. The castigation of most of the Dunces in the *Dunciad* marked an exasperated end of years of forbearance on the side of Pope. After initial errors in attacking Dennis (1711), Philips (1713), and later Curll (1716), little came from Pope's pen in the way of personal attack for twelve years. Meanwhile between 1711 and 1727 over fifty attacks on Pope were printed, besides almost a dozen things by Pope that the poet did not wish printed—including indecent squibs, personal letters, and such a piece as the satirical portrait of Addison (1722). These attacks came from at least seventeen different authors. At least seven newspapers printed anonymous attacks in this period. So far as we know Pope had attacked something like half of these seventeen authors; but in most cases (for instance, Dennis and Gildon) the provocation he offered was slight compared with the return in satire that it yielded. He may have printed retorts never identified as his; but as matters stand, all the known facts make the case for forbearance during the years 1716–26 overwhelmingly in Pope's favour, and overwhelmingly against the Little Senate at Button's, Curll's authors, and the (probable) hirelings of such Whig ministers as Walpole.[1]

Surely we must feel that Pope's laboured determination to ensure that his satires turned out to be poetry punctures the notion that they are the direct product of malice. If he did feel malicious towards his victims-to-be, he did not allow the feeling to interfere with the prime business, the business of being a poet; and malice, surely, is not an emotion that keeps for years. Perhaps he took a pleasure in biding his time? Not when one of his constitution might only have a brief space of life left—'how short a time [I] have to live', he remarked in the preface to the collected *Works* of 1717[2]—and not when the chief pleasure of that interval was the pleasure of writing well: 'to make verses was his first labour,' said Dr. Johnson, 'and to mend them was his last';[3] 'I writ because it amused me,' said Pope, 'I corrected because it was as pleasant to me to correct as to write.'[4]

We can say, then, that Pope had indeed something of the quality of a Persius: his devotion to the art of writing was

[1] *The Best of Pope*, pp. xxxvii f.
[2] Para. 9: cf. Sherburn, *Early Career*, pp. 42 f.
[3] *Lives of the Poets*, iii. 218.
[4] Preface to *Works*, 1717, para. 6. By 'amused' Pope means 'interested', 'fascinated'.

saintly. And from this it followed—or so it was claimed in
Pope's time—that he had the right to decry bad writing. So
much had been declared by Dryden, and the opinion came
weightily from one who had shown himself sensitive to the
problems in personal ethics that satire raises for the satirist:

> these ill-writers, in all justice, ought . . . to be exposed . . . and none
> is so fit to correct their faults, as he who is not only clear from any in
> his own writings, but is also so just, that he will never defame the good;
> and is armed with the power of verse, to punish and make examples of
> the bad.[1]

This was, and is, the justification of the *Dunciad*: except in
so far as it defamed the good—rightly disgusted over Bentley's edition of Milton, Pope no doubt underrated the sort
of textual criticism Bentley practised on the classics, and,
smarting from the reception of his own edition of Shakespeare, made Theobald out to be a very much worse scholar
than he was. But apart from those two, and Defoe (whose
writings we know from other sources he justly esteemed),[2]
Pope, as Dryden had counselled, only attacked writers and
scholars who were inferior. 'The good poets of Pope's day,
from Prior to Thomson, were his friends';[3] and he immediately showed interest in the anonymous author of *London*.
All told, he praised those authors whom posterity is praising.
We cannot say this of all who have satirized literary men:
Byron, for example, scoffed at Wordsworth to the end, and
often at Coleridge and Keats, at the same time lauding figures
who now appear of minor importance.

Not only did Pope claim the *ex-officio* right to satirize bad
writing, he also felt the satire of it to be a duty. The reasonableness of his position has recently been put very well:

> Pope is usually concerned with the offence as well as the offender.
> He lived in an age which still tended to regard everything that appeared
> in print as literature; and even when he is satirizing his scribblers he
> still pays them the compliment of treating their work as bad literature. . . .
> Pope . . . took a firm stand against the upstarts whom he saw invading

---

[1] *Essays*, ii. 22.

[2] Spence, *Anecdotes*, pp. 258 f.: 'The first part of Robinson Crusoe is very good.—
De Foe wrote a vast many things; and none bad, though none excellent, except this.
There is something good in all he has written.'

[3] Sherburn, *The Best of Pope*, p. 458.

the enclosed territory of literature. In the *Dunciad* of 1729 it is partly the *type* that he is attacking: the pedantic scholar like Hearne or Theobald; the weekly journalist like Roome and Concanen; the party hack like Oldmixon; the popular writer like Mrs. Centlivre, Mrs. Haywood, Ned Ward . . . the shameless publisher like Edmund Curll. . . . Such writers *and such writing* seemed to Pope—as, indeed, to John Dennis—to threaten the standards of literature. . . . Men like Swift and Pope, conservative in their outlook, were honestly alarmed for the future of polite letters, and in 1728 there was some reason for alarm.[1]

As Swift put it, 'a damnable poet [is] a public enemy to mankind'.[2]

It may be objected, however, that Pope punished the 'crime'[3] of bad writing with too much severity. He certainly did take every advantage of the power of verse. But the effect of that power must not be exaggerated nor its nature misconceived, especially as it was exercised in the time of Pope. The later seventeenth century and the early eighteenth, ages of criticism, were also ages of satire (so much so that if you did not like satire you admitted as much), and in ages addicted that way the satire supplying the demand always seems partly a business product. Scholars have wasted time trying to account for each of Pope's satiric allusions in terms of individual feeling. They did not see that in an age addicted to satire a satirist is given not only his 'kind' of poetry but much of its subject-matter with it: we might almost say that readers opened a new satire in order to confirm their forecast of its contents. So that when Pope attacked Dennis he was not necessarily doing more than aiming a shaft which the age had put into his hand at a man who already existed as a butt. And the same is true of Pope's satire of Defoe:

As one of the most frequently abused authors of his generation, Defoe takes his place naturally in a satirical portrait gallery; it would have been surprising if Pope had left him out, or failed to mention the pillory.[4]

Expectations were raised, and, to a greater extent than later readers have appreciated, the satisfying of them seemed as

[1] J. R. Sutherland, Twickenham ed., v, pp. xlv f.
[2] Pope's *Correspondence*, iii. 21.
[3] See the 'Advertisement' to the 1729 edition of the *Dunciad* (Twickenham ed., v. 9).   [4] Twickenham ed., v. 437.

much a game as a war: contemporary readers noted the accuracy of the aim and the sharpness of the point rather than the malice boiling in the breast of the archer.

4

If satire is as much a game as a war, and is received as such at least by the general reader, it follows that the test of successful satire is rather literary than personal, aesthetic than moral. Readers do not disapprove of satires because they are immoral so much as because they strike weakly. Dryden laughed at Shadwell because

Thy inoffensive Satyrs never bite;[1]

and Trapp was disappointed in Persius because, unlike Juvenal, 'he wants Poignancy and Sting'.[2] When Pope hisses

Let *Sporus* tremble—[3]

he can do so in public because he knows his satire is good enough as satire to make any person it mentions take notice. We may infer that Pope is cruel as a person, but that the inference is made at all is due to his literary power.

Nor must we exaggerate the personal injury inflicted by poetry when it is great poetry, and especially when it is the sort of great poetry that Pope wrote. If he elected to be a satirist, he saw to it that none of his poetic gifts went unemployed; he directed them all into his satire. This is what makes it unique: it is as if a score of poets had written it, contributing their individual gifts to it as friends and strangers contributed coloured stones to his grotto: it is as if Virgil and Milton, Marvell, Keats, and Tennyson had collaborated with Horace, and Dryden, and Swift. And poetry compounded so variously, though it may not be 'seraphically free From taint of personality', is poetry that is innocent of what is pettily personal. To take two small instances. When the first readers of the *Dunciad* came upon

And Shadwell nods the Poppy on his brows,

[1] *Mac Flecknoe,* l. 200.   [2] *Lectures on Poetry,* trans., 1742, p. 235.
[3] *Epistle to Dr. Arbuthnot,* l. 305.

or

> Narcissus, prais'd with all a Parson's pow'r,
> Look'd a white lilly sunk beneath a show'r,[1]

the historical Shadwell, who took opium, and the historical Lord Hervey (if indeed many contemporary readers spotted Hervey under the pseudonym) are swallowed up in imagery. When in 1742 the young Gray reported to his friend West on the 'greatly admired' *New Dunciad* (i.e. what is now book iv), a poem which, though general in the main, hurts individuals, he speaks of it, not as a torture-chamber, but as a poem containing passages that are 'as fine as anything [Pope] has written'.[2] And when, later, he hopes, in the face of seemingly serious incrimination, that Pope should be found 'an honest Man', he hopes it not because Pope is a satirist, but because he is a poet, 'the finest Writer, one of them, we ever had'.[3]

Moreover, the credit side must have been clear enough to the victims themselves. Even Addison must have seen the compliment within the blame—as G. K. Chesterton saw it in his slight but trenchant essay, 'Pope and the Art of Satire':

It may seem a singular observation to say that we are not generous enough to write great satire. This, however, is approximately a very accurate way of describing the case. To write great satire, to attack a man so that he feels the attack and half acknowledges its justice, it is necessary to have a certain intellectual magnanimity which realises the merits of the opponent as well as his defects. This is, indeed, only another way of putting the simple truth that in order to attack an army we must know not only its weak points, but also its strong points. . . . It is impossible to satirise a man without having a full account of his virtues. It is too much the custom in politics to describe a political opponent as utterly inhumane, as utterly careless of his country, as utterly cynical, which no man ever was since the beginning of the world. This kind of invective may often have a great superficial success: it may hit the mood of the moment; it may raise excitement and applause; it may impress millions. But there is one man among all those millions whom it does not impress, whom it hardly even touches; that is the man against whom it is directed. The one person for whom the whole satire has been written in vain is the man whom it is the whole object of the institution of satire to reach. He knows that such a descrip-

---

[1] iii. 22 and iv. 103 f.
[2] *Correspondence*, ed. Toynbee and Whibley, 1935, i. 189.   [3] Id., p. 229.

tion of him is not true. He knows that he is not utterly unpatriotic,
or utterly self-seeking, or utterly barbarous and revengeful. He knows
that he is an ordinary man, and that he can count as many kindly
memories, as many humane instincts, as many hours of decent work
and responsibility as any other ordinary man. But behind all this he
has his real weaknesses, the real ironies of his soul: behind all these
ordinary merits lie the mean compromises, the craven silences, the
sullen vanities, the secret brutalities, the unmanly visions of revenge.
It is to these that satire should reach if it is to touch the man at whom
it is aimed. And to reach these it must pass and salute a whole army of
virtues. . . .

Mr. Henley and his young men are very fond of invective and
satire: if they wish to know the reason of their failure in these things,
they need only turn to the opening of Pope's superb attack upon
Addison. The Henleyite's idea of satirising a man is to express a violent
contempt for him, and by the heat of this to persuade others and himself that the man is contemptible. I remember reading a satiric attack
on Mr. Gladstone by one of the young anarchic Tories, which began
by asserting that Mr. Gladstone was a bad public speaker. If these
people would, as I have said, go quietly and read Pope's 'Atticus', they
would see how a great satirist approaches a great enemy:

> 'Peace to all such! But were there one whose fires
> True genius kindles, and fair fame inspires,
> Blest with each talent, and each art to please,
> And born to write, converse, and live with ease.
> Should such a man ———'

And then follows the torrent of that terrible criticism. Pope was not
such a fool as to try to make out that Addison was a fool. He knew
that Addison was not a fool, and he knew that Addison knew it. But
hatred, in Pope's case, had become so great and, I was almost going to
say, so pure, that it illuminated all things, as love illuminates all things.
He said what was really wrong with Addison; and in calm and clear
and everlasting colours he painted the picture of the evil of the literary
temperament:

> 'Bear like the Turk, no brother near the throne,
> View him with scornful, yet with jealous eyes,
> And hate for arts that caused himself to rise.
>
> .   .   .   .   .   .
>
> Like Cato give his little Senate laws,
> And sit attentive to his own applause;
> While wits and templars every sentence raise,
> And wonder with a foolish face of praise.'

This is the kind of thing which really goes to the mark at which it aims. It is penetrated with sorrow and a kind of reverence, and it is addressed directly to a man. This is no mock-tournament to gain the applause of the crowd. It is a deadly duel by the lonely seashore.[1]

Even Pope's smaller victims must have been aware of glory. Atterbury, we saw, would not have minded 'to be a little sneer'd at in a Line, or so, for the sake of the pleasure I should have in reading the rest'. The angry and filthy retorts of the victims do not necessarily represent their whole response. An attack by Pope had its advantages: it did at least thrust you into the limelight (it seems that James Ralph provoked an attack for this very reason);[2] and usually it meant money for you ('The *Dunciad* was a gold mine to Curll',[3] and therefore a silver one to his authors). 'There is nothing more dreadful to an author', said Johnson, 'than neglect; compared with which, reproach, hatred, and opposition, are names of happiness.'[4] The feelings of the victims were mixed: reading Dennis's counter-onslaughts

> . . . I must think, do all I can,
> That there was pleasure there.

If the archer, being a poet, seemed less malicious, the victim, wounded by great poetry, seemed less personally injured. 'Like Gods they fight, nor dread a mortal Wound.'

On another ground, also, Pope achieved the integrity that Dryden saw in Persius, when his theme was the splendid civilization of his time. Etherege, Congreve, Addison, and, in later times, Peacock and Tennyson proved equal to attacking the most exquisite civilization where alone it may be attacked effectively—on its own ground. If we read the satires of Robert Gould, from which Pope learned much in general and borrowed much in detail, we see the difference immediately. In his satires on the aristocracy, Gould fails through being burly: a bull cannot satirize a china shop. But Pope's are so appropriately exquisite that they cannot be dismissed as envious. In his *Rape of the Lock*; in the lavish, creative

---

[1] *Twelve Types. A Book of Essays,* 1910, pp. 51 ff.
[2] See Twickenham ed., v. 452.
[3] Id., p. 436.
[4] *Rambler,* No. 2.

ridicule of Timon's villa and garden; in his dismissal of
courtiers as 'tinsel Insects',[1] and of the court chaplain

> With Band of Lily, and with Cheek of Rose;[2]

—in all such passages it is clear that his deprecation does not
spring from lack of power to experience. His power lies in
his sensitiveness to the very splendour and delicacy he rejects. And, moreover, he was himself a practitioner: his own
garden is important in the history of horticulture.

Unless, then, we take the absolute stand and deny point-
blank that any human being has any right to satirize any of
his fellows, we must allow Pope to be a fit punisher of the
vices of bad writing and of bad 'taste'.

5

Most of what I have been saying concerns the state of
affairs in the first half of the eighteenth century. It is now the
second half of the twentieth, and we are therefore free to treat
Pope's satires as if they never caused pain to anyone. I do not
say that we can read them in the way we read, say, Herrick's
Hesperides. They are too complicated for that, and touch
those reaches of our minds where we are least sure of ourselves. But if the present-day reader cannot get all that Pope
put into them, the next best thing is to get what he gets from
general satire—from, say, the fierce but impersonal satire of
Timon of Athens. Even where Pope's poetry attacked living
individuals, it was too complicated merely to serve the purposes of a vendetta. The satires are poetry first of all, and if
readers lose the poetry by attending to the feelings aroused
two hundred years ago in a quarrel they lack the knowledge
to understand, they had better forget that a quarrel was ever
in progress. Pope took great pains to make sure that his
satires were poetry. If he attacked, say, Lord Hervey under
the title of Sporus, he attacked him, so to speak, with Horace,
Juvenal, and Dryden looking on; and with the beloved Virgil
also, whom Dryden revered for the mastery that could trans-
form a string of words into a cat-o'-nine-tails:

---

[1] 'Epilogue to the Satires', dial. ii, 220.
[2] 'The Fourth Satire of Dr. John Donne . . . Versifyed', l. 251 (Twickenham
ed., iv. 47).

. . . Virgil could have written sharper satires than either Horace or Juvenal, if he would have employed his talent that way. I will produce a verse and half of his, in one of his Eclogues, to justify my opinion; and with commas after every word, to show that he has given almost as many lashes as he has written syllables. 'Tis against a bad poet, whose ill verses he describes:—

> . . . non tu, in triviis, indocte, solebas
> Stridenti, miserum, stipula disperdere carmen?[1]

When Pope called Matthew Concanen

> A cold, long-winded native of the deep,[2]

he was attacking a particular bad poet and his particular bad poetry, but, in addition, was and is making the world laugh as freely as Falstaff does—the world that cannot care two straws for any minor poet of two hundred years ago. Readers who can read Pope's satires as if they were reading *Timon of Athens* get so much of this laughter (and other innocent emotions as strong but subtler) that it is a pity to spoil the effect by interposing the smeared glass of a wrong estimate of Pope's moral character. The readers whom Pope deserves are those who are fully alive to the timeless splendours of his poetry and also know as much as possible at first hand of the man and of his age to be aware, as much as possible, of what his poetry meant for himself and his contemporaries. But failing the possession of that specialist historical knowledge, readers can still get what is after all most important in the satires—their timeless splendours.

If readers persist in neglecting the poetry through persisting in not liking its author, it looks as if they are interested

---

[1] *Essays*, ii. 86. See also Joseph Trapp, *Lectures*, ed. cit., p. 91. In Dryden's translation Virgil's lines are represented by:

> Dunce at the best: in Streets but scarce allow'd
> To tickle, on thy Straw, the stupid Crowd.

I recall a remark of the late R. M. Hewitt about Milton on the same lines as Dryden's about Virgil: he adduced the evidence for Milton's power, rather potential than actual, as a satiric poet from a line similar in content to that of Virgil's:

> Grate on their scrannel Pipes of wretched straw.

('Lycidas', l. 124.) Hewitt linked this with the following from Aubrey's account of him: 'Extreme pleasant in his conversation, & at dinner, supper &c: but Satyricall. He pronounced yᵉ letter R very hard;' to which he added the note: 'a certain signe of a Satyricall Witt fr. Jo: Dreyden' (*Early Lives of Milton*, ed. Helen Darbishire, 1932, p. 6).   [2] *Dunciad*, ii. 300.

more in stale literary gossip than in literature, or that they fear that the poetry may 'shock them with [its] truth'[1]—with its truth about themselves. For the only non-literary credentials that we have the right to demand of any satirist who does not attack us by name are not moral credentials at all, but intellectual ones. The only thing that we can properly demand of him is that the scheme of morals offered in his writings is a sound scheme, that what he 'stooped to' was indeed 'truth'.

[1] I borrow this phrase from Pope's Preface to his *Works*, 1717, para. 4.

XII

TRUTH AND SENTIMENT

IN the Advertisement affixed to *An Epistle to Dr. Arbuthnot*
Pope voiced his belief that

If [the poem] have any thing pleasing, it will be That by which
I am most desirous to please, the *Truth* and the *Sentiment*.

On this occasion he was underrating the sensuous pleasure
afforded by the poem, and by all the other poems of his—the
pleasures of metre, of words attended to as words, of imagery
in both its kinds. Usually he did not underrate this sensuous
pleasure, since without it poetry could not be agreed to exist.
On one occasion he pointedly noted the 'evaporation' of the
'spirit' of poetry from translations of *An Essay on Man*,[1] and
at the other end of his career comes the devastating remark
made to the aged Wycherley, whose poems the eighteen-
year-old Pope had undertaken to revise: he ends the list of
his revisions with 'some I have . . . turned more into Poetry'.[2]
For Pope, however, the sensuous pleasures of poetry were
not enough. Horace had asked of it profit as well as delight,
and the profit of poetry may be said to have lain for Pope in
what he here calls 'truth' and 'sentiment'. In this particular
context 'Truth' may be intended to mean biographical fact—
the poem recounts his career among his fellow writers. But
if we generalize and make it apply to his poems all together,
it will mean Nature addressing itself to man's head, while
'Sentiment', in both particular and general, will mean Nature
addressing itself to man's heart. Being a poet, what he liked
most was Truth and Sentiment together. Sometimes he gave
his readers Truth with the addition only of conciseness and
versification:

A *little learning* is a dang'rous thing;[3]

or

. . . Happiness! our being's end and aim![4]

---

[1] *Correspondence*, iv. 484. [2] Id., i. 16.
[3] *Essay on Criticism*, l. 215. [4] *Essay on Man*, iv. 1.

and a score of aphorisms more. If he had always expressed
Truth 'neat', as in these instances, he would never have
thought of himself as a poet, nor would his readers. But
usually in his poems Truth did not exist without Sentiment.
There was plenty of Truth in Clarissa's speech to Belinda,
but it was painful Truth:

> Oh! if to dance all Night, and dress all Day,
> Charm'd the Small-pox, or chas'd old Age away;
> Who would not scorn what Huswife's Cares produce,
> Or who would learn one earthly Thing of Use?
> To patch, nay ogle, might become a Saint,
> Nor could it sure be such a Sin to paint.
> But since, alas! frail Beauty must decay,
> Curl'd or uncurl'd, since Locks will turn to grey,
> Since painted, or not painted, all shall fade,
> And she who scorns a Man, must die a Maid;
> What then remains, but well our Pow'r to use,
> And keep good Humour still whate'er we lose?[1]

There was plenty of Truth in the 'character' of Flavia, but
the head that was thinking was also shaking. And also in the
'character' of Man, but the Truth was felt as confessing alter-
nate grandeur and abasement.[2] The 'character' of Atticus
began in *honnêteté*, a constituent of secondary Nature, but
left that far behind for primary, which, because it was Nature
inverted, caused pain near to the point of tears:

> Who but must laugh, if such a man there be?
> Who would not weep, if *Atticus* were he![3]

Pope seldom gave his readers Truth without Sentiment, confidently believing that if he gave them something worth
thinking about and made them feel about it too, he would
have attained the highest end of poetry.

This being so, he sought to make his poetry of the kind
that the common reader learns by heart. Taking Nature for
his main subject he was assured of readers, and he saw to it
that the verse in which he embodied his subject was economical of words, varied of tone, always claiming to be
spoken (as if it were verse in a play). The result was a wide-

---

[1] *Rape of the Lock*, v. 19 ff.
[2] See above, p. 31.   [3] *Epistle to Dr. Arbuthnot*, ll. 214 f.

spread committal to memory. I have quoted his line about himself:

Composing songs for fools to get by heart,[1]

which snubbed himself and his readers, and yet showed the readers to be responding as he wished. I have alluded else-where to the young convict in our own century who found the routine imposed on the gangs the more bearable because he knew thousands of Pope's couplets by heart, and got pleasure out of saying them over and over.[2] The young convict was in good intellectual company: Wordsworth's annotations of Barron Field's manuscript memoir of him include the statement:

I have ten times more knowledge of Pope's writings, and of Dryden's also, than ever [Hazlitt] had. To this day [c. 1836] I believe I could repeat, with a little previous rummaging of my memory, several thousand lines of Pope.[3]

In his own day and later, readers of Pope's poetry had many lines by heart. Thinking so highly of the feelings, he would have been pleased with a recent interpretation of the old phrase:

When I speak of learning by heart . . . I mean something more than memorizing; and indeed, when the phrase was made it was intended, plainly, to cover something different from any kind of learning by head.[4]

The *Rape of the Lock* has been read by the wide world of readers: even as early as two years after the appearance of the separate revised edition of 1714 it was in the hands of seamstresses.[5] Johnson spoke of its 'readers of every class, from the critick to the waiting-maid'.[6] Pope would have felt his ends attained by this width of continued fame for that poem and most of the rest. Having thought so much of Natural man he would have liked to know how numerous and various were his admiring readers—various but warmly conscious of what they held in common.

[1] See above, p. 136.
[2] *Essays in Criticism and Research*, 1942, p. 102.
[3] *Letters of the Wordsworth Family*, ed. Knight, 1907, iii. 122.
[4] H. W. Garrod, *The Study of Poetry*, Oxford, 1936, p. 7.
[5] See Twickenham ed., ii. 105.   [6] *Lives of the Poets*, iii. 232.

APPENDIX 1

POPE'S POETRY 'ALL OVER MORALITY'

In substantiation of the claim (which happens to have struck some critics as a novel one) that Pope's career as a poet shows no break worth speaking of,[1] I propose to examine a paragraph from a recent book where it is not enough allowed. Writing of the poetry Pope wrote in the last twenty years of a career twice as long, Mr. R. W. Rogers has considered it in relation to the poetry he wrote in the first twenty. This relationship, I think, he misconceives, and mainly because he accepts too much of what Pope himself said of the relationship:

[Pope] publicly stated that what he had written earlier had come to seem inadequate and unsatisfying. Addressing Lord Bolingbroke in the *Essay on Man*, he declared:

> That urg'd by thee, I turn'd the tuneful art
> From sounds to things, from fancy to the heart;
> For Wit's false mirror held up Nature's light . . .
> (iv, ll. 391–3)

In the *Epistle to Dr. Arbuthnot* he again wrote of his development as a poet, boasting:

> That not in Fancy's Maze he wander'd long,
> But stoop'd to Truth, and moraliz'd his song . . .
> (ll. 340–1)

And in the same poem he dismissed his early verse in these terms:

> Soft were my Numbers, who could take offence
> While pure Description held the place of Sense?
> Like gentle *Fanny*'s was my flow'ry Theme,
> A painted Mistress, or a purling Stream.
> (ll. 147–50)

And Mr. Rogers proceeds:

To an extent Pope's descriptions of his earlier work are valid ones. His poetry had been largely experimental, the result of his desire to establish himself in the Virgilian tradition of letters. It was imitative and precocious; and it reflected an intense application to prosody and diction. It was produced by one who had spent his youth in quiet study and who was interested in art primarily for art's sake. His later poetry, on the other hand, was critical and analytic in temper. It was the work of a sensitive and perceptive moralist and commentator upon society. The shift in Pope's literary interests was not, however, quickly

[1] See above, p. 36.

ade. He had studiously cherished his early aspirations; and he was
abandon the sort of work which might lead to an epic and to take
rian kind of poetry which might not endure and which threatened
him in perpetual controversy. A variety of circumstances, personal
gical, conspired to force him, almost in spite of himself, to the
which altered the character of his poetry.[1]

'To an extent', says Mr. Rogers, and we cannot but ask 'To what
extent?' When did the change, if there was a change, take place? and
what was its nature?

From Warton onwards the change Pope says he saw has been assumed to fall between the *Works* of 1717 and the later poems—between
Eloisa to Abelard and the *Dunciad*. This places on one side of the
division the *Pastorals*, *An Essay on Criticism*, the *Rape of the Lock*,
the *Temple of Fame*, *Windsor Forest*, *Eloisa to Abelard*, 'An Elegy on
the Death of an Unfortunate Lady', and, on the other, the *Dunciad*,
An Essay on Man, the *Moral Essays*, the *Imitations of Horace*. If the
'painted Mistress' is Belinda and if the 'purling Stream' is the Thames
as it comes into *Windsor Forest*, those attributions would support Warton. But the gap that is most marked runs between the *Pastorals* and
the rest. Of this gap Pope shows himself conscious at the close of *An
Essay on Criticism*:

> Such late was Walsh—the Muse's judge and friend,
> Who justly knew to blame or to commend;
> To failings mild, but zealous for desert;
> The clearest head, and the sincerest heart.
> This humble praise, lamented shade! receive,
> This praise at least a grateful Muse may give:
> The Muse, whose early voice you taught to sing,
> Prescrib'd her heights,[2] and prun'd her tender wing,
> (Her guide now lost) no more attempts to rise,
> But in low numbers short excursions tries:
> Content, if hence th' unlearn'd their wants may view,
> The learn'd reflect on what before they knew:
> Careless of censure, nor too fond of fame;
> Still pleas'd to praise, yet not afraid to blame,
> Averse alike to flatter, or offend;
> Not free from faults, nor yet too vain to mend.[3]

And that these same 'low numbers' are expressing moral sense is clear
from the passage quoted—Pope's essay on criticism, as I have shown,
is as much an essay on life as on literature.[4] It is just possible that

---

[1] Robert W. Rogers, *The Major Satires of Alexander Pope*, Urbana, Ill., 1955,
pp. 1 f.
[2] Walsh had evidently encouraged Pope towards the epic, which, while still
younger, he had already attempted: he wrote 'Part of an Epic Poem when about
twelve' (Spence, p. 24).   [3] ll. 729 ff.   [4] See above, pp. 140 ff.

Bolingbroke seconded Walsh in urging Pope to write in forms superior to pastoral. Bolingbroke had not seen the *Pastorals* in manuscript, but they were printed in 1709, and soon afterwards Pope and he were fellow members of the Scriblerus Club. However that may be (and the degree of soundness in that suggestion does not affect the argument), the nature of the change as Pope described it in late poems points to an early date—a change 'from sounds' would seem to be a change from poems of which he said, describing the *Pastorals*, 'There is scarce any work of mine in which the versification was more laboured [i.e. elaborate]'.[1] But in any event he does not give a true picture when he speaks of exchanging sounds for things, pure description for sense, fancy for heart, false wit for Nature, for these are not primary differentiae among any poems of his. It would be a thankless task to go through the poems testing them for sounds (the lines that best pleased his ear, those on Mæotis, come not from the *Pastorals* but the *Dunciad*);[2] for things (there may be more things, as opposed to mere 'words', and things more important to man, in the later poems, but if so the later poems begin with the *Rape of the Lock*); for 'pure' description (description exists of necessity in most poems and more of it is necessary in the earlier poems, but even so it is scarcely ever 'pure' to the extent of being picture for picture's sake, having been called for by the theme in whole or part); for satire or 'sense'-that-gives-'offence' (it is fulsomely there in the early lines on Settle[3] and in *An Essay on Criticism*); for fancy (if the sylphs of the *Rape of the Lock* and the rock of ice on which Fame's temple is built are fancy, then also is much of the *Dunciad*). And, to complete this sketch, the 'painted Mistress,' being Belinda, is as much an instance of Nature as any exhibit in 'Of the Characters of Women', and the Thames in *Windsor Forest* bursts the pastoral bounds by being seen as the artery of British commerce, internationalism, and naval greatness.

All of which suggests that if a change did take place, it was before Pope published any poems at all. Mr. Rogers calls the earlier poems Virgilian, but they are as much Horatian. His 'first' poem, the Horatian 'Ode on Solitude', is sufficiently adult, while *An Essay on Criticism*, published when he was twenty-three, is quite as mature as Horace's *Ars Poetica*. And even the pastorals are no more 'art for art's sake' than Virgil's were: the work of a boy, Pope's country poems are adult: as, for instance, in the exclamation:

Just Gods! shall all things yield returns but love?[4]

---

[1] Spence, p. 312.
[2] *Dunciad*, iii. 87 f.: 'Lo! where Mæotis sleeps, and hardly flows/The freezing Tanais thro' a waste of snows.'
[3] See above, p. 82.   [4] 'Autumn', l. 76.

or in the dedication of 'Spring' to Sir William Trumbull:

> You, that too wise for pride, too good for pow'r,
> Enjoy the glory to be great no more,
> And carrying with you all the world can boast,
> To all the world illustriously are lost . . .?[1]

or

> The sprightly Sylvia trips along the green,
> She runs, but hopes she does not run unseen;
> While a kind glance at her pursuer flies,
> How much at variance are her feet and eyes![2]

Elizabeth Barrett Browning declared that

> . . . Pope was sexagenarian at sixteen;[3]

this overlooks the love poetry, which is mature without being super-annuated, but it is better to see Pope as always old than to see him as on one occasion Wordsworth did: Wordsworth's own poetry contains nothing that can rival the authority of Pope's lines on Sylvia in their own category, yet he saw Pope as 'wander[ing] from humanity in his Eclogues with boyish inexperience'.[4] The *Pastorals* include among their concerns a concern with men and women fully grown, and so a concern with right and wrong; even Sylvia presents an ethical problem in miniature (either her feet are right and her eyes wrong, or vice versa; or they demonstrate that right and wrong are never found unmixed in a human being). So that, if these are samples of Pope's *Pastorals*, I need not proceed to demonstrate the moral content of *An Essay on Criticism*, the *Rape of the Lock*, the *Temple of Fame*, or even of *Eloisa to Abelard* and the 'Elegy on the Death of an Unfortunate Lady'. Pope was a moralist from the start. Looking back in 1729, he told Swift that

> My first friendship at sixteen [i.e. in 1704], was contracted with a man of seventy, and I found him not grave enough . . . for me. . . .[5]

And in 1718 Atterbury was to use these words when thanking him for the sight of some verses:

> I like the Lines well: they are Yours, and they are Good, & on both accounts, very welcome to me. You know my Opinion, That Poetry without a Moral is a Body without a Soul. Let the Lines be never so finely turn'd, if they do not point at some Useful Truth, if there be no degree of Instruction at the bottom of them, they can give no true delight to a Reasonable mind; they are

---

[1] ll. 7 ff. [2] Id., ll. 57 ff.
[3] *Aurora Leigh*, 1857, p. 37.
[4] 'Essay Supplementary to the Preface [to the *Lyrical Ballads*]', para. 17.
[5] *Correspondence*, iii. 80.

versus inopes rerum, nugaeque canorae; and as such they may tinkle prettily in the Ear, but will never reach the Heart, or leave a durable Impression behind them. No body that reads your Verses, will blame you on this account for they are all over Morality, from the beginning to the End of them.[1]

Altogether it is plain that we must not take Pope's own account too literally. His poems could never have been called poems of 'fancy' any more than you could liken to a maze poems which, though intricate, are never confusing. In his later poems, therefore, Pope did not 'stoop to Truth' for the first time, but 'stooped' only to more of it.[2]

Mr. Rogers allows Pope to be precocious but does not allow his precocity to be extreme. There is an increase of enrichment, density, intensity as Pope goes deeper into his one subject-matter, and the process begins while he is still a boy. His subject-matter remains the same though differently mixed, his art the same though it becomes more richly skilled. 'How much at variance', he had said of Sylvia in 1709: that is what he says of all the women of the second *Moral Essay*, twenty-five years later, but he says it with much more technical power and a deeper awareness of the richness of the human material that the old proverbial truth interprets.

[1] Id., i. 502.

[2] At that time 'stoop' connoted decisive power— its modern equivalent would be 'swoop'. The stooping of a tiercel-gentle was anything but gentle:

> .. . the partridge sprung,
> He makes his stoop; but, wanting breath, is forced
> To cancilier [i.e. to turn on the wing]; then, with such speed as if
> He carried lightning in his wings, he strikes
> The trembling bird, who even in death appears
> Proud to be made his quarry.

(Massinger, *The Guardian*, I. i.) Cf. also Twickenham ed., v. 255: 'But the Muse ceases not here her Eagle-flight. Sometimes, satiated with the contemplation of these *Suns* of glory, she turneth downward on her wing, and darts like lightning on the *Goose* and *Serpent* kind.'

READING POPE WITH TOO FREE
A MIND[1]

THERE are indications that nowadays Pope is sometimes read without due attention to first principles. A recent book, Rebecca Price Parkin's *The Poetic Workmanship of Alexander Pope*,[2] may be taken as an instance.

The titles of Mrs. Parkin's chapters—'The Implied Dramatic Speaker', 'Irony', 'Parallelism . . .', 'Tonal Variation', and so on—show that she is attempting analysis. (Not complete analysis, however; she has little to say of metre, diction, syntax, or sound.) We judge the success of a method of analysing literature by the light it throws on the object, and in that obvious statement it is the second of the terms that is the trickier. The object is twofold—a text existing on the page and a thing created by the text in the mind of the reader. The critic speaks of the text as his mind possesses it, and the reader of the criticism tests what he reads by reference to his own possession of it, finding that piece of criticism useful which enlarges his sense of possession without making him feel that the critic possesses something at variance with it. How does Mrs. Parkin fare when exposed to these tests?

Both well and ill. She sees, for instance, that in Pope's poems there are shifts from one implied, or stated, audience to another. She sees how frequent these shifts are, and through what a gamut they move. To take instances which, as it happens, she does not use: 'Let *Sporus* tremble——' implies that a third person is hearing or overhearing words supposedly addressed only to Dr. Arbuthnot; and there is that terrific line in the same poem, which uses a device possibly unique in an epistle:

> Hear this! and spare his Family, *James More*!

Another method that helps us see our own mental possession more fully and clearly is that of distinguishing tones which, it is well known, Pope varies more continually than any other English poet. Mrs. Parkin is able to show how much and how often the tone does vary, and it is an interesting sight.

---

[1] See above, p. 190.
[2] University of Minnesota Press; Geoffrey Cumberlege: Oxford University Press, 1956.

But, taking the book as a whole, one cannot feel that Mrs. Parkin's mental image of Pope's poetry could stand a re-examination of the text. She is not yet a thoroughly competent reader of her admittedly difficult poet. There are signs that she could become so, and since Pope is an author that his admirers read (as Lamb said) 'over and over', there is ground for hope that she will. To instance first a small matter. The *Epistle to Dr. Arbuthnot*, she says, 'opens, literally, with a bang'. Did John in fact bang the door? That he closed it softly is evinced by the word *fatigued* which also accounts for the repetition of the opening of the request—the words are only just got out:

> Shut, shut the door, good John!, fatigu'd I said.

This is an instance of a loose attentiveness which has its effect on the larger matters. Another cause of imperfect criticism is that Mrs. Parkin lets the principles that prompt her use of her methods usurp the place of first principles. What is ancillary is made primary. Take, for instance, these remarks from the chapter 'Tonal Variation':

> A basic function of tonal variation, especially in Pope's longer poems, is the prevention of monotony. If Pope had produced in *Windsor Forest*'s four hundred and thirty-four lines nothing but unrelieved description of landscape, he would have been, like his own Dunces, 'Sleepless himself, to give his readers sleep'.

The real subject of these remarks is Pope's means of preventing monotony. That being so, the first thing to speak about is matter. The claims of matter do assert themselves in this passage, but by the method of a false equation, for 'description' (which here means matter) exists in a different category from tonal variation, which is a way of expressing a sense of matter. What becomes of Pope's allegedly great debt to tonal variation if we put Mrs. Parkin's thinking into better shape? 'Pope wished not to be monotonous. He therefore varied his sorts of matter. Varying them, he also varied, as one might expect, the tone in which he spoke of them, writing of bluish hills in a quiet tone, and of world-trade in a pompous tone.' When Mrs. Parkin goes on to say, 'Shifts from one tone to another keep the attention alerted', we wish to revise the predicate and read 'are one of several things that keep . . .'.

And surely the claims Mrs. Parkin makes for tonal variation crumple up when we read 'Tone, after all, cannot be completely distinguished from content. Tone is not only how a thing is said but also in part what is said.' And to come on 'tone' at another angle, what is its value to the critic when it prompts such a remark as this about *Windsor Forest*: 'Notable is the absence of humorous or low tones'—by 'low' tones Mrs. Parkin means tones conveying indecent sense? Notable rather would have been their presence.

In her chapter on Irony Mrs. Parkin claims that

One of the most valuable psychological features of irony is that it helps keep
the reader alert . . . the assertion of an ironic poem cannot be accepted at face
value but must be incessantly scrutinized for double meanings. . . .

There is a danger in this *modus operandi* that Mrs. Parkin does not
allow for. Would it not be better to say: 'Since not all the assertions of
a poem by Pope are necessarily to be taken at face value, the reader must
distinguish those that are from those that are not'? The trouble with
irony has always been the obstacles it raises for the non-ironical expression that cannot but be intermixed with it. The author of a work
containing irony is therefore at the mercy of his reader. Sometimes
Mrs. Parkin finds points of irony that others have missed, and they
were possibly put there by Pope. A particularly interesting example
concerns the last line of *Moral Essays*, iv. Pope has been showing us
how Timon's grandiosities strike him, and goes on to show that,
aesthetics apart, an economic advantage is felt by the poor people in the
neighbourhood:

> Yet hence the Poor are cloth'd, the Hungry fed;
> Health to himself, and to his Infants bread
> The Lab'rer bears: What his hard Heart denies,
> His charitable Vanity supplies;[1]

and ends by saying that in any event the insult to which beauty and
fitness are subjected will not last for ever:

> Another age shall see the golden Ear
> Embrown the Slope, and nod on the Parterre,
> Deep Harvests bury all his pride has plann'd,
> And laughing Ceres re-assume the land.[2]

Mrs. Parkin's comment reads:

Timon has violated the decorum of human economics by turning plowed
fields into pointlessly huge greenswards. But more important in this passage is
what may be called 'elegiac irony', an irony inherent in the human situation.
This irony touches deeper issues than any of the types yet cited. Its effect here,
however, is not so much tragic as humorous, since the tragic stroke is aimed at
the ridiculous figure of Timon. The reader enjoys the prospect of his being
taken down a peg, even though it is by a natural law to which the reader too,
with all things mortal, is subject.

Incidentally, the role of the double meaning of 'laughing' in reinforcing the
irony should be noted. 'Laughing' is meant both in the general sense applicable to all thriving vegetation and in the sense that Ceres, like the reader, is
laughing at the posthumous discomfiture of Timon.[3]

Mrs. Parkin's confidence in her interpretation of 'laughing' may

[1] ll. 169 ff.   [2] ll. 173 ff.   [3] Op. cit., p. 42.

well be justified. It is quite possible that to miss it is to miss realizing Pope's intention. On the other hand it is equally possible that Pope did not intend the double meaning. Each reader must decide for himself according to his own sense of Pope, of Pope's poetry, and indeed of poetry in general. I suggest that there are several reasons why Pope did not want Ceres to be laughing *at* anything. In the first place 'laughing' without the connotation 'laughing at' is beautifully apt for describing Ceres, the goddess associated with corn—'The vallies . . . stand so thick with corn, that they shall laugh and sing.'[1] So satisfying is this innocent sense of 'laugh' and 'laughing', so suitably placed along with 'the golden ear' and its 'nodding', that to add to it something more sophisticated—to add the scornful scoring of a point implied in laughing *at*, even if the larger scorn and scoring of a goddess, is to spoil rather than to supplement happily. That is how I myself interpret Pope's intentions, but, as I say, this is an instance where the reader must judge for himself, having first, of course, tried to qualify for reaching a right judgement.

Another of Mrs. Parkin's instances I think not open to two interpretations—the instance of 'die' as used at the close of the *Rape of the Lock*. Sometimes in that poem 'die' bears the contemporary sense of reach (and pass) the point of sexual consummation. The brilliance of Pope's use of the word in this sense is obvious in the lines:

> Nor fear'd the Chief th'unequal Fight to try,
> Who sought no more than on his Foe to die;[2]

(which plainly states the callous nature of the Baron's attentions to Belinda), and possibly also in another line:

> Nor think, to die dejects my lofty Mind.[3]

It is equally obvious that on another occasion in the poem the word can bear only its primary meaning 'cease to exist', as for instance here:

> And soften'd Sounds along the Waters die;[4]

and

> And she who scorns a Man must die a Maid.[5]

The use of *die* in oblique forms ('dies', 'died') are all in this primary sense. The poem closes with the lines:

> Not all the Tresses that fair Head can boast
> Shall draw such Envy as the Lock you lost.
> For, after all the Murders of your Eye,
> When, after Millions slain, your self shall die;
> When those fair Suns shall sett, as sett they must,
> And all those Tresses shall be laid in Dust . . .

---

[1] Psalm lxv (Prayer Book), 14.   [2] v. 77 f.   [3] v. 99 f.   [4] ii. 50.   [5] v. 28.

On which Mrs. Parkin comments:

By means of a pun on 'die' Pope makes a humorous, down-to-earth sexual allusion in these lines; but it is softened by the reference to Belinda's mortality and the short date of all things sweet and rare.[1]

Pope certainly does make a down-to-earth sense in the lines literally, using the word 'dust'. But surely the context restricts the sense of 'die' to its primary sense. Unless we allow that restriction we ruin the whole effect of sadness and tenderness.

Take another instance. At pp. 17 f. above I have quoted Pope's lines 'Lo! the poor Indian . . .'. Mrs. Parkin's interpretation brings up a matter worth investigation, if only because it is inspired by a note by Professor Mack. It will be best to set out the paragraph afresh, and to place it in its context in *An Essay on Man*, since, of course, it has a place in an argument. Pope has been saying that

> Heav'n from all creatures hides the book of Fate,
> All but the page prescrib'd, their present state.[2]

This 'blindness to the future' he sees as 'kindly giv'n'.[3] Whereupon follow the two paragraphs in question:

> Hope humbly then; with trembling pinions soar;
> Wait the great teacher Death, and God adore!
> What future bliss, he gives not thee to know,
> But gives that Hope to be thy blessing now.
> Hopes springs eternal in the human breast:
> Man never Is, but always To be blest:
> The soul, uneasy and confin'd from home,
> Rests and expatiates in a life to come.
> Lo! the poor Indian, whose untutor'd mind
> Sees God in clouds, or hears him in the wind;
> His soul proud Science never taught to stray
> Far as the solar walk, or milky way;
> Yet simple Nature to his hope has giv'n,
> Behind the cloud-topt hill, an humbler heav'n;
> Some safer world in depth of woods embrac'd,
> Some happier island in the watry waste,
> Where slaves once more their native land behold,
> No fiends torment, no Christians thirst for gold!
> To be, contents his natural desire,
> He asks no Angel's wing, no Seraph's fire;
> But thinks, admitted to that equal sky,
> His faithful dog shall bear him company.[4]

Professor Mack, whose notes on this passage are of great interest, includes among them the critical note:

---

[1] Op. cit., p. 58.   [2] i. 77 f.   [3] i. 85.   [4] i. 91 ff.

There is irony directed against the Indian (cf. the naive materialism of his after-life, and iv. 177–8 [of the poem]) as well as against proud Science. Both (being human) are incapable of understanding God's ways, though the Indian surpasses proud Science in trusting them.[1]

Turning to the passage referred to in the fourth epistle we read:

> Weak, foolish man! will Heav'n reward us there
> With the same trash mad mortals wish for here?
> The Boy and Man an individual makes,
> Yet sigh'st thou now for apples and for cakes?
> Go, like the Indian, in another life
> Expect thy dog, thy bottle, and thy wife:
> As well as dream such trifles are assign'd,
> As toys and empires, for a god-like mind.
> Rewards, that either would to Virtue bring
> No joy, or be destructive of the thing:
> How oft by these at sixty are undone
> The virtues of a saint at twenty-one!
>   To whom can Riches give Repute, or Trust,
> Content, or Pleasure, but the Good and Just?
> Judges and Senates have been bought for gold,
> Esteem and Love were never to be sold.
> Oh fool! to think God hates the worthy mind.[2]

It would be interesting to discuss whether or not we are to allow for this passage when reading the passage in Epistle I. As we read that Epistle for the first time we cannot allow for it, and it is even possible that Professor Mack is the first person to see that a cross-reference may be called for. Perhaps it is not to the point to note that Epistle I was originally published eleven months before Epistle IV. But even if we do allow that Pope intended us to bear in mind what he later said of the Indian while we are reading what he first said of him, it does not much affect the sense of the passage in Epistle I. That sense, surely, is something like this: 'Man should pitch his hopes low especially as to his fortunes in the life to come. The Indian commendably pitches them low: not having book-learning ("Science" still meant primarily "knowledge" at this time), he only asks a continuation of what he likes most in his present life. That preference includes an absence of white men, who enslave him and torment him like fiends ("poor" as he is) in their greed for wealth. (At the same time as we are asked to admire the humility of the Indian, Pope asks us to be aware of the contrast, that is, to be ashamed of ourselves.) We have "science" and it has made us "proud", we are "Christian" and yet thirst, and not for God and righteousness (Professor Mack notes the Biblical references), but for

---

[1] Op. cit., p. 47.

[2] ll. 173 ff.

gold. With everything to induce in us shame and so the humblest of
hopes about the after-life when our life on earth will be judged, we
indulge hopes that could not well be higher! We expect to be angels
and seraphs! What a painful irony it is to Christians (unless they are
truer to their alleged ideal) that an Indian who never heard of Christ
should be so much nearer the real Christian in point of humility, that
virtue which Christ so highly valued.' Something like this is Pope's
sense in the passage when taken in itself; and if we take it alongside
that later passage, we go on to say that Pope thinks that the Indian's
heaven is too merely earthly and so making no allowance for some
likely sort of change, a sense that can be added without upsetting the
main sense of the former paragraph. Pope's sense is complicated, but
rather because it is saying much than because it is saying something
indeterminate. We see where he stands. Mrs. Parkin makes the following comments on the passage:

It might almost be said that here irony floats on the ambiguity. Half of the
irony is directed against the poor Indian; half against the Christian who thinks
himself, but who in some respects at least is not, superior to the Indian. It is
not easy to say whether in these lines we are being told that it is good or bad to
ask for an angel's wing or a seraph's fire. The fact is, we are being told both.
On the one hand, it seems that the Indian is being praised for his common
sense in resting content with natural being and not desiring such chimeras as
angelic wings and seraphic fires. The Christian who insists on these is con-
demned as arrogant and a fool. On the other hand, it would seem that it is the
savage, poor and untutored, with his idea of paradise as physical comfort and
security, who is being satirized; whereas the Christian is being commended for
his less material aspirations.

Actually, both of these things are being done at once. The result of this
paradoxical procedure is a closer approach to completeness of statement. The
insight here seems more complex, more conscious of the inadequacy resulting
from the expounding of one viewpoint *or* the other, than would have been true
if the poet had confined himself to an unambiguous, non-ironic statement.

When this particular instance of ambivalent irony is related to the central
meaning of the *Essay on Man*, it is seen to be especially significant. In one sense,
the untutored Indian's attitude is superior to the Christian's; and in another
sense, the latter's to the former's.

The important point is that both are satirized, both are fallible, both have
need to submit to a reality greater than they.[1]

I do not see any ambiguity. Pope is making two statements, which
we do not need to bring together. If we do, they remain separate.
The first allots praise to the Indian for his moral character, and blames
those Christians who are too proud to hope humbly. The second cites
the Indian as an example of the men who lack what might be called

[1] Op. cit., pp. 47 f.

theological imagination—the power to conceive of an after-life in other than earthly terms. There is no conflict between moral character and the lack of a theological imagination. The two things belong to different categories. Pope's final word to both the Indian and the Christian occurs before either are mentioned, in the paragraph I began by quoting: 'Wait the great teacher Death . . .'.

The best comment on Mrs. Parkin's way of reading Pope is the first note among those he added to his translation of the *Iliad*. His object here is the criticism of Homer's text, but there is a wider object also. I quote the first paragraph all but the last of its sentences, since it is both so brilliant and so little known:

It is something strange that of all the Commentators upon *Homer*, there is hardly one whose principal Design is to illustrate the Poetical Beauties of the Author. They are voluminous in explaining those Sciences which he made but subservient to his Poetry, and sparing only upon that Art which constitutes his Character. This has been occasion'd by the Ostentation of Men who had more Reading than Taste, and were fonder of shewing their Variety of Learning in all Kinds, than their single Understanding in Poetry. Hence it comes to pass that their Remarks are rather Philosophical, Historical, Geographical, Allegorical, or in short rather any thing than Critical and Poetical. Even the Grammarians, tho' their whole Business and Use be only to render the Words of an Author intelligible, are strangely touch'd with the Pride of doing something more than they ought. The grand Ambition of one sort of Scholars is to encrease the Number of *Various Lections*; which they have done to such a degree of obscure Diligence, that we now begin to value the first Editions of Books as most correct, because they have been least corrected. The prevailing Passion of others is to discover *New Meanings* in an Author, whom they will cause to appear mysterious purely for the Vanity of being thought to unravel him. These account it a disgrace to be of the Opinion of those that preceded them; and it is generally the Fate of such People who will never say what was said before, to say what will never be said after them. If they can but find a Word that has once been strain'd by some dark Writer to signify any thing different from its usual Acceptation, it is frequent with them to apply it constantly to that uncommon Meaning, whenever they meet it in a clear Writer: For Reading is so much dearer to them than Sense, that they will discard it at any time to make way for a Criticism. In other places where they cannot contest the Truth of the common Interpretation, they get themselves room for Dissertation by imaginary *Amphibologies*, which they will have to be design'd by the Author. This Disposition of finding out different Significations in one thing, may be the Effect of either too much, or too little Wit: For Men of a right Understanding generally see at once all that an Author can reasonably mean, but others are apt to fancy Two Meanings for want of knowing One.

Swift had taken up the same sort of position in *A Tale of a Tub*:

The Author is informed, that the Bookseller has prevailed on several Gentlemen, to write some explanatory Notes, for the goodness of which he is not to answer, having never seen any of them, nor intends it, till they appear in Print, when it is not unlikely he may have the Pleasure to find twenty Meanings, which never enter'd into his Imagination. . . .

For, *Night* being the universal Mother of Things, wise Philosophers hold all Writings to be *fruitful* in the Proportion they are *dark*; And therefore, the *true illuminated* (that is to say, the *Darkest* of all) have met with such numberless Comentators, whose *Scholiastick* Midwifry hath deliver'd them of Meanings, that the Authors themselves, perhaps, never conceived, and yet may very justly be allowed the Lawful Parents of them: The Words of such Writers being like Seed, which, however scattered at random, when they light upon a fruitful Ground, will multiply far beyond either the Hopes or Imagination of the Sower.[1]

Pope's preference for one meaning over two, one at least of which he regards as wrong, seems to come oddly from a poet who delighted in puns. On second thoughts, however, the preference interprets the way he regarded puns. For him a pun added to the primary sense without despoiling or contradicting it.

---

[1] *Tale of a Tub*, pp. 20 and 186. Some hundred and fifty years later Mallarmé deliberately placed himself on the side of this kind of critic, but here are Swift and Pope witnessing to the existence of the kind in their own time, and standing in opposition to such critics as belong to it.

INDEX II

NAMES OF PERSONS AND WORKS

(Works are listed by authors and editors only, when these are known; otherwise, by title.)

Abbott, Edwain, *Concordance to the Works of Alexander Pope, with an Introduction by E. A. Abbott*, 62, 167, 181, 182.

Abelard, Pierre, *see* Index I, *Eloisa to Abelard.*

Addison, Joseph, 116, 132 n., 138, 240; as 'Atticus', 122, 170, 173 n., 218, 219, 234, 238, 239 f., 245; *Cato*, 121; *Letter from Italy,* 211. See also *Spectator* (18th century).

Ainley, Henry, 189.

Allen, Ralph, 42, 197.

Allingham, William, 177 n.

Amelia, Sophia Eleonora, Princess of England (daughter of George II), 178.

Anne, Queen of England, 96 n., 148, 156, 182.

Arbuthnot, John, 60, 199, 229, 252. *See also* Index I, *Epistle to Dr. Arbuthnot.*

Ariosto, Lodovico, 206.

Aristotle, 20, 46, 79, 80, 122 f., 232 n.; *Poetics*, 19, 66 n., 127 n.

Arnold, Matthew: Preface to *Poems* (1853), 23, 118; 'Sohrab and Rustum', 118.

Arthos, John, *Language of Natural Description in Eighteenth-Century Poetry*, 165 n.

Asquith, Margot, 220.

Atterbury, Francis, *see* Rochester, Bishop of.

Aubrey, John, 242 n.

Ault, Norman: ed. Pope's *Prose Works*, 214 n.; *New Light on Pope*, 227 n.

Austen, Jane, 206.

Ayrton, William, 147 n.

Bacon, Francis, 172.

Baker, David Eskine, trans. Voltaire's *Metaphysics of Sir Isaac Newton*, 15 ff.

Ball, F. Elrington, ed. *Correspondence of Jonathan Swift*, 38 n.

Bathurst, Allen, Earl Bathurst, 31, 221. *See also* Index I, *Moral Essays*, III, 'Of the Use of Riches. To Bathurst'.

Bavius, 122.

Beckett, Samuel, 10.

Bentley, Richard, ed. of Milton, 235.

Berenger, Richard, 12.

Berkeley, George, 6, 98, 105, 106.

Bethel, Hugh, 48, 135.

Bible, 9, 172, 257. *See also* Ecclesiastes, Genesis, Jesus Christ, Proverbs, Psalms.

Blackmore, Richard, 97, 178; *Prince Arthur*, 179.

Blackwood, John, 23.

Blake, William, *Poetical Works* (ed. John Sampson), 106.

Blondin, Charles, 115.

Blount, Martha, 37, 38, 59, 112, 116 n., 169 n., 199 ff., 225, 226 f., 229.

Blount, Teresa, 112, 116 n., 199 f., 202 f., 225.

Boileau-Despréaux, Nicolas, 26, 87; *Lutrin*, 87.

Bolingbroke, Henry St. John, Viscount, 33 ff., 37, 43 n., 105, 147 n., 171, 247, 249.

Boswell, James, 17; *Life of Johnson*, 8, 11 f., 29, 32, 106 n., 109 n., 115 n., 192 n.

Bouhours, Dominique, 75.

Bowles, William Lisle, 218; ed. *The Works of Alexander Pope* (1806), 214 n.

Boyer, Abel, 179.

Boyle, John, *see* Orrery, Earl of.

Boyle, Richard, *see* Burlington, Earl of.

Boyle, Robert, *Occasional Reflections upon Several Subjects*, 80.

Breval, J. D., 178.

Brontë, Emily, 102 f., 210.